WITHDRAWN

THE IMPORTANCE OF PLACE IN THE AMERICAN LITERATURE OF HAWTHORNE, THOREAU, CRANE, ADAMS, AND FAULKNER

American Writers, American Culture, And The American Dream

Robert Glen Deamer

Studies in American Literature
Volume 7

The Edwin Mellen Press
Lewiston/Queenston/Lampeter

Library of Congress Cataloging-in-Publication Data

Deamer, Robert Glen.
   The importance of place in the American literature of Hawthorne,
Thoreau, Crane, Adams, and Faulkner : American writers, American
culture, and the American dream / Robert Glen Deamer.
      p. cm. -- (Studies in American literature ; v. 7)
   Includes bibliographical references.
   ISBN 0-88946-163-5
   1. American literature--History and criticism. 2. Setting
(Literature) 3. Myth in literature. 4. Regionalism in literature.
5. Romanticism--United States. I. Title. II. Series: Studies in
American literature (Lewiston, N.Y.) ; v. 7.
   PS169.S45D4 1990
   810.9'22--dc20
                                                               89-13683
                                                                   CIP

   This is volume 7 in the continuing series
   Studies in American Literature Volume 7
   ISBN 0-88946-163-5
   SAL Series ISBN 0-88946-166-X

A CIP catalog record for this book
is available from the British Library.

                    The Edwin Mellen Press
Box 450   Box 67
Lewiston, New York   Queenston, Ontario
U.S.A. 14092   CANADA L0S 1L0

                    The Edwin Mellen Press, Ltd.
                    Lampeter, Dyfed, Wales
                    UNITED KINGDOM SA48 7DY

            Printed in the United States of America

For Eleny

TABLE OF CONTENTS

SECTION IV -- THE SOUTH: WILLIAM FAULKNER

Chapter 11
The Adamic Hero and the Southern Myth:
Faulkner's Isaac McCaslin and Quentin Compson

SECTION V -- THE LOSS OF PLACE: AMERICAN FICTIONISTS, AMERICAN OBSERVERS IN ENGLAND

Chapter 12
The American Dream and the Romance Tradition in American Fiction:
A Literary Study of Society and of Success in America

Chapter 13
American Observers in England, 1820-1920: A Cross-National
Perspective on American Culture and the American Character

ACKNOWLEDGMENTS

Several chapters in this book have grown from doctoral studies within the American Studies program at the University of New Mexico. James Barbour directed, most helpfully, a project allowing me to pursue my interest in Thoreau's mysticism and in Thoreau's doctrine of wildness. Joel M. Jones directed a project under which I examined the cultural implications of the Romance tradition in American fiction. Ferenc Szasz agreed to my writing of a paper on Hawthorne's relation to New England Puritanism. David A. Remley directed a project under which I investigated the relationships between the American dream and the initiation theme in American fiction. Professors Jones, Szasz, and Remley also served as readers and critics of my dissertation on "The American Dream."

To George Arms, my debt is, quite simply, immeasurable -- not just for the high standards and the inspiration of his seminar on Henry Adams and Stephen Crane, but also for numerous favors and kindnesses over the years since that seminar at the University of New Mexico in the Spring of 1972. Chapters 5, 8, and 10 all derive from work originally done for Professor Arms' seminar.

Research for Chapters 6 and 9 was sponsored by a National Endowment for the Humanities fellowship for a 1978 summer seminar at the University of Kansas -- directed by Stuart Levine, Editor of *American Studies*. It is a pleasure to acknowledge my debt to Professor Levine and to the members of this seminar for a stimulating and educative summer.

Professor Merrill Lewis of Western Washington University read an earlier version of my chapter on Thoreau and provided excellent, penetrating advice toward a stronger essay. Professor Thomas D. Clark of Indiana University East carefully read and edited an earlier version of Chapter 12, and offered valuable suggestions for its improvement. Professor Thomas J. Lyon of Utah State University, Editor of *Western American Literature*, advised and encouraged me toward a stronger essay on Stephen Crane's Western stance.

As I began the final writing and revising needed to make this book, Dr. Herbert Richardson, Editor of The Edwin Mellen Press, offered excellent organizing suggestions.

One other debt -- to Eleny K. Deamer, my wife -- is evidenced by another page.

Publication Acknowledgments

Some chapters of this book were originally published, in somewhat different versions, as follows:

"Thoreau: Walking Toward England." In *The Westering Experience in American Literature: Bicentennial Essays*. Ed. Merrill Lewis and L. L. Lee. Bellingham: Western Washington University Press, 1977. Pp. 85-93.

"Hawthorne's Dream in the Forest." In *Western American Literature*, 13 (Winter , 1979), 327-339.

"The Westering Experience in Fulton County, Indiana: An Historical Study in Midwestern American Culture." In *MidAmerica VIII*. Ed. David D. Anderson. East Lansing, Michigan: The Midwestern Press, 1981. Pp. 151-160.

"Stephen Crane and the Western Myth." In *Western American Literature*, 7 (Summer, 1972), 111-123.

"Remarks on the Western Stance of Stephen Crane." In *Western American Literature*, 15 (Summer, 1980), 123-141.

"The American Dream and the Romance Tradition in American Fiction: A Literary Study of Society and Success in America." In *Journal of American Culture*, 2 (Spring, 1979), 5-16. And in *Onward and Upward: Essays on the Self-Made American*. Ed. Thomas D. Clark. Bowling Green, Ohio: Bowling Green University Popular Press, 1979. Pp. 5-16.

CHAPTER 1

Dreams and Directions:
American Myths of Place

It is not down on any map; true places never are.
-- Melville, *Moby Dick*

I learned this, at least, by my experiment: that if one advances confidently in the direction of his dreams, and endeavors to live the life which he has imagined, he will meet with a success unexpected in common hours.
-- Thoreau, *Walden*

This is a book about place in America. More exactly, it is a book about American myths of place and about the ways in which certain American places have, historically, become associated with certain American myths. Most importantly, perhaps, it is a book which seeks to show how the myths associated with certain American places are vividly dramatized in the writings and often in the very lives of some of our major literary, historical, and philosophical figures.

As a study of American myths of place, this book is, intrinsically, also a study of the culture which has given rise to, and which continues to support, these myths -- for my focus is upon myth as a *collective* belief which usually has as much, or more, to do with a culture's aspirations and wish fulfillments as it has to do with realities. And it is a study of the American dream -- to the extent that the American dream is, as I hold, a cluster of myths which happen, mainly, to be myths of place. I am of course making no claim to having covered all American places which have generated certain myths -- which myths do themselves, as I believe, give rise to certain distinct, unique consciousnesses. And certainly I am making no claim to having described *all* of the myths comprising the American dream. But there is an effort here to study with thoroughness the myths of place which are identified and considered.

There is an effort, also, to show how American myths of place are in essentially historical ways indigenous not simply to certain geographical areas but also to the geographical relation, or *direction*, held by these areas with respect to the rest of the United States and, equally importantly, to Europe -- and especially to England.

New England as a myth of place -- as a region with a distinct consciousness and point of view -- clearly begins, for example, with England. For while Emerson's dictum that "The American is only the continuation of the English genius into new conditions, more or less propitious,"[1] does not directly apply to all American places, it definitely *does* apply to New England. "The true Bostonian" -- as Henry Adams affirmed -- "always knelt in self-abasement before the majesty of English standards; far from concealing it as a weakness, he was proud of it as his strength."[2]   Even Thoreau, whose aversion -- Emerson said -- "from English and European manners and tastes almost reached contempt,"[3] unknowingly affirmed in his literature and embodied in his life (as the following chapter aims to show) the essential values and the essential traits which Emerson himself discovered and praised in the English gentleman.   And it was by way of cogently questioning and qualifying the American westering experience which his countrymen were so restlessly pursuing that Thoreau himself ended up affirming the values and embodying the traits of the Englishman.   I mean, in other words, to say that New England as a myth of place embodies a deep tension and contradiction between America's Western and Adamic myths of separation, freedom, and self-creation and the refined, aristocratic values, customs, and traditions of English society and English culture.   What emanates from New England as place, and what vivifies the New England consciousness, is a continuous qualifying of the blatant, strident celebration of America's Western myth such as one finds, for example, in the American Midwest.   Even in Concord, Emerson claimed to have found but one *man*:   Henry David Thoreau.   The only other place where it is clear that Emerson found *men*, and there in good number, was England -- this in spite of his own electric urgings of his countrymen toward manly independence and "Self-Reliance."

Historically, then, the New Englander, and especially the New England writer, was in truth a *new* Englander -- which is to say that while he was of course fully conscious of his American-ness (of his status as a new man in a new world), he found himself yearning at the same time toward the attractive, refined society and culture of his Old Home. In spite of his almost strident patriotism, for example, a disillusioned Hawthorne found himself writing from England (in 1857) to his friend Horatio Bridge and confessing that he would not really regret what seemed to be an imminent dissolution of the Union. For "we have no country -- at least, none in the sense an Englishman has a country. I never conceived, in reality, what a true and warm love of country is till I witnessed it in the breasts of Englishmen. The States are too various and too extended to form really one country."[4] Perhaps the most revealing aspect of this statement is the fact that it comes from a New Englander who, temperamentally, rivalled Thoreau in his steadfast determination to resist the Anglophilia so typical of the New England and particularly of the Boston area. And the last chapter of this book will show that in *Our Old Home* Hawthorne adamantly continued his resistance to Anglophilia. Yet it bears remembering that *as an artist* Hawthorne began his career with a remarkable story, "My Kinsman, Major Molineux," which is unique in American literature as a nightmare vision of the American Revolution as an act of parricide. Tellingly enough, too, one witnesses Hawthorne struggling at the end of his career to complete a romance about a lost American heir to an English estate. And while Emerson immortalized "the spirit of '76" in his "Concord Hymn," he also concluded his book on *English Traits* with the assertion that "The American system is more democratic, more humane; yet the American people do not yield better or more able men" and with the further assertion that "The [English] power of performance has not been exceeded--the creation of value. The English have given importance to individuals, a principal end and fruit of every society. Every man is allowed and encouraged to be what he is."[5]

Why then did we have a Revolution? This is the question quickening the New Englander's conscience and consciousness which could be answered only tragically, or not at all. As a following chapter aims to show, it is a question implicit, too, in Hawthorne's "My Kinsman, Major Molineux," a story written long before Hawthorne actually travelled to England. There is, quite simply, in "My Kinsman, Major Molineux" a vivid dramatization of the American Revolution as a "Faustian pact, [a] bargain with the Devil," which Leslie A. Fiedler claims "our authors have always felt as the essence of the American experience."[6]   For surely "My Kinsman, Major Molineux" is rivalled only by "Young Goodman Brown" and by *The Scarlet Letter* as being the most *gothic* of Hawthorne's works, and, more than either of these, it is a graphic illustration of Fiedler's thesis that "the guilt which underlies the gothic and motivates its plots is the guilt of the revolutionary haunted by the (paternal) past which he has been striving to destroy; and the fear that possesses the gothic and motivates its tone is the fear that in destroying the old ego-ideals of Church and State, the West has opened a way for the inruption of darkness: for insanity and the disintegration of the self."[7]

It is, however, not simply the image and the heritage of England which stands behind and largely defines New England as a myth of place: it is also New England's Puritan heritage. Just as the New Englander's response to America's westering dream -- to the Adamic myth of freedom and rebirth in a pristine natural world *beyond* the frontier -- found him knowingly or unknowingly, willingly or unwillingly, turning to the English gentleman as an embodiment of the ideal man and the ideal way of living after all, so too did New England's Puritan heritage condition for the New Englander any unqualified celebration of the American myth of the West. The world views, or ontologies, inhering in American Puritanism and in the American Western myth could not, in fact, be more sharply or more completely opposed -- even though the Puritans themselves were confronted by at least one antinomian, westering-minded colonist -- Anne Hutchinson -- who questioned the Puritan ontology. Most compellingly of all, of course, one sees the tensions and contradictions between America's Puritan heritage and America's Western and Adamic myths dramatized in the life and writings of Nathaniel Hawthorne. While Thoreau, for example, cogently and tellingly questioned the *quality* of his countrymen's westering experience, Hawthorne somberly and tragically questioned even the human *possibility* of America's westering dream -- a dream which, as Hawthorne well knew, his own Puritan ancestors would have seen not just as hopelessly naive but as evil, and as essentially mad. Yet, as Chapter 3 is meant to show, one side of Hawthorne's own nature -- the creative, artistic side -- did in fact dream the American westering dream, created compelling, independent, strong-willed heroines who followed the footsteps of Anne Hutchinson. And in at least one dramatic action of his own life, Hawthorne went a step further in new-world hopefulness than even Emerson or Thoreau: when he joined the utopian experiment of Brook Farm.

I see the New England place-myth, of all the American myths of place, as being the most richly complex and ambivalent and suggestive in the stance that it takes toward the world and toward the American dream. In many ways this complexity and tension and suggestiveness is epitomized, for example, in the antitheses which Henry Adams develops between "Quincy" and "Boston" in the early chapters of *The Education of Henry Adams*. The boy of Quincy relished nature, wildness, and what Thoreau celebrated and praised as "a *purely* sensuous life"[8] with an intensity equalling that of Thoreau himself. "To the boy Henry Adams, summer was drunken"; it was "tropical license," "sensual living," "the multiplicity of nature." Summer was country and Quincy. The counter-image and counter-balance ("only seven miles away") was Boston: Boston State House, Beacon Hill, Mount Vernon Street, the First Church -- all embodying "that eighteenth-century inheritance which [Henry Adams] took with his name."[9] For Henry Adams, the "two modes of life and thought, balanced like lobes of the brain," imaged by these two place-symbols -- Quincy and Boston -- came as no chance occurrence: they were themselves indigenous to, and inseparable from, the climate and the place of New England itself:

> The chief charm of New England was harshness of contrasts and extremes of sensibility -- a cold that froze the blood, and a heat that boiled it . . . . [T]he charm was a true and natural child of the soil, not a cultivated weed of the ancients. The violence of the contrast was real and made the strongest motive of education. The double exterior nature gave life its relative values . . . . Town [Boston] was winter confinement, school, rule, discipline; . . . above all else, winter represented the desire to escape and go free. Town was restraint, law, unity. Country, only seven miles away, was liberty, diversity, outlawry, the endless delight of mere sense impressions given

by nature for nothing, and breathed by boys without knowing it.[10]

Telling and effective as these counter-images and place-symbols are, we should nevertheless remember, as Adams himself confesses, that they are not entirely exact and true: the Adams tradition, "that eighteenth-century inheritance which [Henry Adams] took with his name," really belonged after all to Quincy, and not to Boston. It was at Quincy, for example, that "the President," John Quincy Adams ("close on eighty"), led his rebellious six-year-old grandson "near a mile on a hot summer morning over a shadeless road . . . to school." In other words, Quincy represented not only "the multiplicity of nature" but also Henry Adams' own eighteenth-century Puritan inheritance of resistance, truth, duty, and law. "Resistance to something was the law of New England nature" -- and what becomes clear to the growing boy who, at ten, had already learned why "the dead President," his grandfather, "would have been out of place" at his own Eulogy delivered "to an assemblage of Bostonians in the heart of mercantile Boston" is that the resistance is to Boston itself: "Quincy had always been right, for Quincy represented a moral principle -- the principle of resistance to Boston."[11]

Boston was to be resisted because of its tendency too easily to compromise the values and the standards of New England's Puritan heritage. It was in Boston, and not in Quincy, that the Puritan was giving way to the Yankee -- moral principles succumbing to acquisitive, mercantile self-interests. In directly personal terms, Boston was for Henry Adams identified with "the other grandfather" -- not with the intensely principled, restless-minded former President who had been "the eighteenth century, as an actual and living companion," but with the wealthy Brooks grandfather who died "bequeathing what was supposed to be the largest estate in Boston." More directly and more personally still, "the inherited feud between Quincy and State Street" was epitomized in Adams' father's political resistance to "the slave-power [which] over-shadowed all the great Boston interests." The entire family of Charles Francis Adams, for that matter, was of course "anti-slavery by birth, as their name was Adams and their home was Quincy"; and as for the boy of only ten: "his face was already fixed, and his heart was stone, against State Street." There is clear significance, too (and for a writer as highly conscious as Adams *this* had to be a fully conscious action), in the fact that the grown-up Henry Adams did not use the Brooks part of his christened name. And no reader of *The Education* can take very seriously the author's wondering if the boy, had he known what the future had in store, might "have quitted his eighteenth-century, his ancestral prejudices, his abstract ideals, his semi-clerical training, and the rest, in order to perform an expiatory pilgrimage to State Street, and ask for the fatted calf of his grandfather Brooks and a clerkship in the Suffolk Bank."[12]

This intense opposition and conflict as imaged by the Quincy/Boston place-symbols is immensely important not just for what it reveals about Henry Adams' -- and New England's -- own heritage, and not just for the far-reaching influences that it exerted on Adams' own life and writings, but also because of the ways that it relates the New England myth of place to the other American myths of place which are studied in this book. And it is Henry Adams himself -- as a classic American historian -- who helps to explain what I mean. For in his *History of the United States of America during the Administrations of Jefferson and Madison* Adams comprehensively and penetratingly examines the historical and cultural consequences of an entire nation's obsessive commitment to Wealth and to Progress, to economic aggrandizement and to self-interested enterprise, such as his own ancestors had as a matter of duty and principle resisted in Boston. The relation between Boston and the Midwest, and the Far West, and even the South, came, as Adams incisively demonstrates, with the kind of colonization, with the kind of westering experience, which characterized the new Jeffersonian, democratic, progressive society of 1800:

> From Lake Erie to Florida, in long, unbroken line, pioneers were at work, cutting into the forests with the energy of so many beavers, and with no more express moral purpose than the beavers they drove away. The civilization they carried with them was rarely illumined by an idea; they sought room for no new truth, and aimed neither at creating, like the Puritans, a government of saints, nor, like the Quakers, one of love and peace; they left such experiments behind them, and wrestled only with the hardest problems of frontier life . . . . Greed for wealth, lust for power, yearning for the blank void of savage freedom . . . -- these were the fires which flamed under the caldron of American society.[13]

It can be argued -- as my chapter on the westering experience in Fulton County, Indiana, does in fact argue -- that the fires which Adams saw flaming in 1800 have, since then, flamed continuously in American society, to greater or to lesser degrees in certain American places. And it is, I believe, the extents to which these flames are either accepted, and even celebrated, or resisted and protested against that defines the major American myths of place which, historically, were created by the Westward Movement of American pioneers. Philosophically, ontologically, that is to say, Thoreau was certainly right in affirming that "frontiers are not east or west, north or south" but "wherever a man *fronts* a fact";[14] historically, though, as Thoreau himself was keenly aware, the *direction* of the frontier in America was unquestionably westward. And it is, in a very direct and basic way, Americans' stance toward the frontier, toward the West, and toward their own westering experience that has defined their character, their culture, and their myths of place. There is, for example, an absolute, irreconcilable difference between Henry David Thoreau's New Englander's view that the West "is but another name for the Wild" (that is, for an intense, original *way* of living) and Frederick Jackson Turner's Midwesterner's view that, historically, "The West was another name for opportunity."[15] Thoreau's principled resistance to the acquisitive, materialistic character of America's Westward Movement and his moral and metaphysical definition of the true West as a proper *way* of living ("a life of simplicity, independence, magnanimity, and trust")[16] characterized not only Thoreau but also the life-stance inhering in the New England place-myth generally. Sadly, and even tragically, Turner's belief that what the West *actually* meant to historic westering Americans was "free land" and "opportunity" has, on the evidence, been eminently true of Turner's own Midwest.

While Turner would not have taken kindly to Henry Adams's assertion that the American colonization of 1800 was characterized by pioneers "in long, unbroken line . . . cutting into the forests with the energy of so many beavers, and with no more express moral purpose than the beavers they drove away," he would have been hard put to have shown what in his own writings -- in his own analyses of the American westering experience -- argued against Adams's assertion. For if "the Great West" is defined as "an area of free land" (or, more exactly, as that region which, historically, experiences "the transforming influences of free land") and if the pioneering experience itself is defined in terms of free, equal economic "opportunity" -- and these *were* Turner's definitions[17] -- then man's relation to land becomes profane and society itself becomes sterile, secularized, and, as Henry Adams charges in his *History*, without moral purpose. Democracy, as Turner so fondly stressed, may indeed develop in direct response, or proportion, to the freedom of opportunity provided by the free lands -- but it will be the barren, strictly economic democracy tellingly defined by Richard Hofstadter as "a democracy in cupidity."[18] There are times, to be sure, when Turner himself seems to be on the verge of identifying and exposing the moral issues and questions intrinsic to his conception of the historic frontiersman and of the historic frontier experience -- as when he notes that the West was "a region of ideals, mistaken or not"; or when he notes that the buoyant, self-confident, and self-assertive drive of the West toward "a new type of democracy" contained "elements of evil and elements of good."[19] Essentially, though, Turner not only approved of but also celebrated the ideal which he claimed was "the Western man's ideal": the "self-made man."[20] This bears stressing for the simple reason that Turner *is* in point of fact right in what he says about the history of the American westering experience -- at least insofar as that experience applies to the American Midwest. What must be seen as a willful avoidance on Turner's part of the shallowness of the ideals generated by, or inhering in, the historic frontiersman's rush for "free lands" does not alter the fact that these were, and are, ideals indigenous at least to the American Midwest. Certainly the ideal of the self-made man and its concomitant ideals of enterprise, progress, wealth, and material success are the ideals which energized the pioneers of Fulton County, Indiana -- as revealed by the narratives of original settlers studied in Chapter 7. As a resident of Fulton County, and as a self-employed businessman in its county seat of Rochester, I can say with confidence that such values still drive, still define this society. To Thoreau's question ("What aims more lofty have they than the prairie dogs?"),[21] to Adams's question -- or, that is, to New England's question -- of the moral purpose of nineteenth-century Midwestern pioneering, Fulton County people appear only to have the gospel preached by an original settler and early sheriff, Benjamin C. Wilson: "It is progress and improvement that makes wealth." And of course it was Wilson's Midwestern American dream, voiced in 1875, that "the coming generation will far excel the present in wealth and personal enterprise."[22] Fulfillment of the dream, significantly enough, was to be looked for in the form of a train ("a through-line railroad") -- the same train which Thoreau saw muddying Walden Pond, which Faulkner saw destroying the Mississippi wilderness, and which Stephen Crane saw robbing the dignity of a heroic marshal of Yellow Sky.

The point is simply the aridity of a democracy of strictly economic individualism and of a society -- the society of the American Midwest -- committed to the ideal of the self-made man. It is significant that as major an apologist of nineteenth-century American colonization and of the American frontier as Turner saw no hero, no social ideal, engendered by America's westering experience *other* than the self-made man. For clearly the Midwestern ideal of the self-made man is a sharply limited, a shallow ideal -- especially in its contrast to the New England ideal of the gentleman: the *English* gentleman, that is -- the man whom American observers in England found uniting Thoreau's "wildness" (strength, energy, independence, originality) *and* refinement (manners, taste, learning). "They [Englishmen] are oppressive with their temperament," said Emerson in *English Traits* -- "and all the more that they are refined."[23] As for Turner's westering self-made man, however, he is really a member of that American progress-minded class of men whom John Crowe Ransom -- speaking in defense of the American South -- has cuttingly, but accurately, referred to as "men still fascinated by materialistic projects, men in a state of arrested adolescence."[24] "Arrested adolescence," moreover, is just part of the problem: for the self-made man's commitment to "progress and improvement" and to "wealth and personal enterprise" such as Benjamin C. Wilson urged upon his fellow citizens of Fulton County is really, as Ransom stresses, a commitment to industrialism (the railroad which Wilson longed for) -- or, that is, to "a pioneering on principle, and with an accelerating speed."[25]

Part and parcel of the continuous, accelerating "pioneering on principle," which I believe not only characterizes but *is* the place-myth of the American Midwest, is the Midwest's commitment to agriculture *as* business -- a commitment so strong, in fact, that a word has been coined and, in the Midwest, is commonly used to define the concept: agribusiness. Not even Turner, it bears pointing out, was given to any eulogizing of the American farmer from a Jeffersonian, agrarian point of view -- this in spite of (or perhaps because of) Turner's emphasis upon the "free lands" aspect of the frontier experience, and in spite of the fact that the heart of the pioneering process was, for him, the first settlement by farmers. Turner, in short, saw the farmers as capitalists, as businessmen. He saw correctly. This is to say that a Jeffersonian, agrarian democracy has not historically been a part of, and is not today a part of, the myth of the American Midwest. As a practicing Realtor in Fulton County, Indiana, who, on a nearly daily basis, witnesses farms being conveyed -- by sheriff's or marshall's sales or otherwise -- to various lending institutions and agencies, I know for a fact that a truly agrarian tradition is neither respected nor *lived*, has actually never existed, in this Midwestern place. Of all the place-myths examined in this book, the myth of the Midwest is the thinnest, the least complex, the least fructifying -- embodying as it does a mindless and a vain pioneering on principle rather than an effort (as with New England) to extend and to integrate the metaphorical meanings of the frontier; or (as with the Far West) to go *beyond* the frontier; or (as with the South) to repudiate the frontier and pioneering on principle in favor of a conservative, refined, tradition-centered, European- and English-oriented way of living.

Perhaps the heart of the Midwest's problem is the problem which Emerson identified and warned Americans against in "Self-Reliance": "Virtues are, in the popular estimate, rather the exception than the rule. There is the man *and* his virtues. Men do what is called a good action...much as they would pay a fine in expiation of daily non-appearance on parade. Their works are done as an apology or extenuation of their living in the world."[26] Playing, at an ever-accelerating rate, the game of success and progress -- pioneering on principle -- is, in the American Midwest, the self-made man's expiation for living in the world. It is a severe price for something which, as Emerson stressed, should be an intrinsic right. Precisely to avoid this price, American history, American culture, and the lives and works of major American writers all reveal a need and an effort to generate, to create other American myths of place. Stephen Crane, for example, had several quests in mind when he left for the West -- the Far West -- in 1895: he wanted, as he said, "to be in a blizzard of the plains" and to "see a cowboy ride";[27] he also clearly wanted to experience physical danger and to test himself against it. These wishes and others were more than rewarded. One thing that Crane was clearly *not* seeking, however, was to become a progressive, competitive, successful self-made man. As my chapters on Stephen Crane -- especially "Stephen Crane and the Western Myth" -- aim to show, a central impulse behind Crane's very journey to the West was a wish to escape what he called in his Galveston sketch "the great elemental facts of American life."[28] He was seeking a true West -- correctly defined, I believe, by Leslie A. Fiedler as an "alteration of consciousness"[29] -- and not a *mid*-West. It was the Midwest and the Midwestern myth of Progress, "the march of this terrible century" (symbolically epitomized for Crane by "the terrible and almighty trolley car"),[30] that he was quite literally fleeing. The flight was successful: Crane did in fact find -- that is, he *experienced* -- the true West, the Far West, which he was seeking. This profoundly changed his vision and his literature, causing him to develop an essentially Western stance toward the world and to formalize -- both in his life and in his writings -- his own resolute, heroic code of life. This is to say that the "moody," "profoundly discouraged," "deeply despondent" young man wearing "grey clothes" ("a flannel shirt and a slovenly apology for a necktie" and even "gloves") whom Willa Cather saw and sought out during the few days that he spent in Lincoln, Nebraska, in February of 1895 was a man who was not yet in, who had not yet attained, a Far West -- as Cather herself (then "just off the range" and a Junior at the University) clearly realized.[31] The strikingly changed and energized young man whom Ford Madox Ford witnessed, a couple of years later, wearing "cowboy breeches and no coat," "wagg[ing] in his hand an immense thing that he called a gun and that we should call a revolver," and "boast[ing] about what heroes in the Far West were capable of" -- dreaming, perhaps, even then of the ranch in Texas that we know he later wanted to buy

-- was a man geographically in England, at Oxted, Surrey. Emotionally and philosophically, and creatively too, he was, however, in the American Far West. The New York Kid, a clear Crane-surrogate in Crane's fine Western story "The Five White Mice," is in simple fact not really different from the "almost fabulous Billy the Kid" who appeared before Ford in England. Nor was Crane's "almost fabulous" Western role-playing the mere posturing which Ford mistakenly claimed. It embodied a Western-change in Crane's vision of life; it dramatized his newly adopted Western stance toward the world.

The life and the writings of Stephen Crane illustrate, in other words, that the myth of the West -- the *far* West -- is the least geographically definable of American myths of place. It is indeed the "alteration of consciousness" argued by Fiedler in *The Return of the Vanishing American*; it is achieved more than it is found; it is an escape *and* a confrontation; it is Thoreau's ideal man (pre-eminently the "I" of *Walden*) "fronting a fact"; it is Stephen Crane confronting new landscapes, new peoples, and new cultures as he travelled from Lincoln, Nebraska, to San Antonio and on to Mexico City. To follow Crane from Lincoln to San Antonio and to Mexico City -- that is, to read closely the writings, including the letters, evoked and inspired by this journey -- is quite literally to transcend the Midwest and to discover the Far West. As with Thoreau and with Crane, however, there must be a yearning desire and a courageous, disciplined effort to achieve a true, or a far, West. There must be a willingness to go beyond the Midwestern myth of progress, of pioneering on principle, beyond the frontier itself -- toward a truly westering experience. For what Thoreau realized while living at Walden and what Crane realized while living in England is that the American dream of the West does not inhere in a literal frontier: it inheres in a spiritual *crossing* of the frontier, in a fronting of primordial reality, in an achieved change in consciousness. I see this as the essential, paramount difference between the myths of the Midwest and of the Far West. The last goal or quest in the minds of Fulton County, Indiana, pioneers -- except for one family from Virginia -- as Chapter 7 aims to show, was achieving a change of consciousness; and in the narratives of original settlers we see, accordingly, no aspiration whatever toward the creating of any new relation to the world: to the new land or even to the original inhabitants -- the Potawatomi Indians

-- of the new land. Their impulse, their goal was just the opposite: to transform the new land, the Territory, into their preconceived notion, or image, of what an improved, progressive, mercantile America should be. And William A. Ward's anguished memory of witnessing, as a boy of nine, "boyhood playmates and staunch friends" being marched single-file through the little frontier town of Rochester -- "driven like cattle from their native land, to a place [Kansas] selected for them by the Government" -- is but an exception proving the rule. "For more than a mile I followed them [the Potawatomi] out of town fully determined that I would go with them, my mother following and as much determined that I should return home."[32] Whether he knew it or not, Ward had gone, at this point, at least half of the way toward becoming an archetypal American protagonist, a Thoreau or Leatherstocking or Huckleberry Finn or Isaac McCaslin: certainly the episode which he recalls is an arresting historic parallel to the archetypal story which Fiedler claims for our classic literature: "the old, old fable of the White outcast and the noble Red Man joined together against home and mother, against the female world of civilization."[33] But, again, Ward's story is, simply and tragically, the poignant exception proving the rule: in clear accordance with the settlers' wishes, the Potawatomi were efficiently and entirely removed from Fulton County, and it is not recorded than any white settler other than this nine-year-old boy lamented the Removal or wished to join the Indians in *their* westering experience -- a Trail of Death -- as they were marched to Kansas. The settlers wanted the Indians' lands (Turner's "free lands"), of course; but it is equally clear, I believe, that the Indian people embodied a different world-view, a different ontology and a different consciousness, which was frightening, which the settlers had neither the open-mindedness nor the courage to confront. This, again, is in striking contrast to the open, courageous, magnanimous *Western* stance toward life and toward alien peoples and cultures which Stephen Crane achieved as he journeyed through Nebraska, Texas, and Mexico. The Indians of Mexico, for example, Crane found, approvingly, to be "utterly distinct": "The Indian remains the one great artistic figure . . . . [H]e fits into green grass, the low white walls, the blue sky, as if his object was not so much to get possession of some centavos as to compose the picture . . . . [Y]ou can imagine anything at all about him[,] for his true character is impenetrable." And because of the Indians' different life-stance, consciousness, and world-view, their "faces" -- as Crane perceived -- "have almost a certain smoothness, a certain lack of pain, a serene faith. I can feel the superiority of their contentment."[34]

I do not wish to argue, as Leslie A. Fiedler does, that achieving a truly westering experience, a true *crossing* of the frontier into the Far West, necessarily means entering "the world of the Indian: the world not of an historical past, but of the eternally archaic one."[35] I do, however, wish to argue that the unique consciousness emanating from the American myth of the Far West is vivified by the view of the world and of reality characteristic of many American Indian cultures -- by which I mean an unsentimental, sacral view of primordial energy *as* reality; a religious view which sees man's sensuous and aesthetic apprehension of the external, elemental, natural world not as a symbol of God, but as God. It is precisely the view implicit in Thoreau's impatient questioning if we are "to be put off and amused in this life, as it were with a mere allegory"[36] -- proving again, as he so often did, that one can be a Westerner without actually living in the West. And it is the view dramatized in Stephen Crane's superlative Western story titled "A Man and Some Others" wherein primordial reality and primordial energy inhere both in the vast, open, unhumanized Western landscape ("mesquit spread from horizon to horizon") -- a landscape "which surely bears a message of the inconsequence of individual tragedy" -- *and* in the defiant blaze of passion with which a "grimy sheep-herder" named Bill embodies "the dignity of last defeat, the superiority of him who stands in his grave."[37] Clearly, there is in the mythic American Far West *no* expiation for living in the world; there is, instead, rough, intense, vital, courageous, self-reliant living in a real -- which is to say, an elemental, natural, primordial (as opposed to a merely social or "civilized") -- world. This is to say, too, that in the final analysis there *is*, after all, a geographic definition, or dimension, to the myth of the Far West; for the fronting -- which is to say, the *experience* -- of primordial reality which is intrinsic to the Far West place-myth does not easily occur in the farmers' and merchants' world east of the Mississippi: in garden-like farms and in commercialized cities. It has yet to be claimed that cowboys can be found in Massachusetts or in Illinois -- still less in Mississippi or in Georgia. The

cowboy belongs to the open range, to deserts, to plains, and to mountains --
as Jack Potter cannot *be* Jack Potter in the Eastern, civilized world of the
"great Pullman" or as Stephen Crane himself could not forego his yearning to
touch primordial reality in order to become a "man of fashion" for Nellie
Crouse. And of course the cowboy with his rough, primitivist, unsentimental,
masculine, unaffected, and magnanimous way, or code, of life stands as an
archetype, or as an avatar, at the center of the myth of the Far West -- just as
New England's English gentleman, the Midwest's self-made man, and the
South's Cavalier gentleman embody and symbolize the aspirations, ideals,
and values of the place-myths with which they are associated.

In its religious, Thoreauvian view of man's capacity to front and to
apprehend sacred reality, and in its bold insistence upon man's capacity for
courageous, magnanimous, heroic conduct, the myth of the Far West is
finally, too, the most hopeful of American myths of place. As myth, the Far
West embodies a tough-minded, realistic, anti-social, anti-cultural but at the
same time strongly affirmative and religious view of man's capacities and of
life's possibilities. It is tempting, then, especially for Americans, to say that
the myth of the Far West is the American myth of place which most nearly
accords with the American dream itself -- but of course we need to remind
ourselves, and this book aims to illustrate, that the American dream is such a
cluster of divergent, conflicting, and even desperately unacknowledged myths
that it is impossible to make such a claim with any certainty. What *can* be
said with reasonable certainty is that the inherent hopefulness of the Far
West place-myth derives substantially and directly from the Adamic vision of
life -- a vision of transcendence, of an absolute West of spiritual rebirth, of an
achieved new innocence and new consciousness -- which, since Thomas
Jefferson at least, has been *one* of the ways that Americans have visioned and
yearned for the American West.

Exactly this Adamic vision of life, of Thoreau's "waking dream"
(defined in *A Week on the Concord and Merrimack Rivers* and achieved in
Walden), of the rebirth into "new youth" which D. H. Lawrence famously
defined as "the true myth of America,"[38] is what is lost in the American myth
of the South. It is, if we look to the fictional world of our greatest Southern
writer: William Faulkner. For in spite of the fact that Faulkner has,

amazingly enough, in his story of "The Bear" created one of American literature's greatest dramatizations of an initiation into the Adamic vision of life (surpassed, in my own opinion, only by Thoreau's *Walden*), the vision of life that is finally rendered in Faulkner's fiction (and this includes "The Bear") is an anguished, despairing, tragic vision of man as time-bound, entrapped, and doomed. It is only as a boy, we should remember, that Isaac McCaslin touches primordial reality, achieves "pride and humility," a new consciousness, and a rebirth into innocence and grace. Part 4 of "The Bear" itself and the following story in *Go Down, Moses*, "Delta Autumn," make it painfully clear that *as a man* Isaac was as trapped and as doomed and victimized by time and by history as any other Faulkner character, including Quentin Compson. The *doom*, as Jean-Paul Sartre, Robert Penn Warren, and other important Faulkner critics have pointed out, is consciousness itself: consciousness, that is, of *time* -- a consciousness which, to be sure, should be sharply distinguished from the Adamic, transcending, sacral, and *Western* consciousness such as Isaac achieved when, in the wilderness, he relinquished his watch and compass, leaving both time and (geographic) place, and gained a vision of Old Ben. Isaac's consciousness of transcendence was a temporary experience; his consciousness of time -- by definition, for Faulkner, a consciousness of the *past*, of *was* -- became permanent: this is where fate and doom and tragedy appear in Faulkner's view of the world. For while man may be said to live within time, it is equally and -- for Faulkner -- more importantly true that man carries time *within himself*,[39] within his consciousness. Indeed Faulkner for his part has expressed a disbelief in the existence of time at all "except in the momentary avatars of individual people."[40] Thus, as Mr. Compson tells his son Quentin III, "a man is the sum of his misfortunes"; and "was" is "the saddest word of all there is nothing else in the world its not despair until time its not even time until it was."[41] This is simply a boxed-in, tragic ontology which locates time and reality within the human consciousness; which, as Sartre has stressed, sees man's *present* as "unspeakable," "essentially catastrophic," "leaking at every seam";[42] and which decisively destroys man's dream of freedom, of hope, of any sense of a future. "One day" (as Mr. Compson himself admits) "you'd think that misfortune would get tired, but then time is your misfortune."[43]

On the evidence, clearly, of William Faulkner's vision, of his ontology of time, it can be said that the Southerner's expiation for living in the world -- living, that is, in the American South -- is not the material, economic success required by the Midwestern place-myth of its archetypal hero, the self-made man (precisely to *this* ideal does the myth of the South stand as a cogent rebuke): the expiation of the Southerner is consciousness itself. In each case -- Midwest and South -- the price is of course extreme. For however different they may be as social and as psychological processes, the self-made man's expiatory success and the Southerner's expiatory time-consciousness are equally absolute as life-denying entrapments. "I do not wish to expiate," as Emerson famously said, "but to live."[44] How ironic and how moving, too, it is, then, that the *myth* of the South -- as cogently elucidated, for example, by the Southern writers of *I'll Take My Stand: The South and the Agrarian Tradition* -- is an affirmation of the South's "genuine" and "native humanism" ("a culture, the whole way in which we live, act, think, and feel")[45] and a repudiation of the prevailing American tendency to expiate rather than to live! It is moving because -- in my own estimation, at least -- the *myth* is true: the Southern Agrarians were right in insisting, as their New England alter ego Emerson also did, that the end of life is living, not expiating. And, indeed, the true Southerner's special expiatory time-consciousness comes into play precisely from his tenacious belief -- as with Faulkner and with the Agrarians -- not only that the Southern myth is true as a cluster of essential human ideals but also that it is true as history: that the image of the older South which they hold up as a rebuke to the prevailing American way of life *did* in fact exist in the historical Southern past. Hence the Southerner's obsession with, his preference of, the past and -- as with Faulkner's characters, at least -- his inevitable, continuous living of his past (his personal past *and* his regional past) even in his present.

Although Southerners themselves may be entrapped, doomed, by the special time-consciousness -- by time, that is, *as* consciousness -- which is the essential experience rendered in Faulkner's fiction, it is by no means Southerners *only* who are obsessed with the place-myth of the South. Wordsworth, when Emerson visited him in England in 1833, "had much to say of America" -- and he had reservations, too, about the direction that the

American democratic experiment was taking: he feared (as Emerson quotes him) that Americans "are too much given to the making of money" and that "they lack a class of men of leisure -- in short, of gentlemen -- to give a tone of honor to the community."[46] And even as Wordsworth spoke, Americans, both North and South, were busy constructing the legend of the Southern Cavalier gentleman and the myth of an agrarian, aristocratic, genteel South -- constructing the legend and the myth precisely as a counter-image to the grasping acquisitiveness against which Wordsworth warned, and which discerning Americans were beginning to see as the main characteristic of the American westering experience north of the Ohio. Since the morally directionless American colonization of 1800 (as described in Henry Adams' *History*), that is to say, Americans have *needed* the myth of the South just as they have always *needed* the myth of the West -- though for very different and, indeed, opposing reasons. For, at bottom, what the Southern place-myth really embodies is a repudiation of America's historic and prevailing dream of separation from traditional European -- and especially from English -- culture. "The South" -- John Crowe Ransom insists in his lead essay for *I'll Take My Stand* -- "is unique on this continent for having founded and defended a culture which was according to the European principles [establishment, leisure, gentility, amiable and distinguished living] of culture." Further: "England was actually the model employed by the South."[47] Quite aside from the fact that there *is* a historical basis for Ransom's claim, Americans have always (secretly, and sometimes not-so-secretly) been pleased to think of the South in these terms. Since the American Revolution itself, there has, in fact, been a genuine ambivalence within the American mind toward the American dream of separation from the past and from the European principles of culture as described in Ransom's essay -- an ambivalence manifesting itself in a secret, guilt-ridden yearning toward a more distinctive, aristocratic society and way of living. Quite at the same time, of course, there has always been in our society and in our history a vibrant yearning toward the *transcendence* of history and of civilization as embodied in our Adamic and our Western myths. Stephen Crane, it is worth remembering -- profoundly influenced and inspired as he clearly was by our Western myth, and given as he was (after his Western trip) to dramatic

Western role-playing -- displayed at the same time an intense, life-long consciousness of and a deep, usually secret pride in his personal and ancestral status as a gentleman *déclassé*.

Because of its strong orientation toward English culture, the Southern place-myth points, of course, directly to the New England place-myth, which itself has always embodied what Hawthorne called in *Our Old Home* "an unspeakable yearning towards England."[48] Two of the contributors to *I'll Take My Stand*, John Crowe Ransom and Stark Young, laud New England as at least one other American region embodying and defending the way of living and the quality of life -- the "genuine" and "native humanism" -- that the Agrarians themselves were defending for the South. And Thoreau's stricture, in *Walden*, that "There are nowadays professors of philosophy, but not philosophers"[49] summarizes in one sentence practically the entire argument which the Southern Agrarians wanted to make against the disintegrative, dehumanizing effect of America's prevailing commitment, or capitulation, to business, to industrialism, and to Progress. As with Thoreau, what the Agrarians cogently called for was a return to first principles: to a recognition that any serious talk about, any real concern for, *culture* is going to have to get back to the quality of the individual lives that the members of a given society actually live; that a true culture, a genuine humanism, cannot -- as Americans so desperately want to believe -- be created "by pouring in soft materials from the top" ("by all sorts of cultural institutions and endowments")[50] instead of by making the needed change in the very base of the problem: the life-pattern itself. "[I]t is admirable to profess" (that is, "to solve some of the problems of life, not only theoretically, but practically") -- as Thoreau insisted -- "because it was once admirable to live."[51] And the impressive and enviable strength of English culture came, as Emerson clearly saw, from its inherence in the distinctive people themselves and in their way of living: "Their culture is not an outside varnish, but is thorough and secular in families and the race."[52]

In the long run, a study of the vibrant myths of place which inhere in the American experience brings one to a recognition that a strong sense not only of place but also of the *loss* of place -- of severe isolation and of intense loneliness -- likewise inheres, historically and until today, in that experience. And as with our American myths of place, the American sense, or experience, of the loss of place is closely associated with and directly related to the American dream itself. This, at least, is what I aim to show in my study (Chapter 12) of the relationships between the American dream and the Romance tradition in American fiction. Certainly the central tradition in our classic fiction embodies -- which is to say that the fiction itself consistently renders -- an extreme sense of *dis*placement in American life. Huckleberry Finn -- himself the result, as Leslie A. Fiedler rightly contends, "of a terrible break-through of the undermind of America itself"[53] -- no doubt epitomizes the sense of absolute loneliness and the defiant, desperate flight from civilization which characterize the protagonist-heroes of classic American fiction. But Huck is far from alone. This, in itself, speaks urgently and despairingly to our American myths of place and to our American dream -- reminding us that our major fictionists, even when they have most sincerely and most strenuously tried, have been consistently unable to affirm, to fully render, or, in short, to *believe* in the aspirations and the ideals emanating from the place-myths which inhere in the American dream. It is not surprising, of course, that our classic fictionists refuse to affirm a myth as culturally and as humanistically disintegrative as the Midwestern myth of success and of the self-made man. The very intensity with which our fictionists, in their Romances, repudiate the Midwest's myth of material success is, however, surely directly related to the fact that our writers have been, more often than not, haunted and trapped and hurt by this myth in their own lives.

Disturbingly, though, it is not just the place-myth of the Midwest which our classic fiction denies. The intrinsically hopeful and affirmative values and possibilities embodied in the place-myth of the Far West, for example, while not willfully denied, are simply shown to fall short of fulfillment, are not rendered or dramatized as viable human possibilities. The achieved rebirth into an absolute West of transcendence and of "new youth" which Thoreau celebrated in *Walden* is not experienced by any classic protagonist-hero of American fiction. Similarly, the humanistic cultural values embodied in our Southern and in our New England place-myths are in no way willfully denied, but are (as with Faulkner and with Hawthorne) rendered as *lost* to an irretrievable past.

Perhaps, too, as both our Southern and our New England place-myths strongly suggest, that irretrievable past which is the true home of the American dream lies not in America at all, but in England. Such a discovery -- and it *is* the discovery of the famous American observers who are studied in the last chapter of this book -- creates, needless to say, a sense of displacement entirely equal to the experience of homelessness which lies at the heart of our classic fiction. The *English*, as American observers from Irving to Santayana immediately saw, have a home, are dedicated to home-life, to domesticity, and to privacy. The absolute dedication of the English to home-life and to distinction in one's *private* life clearly struck American observers as a pre-eminent, if not *the* pre-eminent English trait; and, in response, they came acutely to feel, to understand, that such a dedication is lacking in American life. It is clear, too, that the American observers -- like our American fictionists, or like the Southern Agrarians, or like New England writers and autobiographers such as Thoreau and Adams -- came to realize that the lack of dedication in America to home-life, to privacy, and to distinguished living is directly related to the burden and to the demands of American democracy itself. I mean, again, the burden and the demands of American democratic and economic individualism, of the Midwestern and Turnerian ideal of the self-made man -- though the point, here, is the extreme sense of placelessness and of alienation which American or Turnerian democracy produces. Without knowing so, as I argue in the following chapter, Thoreau was yearning toward England as he sought and wisely decided to create in himself the ideal man and the ideal way of living which -- as he well knew -- American democracy was not yielding; the last chapter of this book shows other famous Americans yearning in the same direction, and for the same reason, and that very knowingly indeed.

In what direction, then, does the American dream lie? This book does not pretend to know -- though it will be clear that its author has his own preferences among the American myths of place which the following chapters examine. As long as Americans continue to question and to wonder about the place-myths which inhere in the American dream, the dream itself will, as dreams should, remain fluid, open to new possibilities, and resisting of final definition.

Chapter 1

Notes

1. Ralph Waldo Emerson, *The Selected Writings of Ralph Waldo Emerson* (New York: The Modern Library, 1940), p. 541. (From *English Traits*.)
2. Henry Adams, *The Education of Henry Adams* (New York: The Modern Library, 1931), p. 19.
3. Emerson, p. 899. (From "Thoreau.")
4. *The Portable Hawthorne*, ed. Malcolm Cowley (New York: The Viking Press, 1948), p. 626.
5. Emerson, pp. 686, 687.
6. Leslie A. Fiedler, *Love and Death in the American Novel*, 2nd ed. (New York: Dell, 1966), p. 27.
7. *Ibid.*, p. 129.
8. Henry David Thoreau, *A Week on the Concord and Merrimack Rivers* (New York: The American Library, 1961), p. 324.
9. Adams, *The Education*, pp. 8, 9, 3, 7.
10. *Ibid.*, pp. 7-8.
11. *Ibid.*, pp. 12, 13, 7, 21.
12. *Ibid.*, pp. 20, 23, 24, 25, 22.
13. Henry Adams, *History of the United States of America during the Administrations of Jefferson and Madison*, ed. Ernest Samuels (Chicago: The University of Chicago Press, 1967), p. 129.
14. *Walden and Other Writings of Henry David Thoreau*, ed. Brooks Atkinson (New York: The Modern Library, 1937), p. 410.
15. *Ibid.*, p. 613; *Frontier and Section: Selected Essays of Frederick Jackson Turner* (Englewood Cliffs, N.J.: Prentice-Hall, 1961), p. 69.
16. *Walden and Other Writings*, p. 13.
17. *Frontier and Section*, pp. 37, 63, 69.
18. Richard Hofstadter, *The American Political Tradition and the Men Who Made It* (New York: Vintage, 1948), p. viii.
19. *Frontier and Section*, pp. 70, 67.
20. *Ibid.*, p. 69.
21. *The Writings of Henry David Thoreau* (Boston: Houghton Mifflin, 1906), VI, 210.
22. "Fulton County--What I know about its early settlements," *Fulton County Historical Society Quarterly*, 10 (August, 1974): 23, 24.
23. Emerson, p. 685.
24. John Crowe Ransom, "Reconstructed but Unregenerate," in *I'll Take My Stand: The South and the Agrarian Tradition* (New York: Harper & Row, 1962), p. 5.
25. Ransom, p. 15.
26. Emerson, p. 149.
27. Thomas Beer, *Stephen Crane: A Study in American Letters* (New York: Alfred A. Knopf, 1923), p. 113.
28. *Stephen Crane in the West and Mexico*, ed. Joseph Katz (Kent, Ohio: Kent State University Press, 1970), p. 31.

29. Leslie A. Fiedler, *The Return of the Vanishing American* (New York: Stein and Day, 1968), p. 175.
30. *Stephen Crane in the West and Mexico*, p. 36.
31. "When I Knew Stephen Crane," in *Stephen Crane: A Collection of Critical Essays*, ed. Maurice Basan (Englewood Cliffs, N.J.: Prentice-Hall, 1967), pp. 14, 15, 13, 12.
32. "Doings in Fulton County," in *Home Folks: A Series of Stories by Old Settlers of Fulton County, Indiana* (Marceline, Mo.: Walsworth, n.d.), I, p. 6.
33. Fiedler, *The Return*, p. 177.
34. *Stephen Crane in the West and Mexico*, pp. 65-66, 77.
35. Fiedler, *The Return*, p. 175.
36. Thoreau, *A Week*, p. 325.
37. *The Western Writings of Stephen Crane*, ed. Frank Bergon (New York: The New American Library, 1979), pp. 72, 79, 85.
38. *Studies in Classic American Literature* (Garden City, N.Y.: Doubleday, 1951), p. 64.
39. Cf. Olga W. Vickery, *The Novels of William Faulkner: A Critical Interpretation*, 2nd ed. (Baton Rouge: Louisiana State University Press, 1964), p. 260.
40. Taken from Faulkner's 1956 interview with Jean Stein. Quoted in Frederick J. Hoffman, *William Faulkner*, 2nd ed. (New York: Twayne, 1966), p. 21.
41. *The Sound and the Fury* (New York: The Modern Library, 1946), p. 197.
42. Jean-Paul Sartre, "On *The Sound and the Fury*: Time in the Works of Faulkner," in *Faulkner: A Collection of Critical Essays*, ed. Robert Penn Warren (Englewood Cliffs, N.J.: Prentice-Hall, 1966), pp. 90, 88.
43. *The Sound and the Fury*, p. 123.
44. Emerson, p. 149.
45. *I'll Take My Stand*, p. xxvi. (From the twelve Southerners' introductory "Statement of Principles.")
46. Emerson, p. 532. (From *English Traits*.)
47. Ransom, p. 3.
48. *Our Old Home* (Boston and New York: Houghton Mifflin, 1907), p. 19.
49. *Walden and Other Writings*, p. 13.
50. "Introduction: A Statement of Principles," *I'll Take My Stand*, pp. xxv-xxvi, xxv.
51. *Walden and Other Writings*, p. 13.
52. Emerson, p. 685. (From *English Traits*.)
53. Fiedler, *Love and Death*, p. 286.

SECTION I

NEW ENGLAND:
THOREAU, HAWTHORNE, ADAMS

CHAPTER 2

Thoreau: Walking Toward England

In the address which he made at Thoreau's funeral, Emerson spoke of his friend's preference for America and for the American West, saying:

> No truer American existed than Thoreau. His preference of his country and condition was genuine, and his aversation from English and European manners and tastes almost reached contempt. He listened impatiently to news or *bonmots* gleaned from London circles; and though he tried to be civil, these anecdotes fatigued him. The men were all imitating each other, and on a small mold. Why can they not live as far apart as possible, and each be a man by himself? What he sought was the most energetic nature; and he wished to go to Oregon, not to London.[1]

Emerson, of all people, should have been aware of the immense irony in these remarks -- as indeed he probably was, secretly. For whatever Thoreau may have thought of England in contrast to America, Emerson had *been* there, twice; had written a penetrating study, *English Traits*, of English culture and of the English character; and *knew* that if there was a place where "men were all imitating each other" it was America, not England -- that if one sought "the most energetic nature" he should go to London, not to Oregon. And--irony of ironies -- Emerson undoubtedly was also aware that if ever an American existed who -- in his self-sufficiency, eccentricity, independence, bluntness, manliness, refinement, and love of nature and of vitality -- resembled the Englishman, it was Henry David Thoreau. Yet as important and revealing as these ironies are, no student of Thoreau or of Thoreau's relation to American culture has taken note of them. Instead of examining the astonishing evidence in Emerson's book that Thoreau's traits were, after all, *English Traits*, scholars have been content to accept the stereotype of Thoreau as the quintessential, Westward-looking American which Emerson presented in his funeral oration. Needless to say, the acceptance of this stereotype is a severe hindrance to any understanding of the real significance that Thoreau's life and writings have within the general context of American history and culture, and within the specific context of the American myth of the West. For if we persist in ignoring the fact that, whatever *he* may have thought, Thoreau was really an archetypal Englishman rather than an archetypal American frontiersman, we will continue to miss one of the most important and most provocative ironies of the entire American westering experience: the fact that the virtues of the legendary heroes (Frontiersmen, Mountain Men, Cowboys) in America's Western Myth are -- as a long line of famous American observers (including such major American writers as Irving, Cooper, Emerson, Hawthorne, and Henry James) discovered[2] -- actually embodied in that Old World social ideal, the English gentleman.

This is all the more important because, as Emerson suggested and as Edwin Fussell has definitively shown,[3] Thoreau *was* obsessed with the metaphorical and mythical meanings of the American West. "Let me live where I will" -- he announced in "Walking" -- "on this side is the city, on that the wilderness, and ever I am leaving the city more and more, and withdrawing into the wilderness. I should not lay so much stress on this fact, if I did not believe that something like this is the prevailing tendency of my countrymen. I must walk toward Oregon, and not toward Europe. And that way the nation is moving, and I may say that mankind progress from east to west" (*W*, V, 218).[4] Yet however literally true this may have been for his countrymen, we know that taking to the woods -- walking, that is, "toward Oregon, and not toward Europe" -- was a metaphor rather than a fact for Henry Thoreau. He was, in reality, contemptuous of America's Westward Movement -- its blatantly pecuniary motives were, he felt, epitomized by the California Gold Rush ("What a comment, what a satire, on our institutions!" [*W*, IV, 464]) -- and in a personal letter of the same period as "Walking" he bluntly asserted that:

> The whole enterprise of this nation, which is not an upward, but a westward one, toward Oregon, California, Japan etc., is totally devoid of interest to me . . . . It is not illustrated by a thought; it is not warmed by a sentiment; there is nothing in it which one should lay down his life for, nor even his gloves . . . . It is perfectly heathenish, -- a filibustering *toward* heaven by the great western route. No; they may go their way to their manifest destiny, which I trust is not mine [*W*, VI, 210].

We know, too, that when, near the end of his life, and in an attempt to regain his health and to save his life, Thoreau really did travel West he was in no way invigorated or inspired by his actual westering experience. All of which is to say that Thoreau was in search of a West, all right, but that it was *his* West,[5] the West of an inner rather than a literal geography. Indeed, one of the most striking features of Thoreau's genius is unquestionably his perception, long before the frontier had actually closed, that if Americans were ever to realize the American dream of the West they would have to recognize that -- whatever Frederick Jackson Turner later may have thought -- the dream is not inherent in the literal frontier. This is a point worth stressing because most American writers, especially American fictionists, have to this day felt a typically American need to define the mythic West spatially, geographically, in terms of a literal place. Thus, for example, we witness Ernest Hemingway taking off for the *Green Hills of Africa*, and explaining that his journey was necessary because

> A continent ages quickly once we come. The natives live in harmony with it. But the foreigner destroys . . . . A country was made to be as we found it . . . . Our people went to America because that was the place to go then. It had been a good country and we had made a bloody mess of it and I would go, now, somewhere else and as we had always had the right to go somewhere else and as we had always gone . . . . Let the others come to America who did not know that they had come too late . . . . Now I would go somewhere else. We always went in the old days and there were still good places to go.[6]

Perhaps "we had always had the right to go somewhere else" (and certainly "we had always gone"), but Thoreau, at least, knew, and knew at the very time that Americans were most excitedly and most energetically pushing westward, that the frantic American search for "good places," for new frontiers and for fresh (economic) starts, is not an act of freedom, but of its opposite. As he explained in *A Week on the Concord and Merrimack Rivers*,

> The frontiers are not east or west, north or south; but wherever a man *fronts* a fact, though that fact be his neighbor, there is an unsettled wilderness between him and Canada, between him and the setting sun, or, farther still, between him and *it*. Let him build himself a log house with the bark on where he is, *fronting* IT, and wage there an Old French war for seven or

seventy years, with Indians and Rangers, or whatever else may come between him and the reality, and save his scalp if he can [*W*, I, 323-324].

And once he had made his own brave, fructifying decision to "front only the essential facts of life" (*W*, II, 100), Henry Thoreau went, as the world knows, not at all to Oregon, but to Walden Pond, one mile from venerable Concord.

This is clear enough. Yet we should not overlook the fact that -- however challenging was Thoreau's gleeful demonstration that the ideal man, the man of courage, discipline, and integrity, is not the actual frontiersman but the man who "fronts a fact"; and however appropriate were his caustic reminders to his countrymen that the only travel of real value is inward rather than westward ("I have travelled a good deal in Concord") -- the joke was still (as Emerson knew, or should have known) to a considerable extent upon Thoreau himself. For if Thoreau succeeded in showing Americans (those with the courage to read him, at least) how small-minded and timid they were in their attitude toward the American geographic West, he did not thereby free himself from a rather severe parochialism of his own when it came to his understanding of and his evaluating of American culture and the American character. If, as I have suggested, Thoreau *had* travelled to England with Emerson, he would have *found* that ideal man -- the man in whom wildness and refinement are united -- for whom he had searched in vain in American society and in American history.[7] Since the ideal man was not to be found in American society or in American history, Thoreau, with his usual self-sufficiency, wisely decided, we know, to create such a man in himself (pre-eminently, of course, in the idealized, poetic self which speaks in *Walden*). However, what better characterizes Thoreau's essential attitude toward life, for example, than Santayana's description of the Englishman as one who lives "in and by his inner man" and who "thinks the prize of life worth winning, but not worth snatching"? Certainly Thoreau lived and wrote out of a belief, like the Englishman's, that "If you snatch it, as . . . Americans seem inclined to do, you abdicate the sovereignty of your inner man, you miss delight, dignity, and peace; and in that case the prize of life has escaped you."[8] And as for those precise *English Traits* -- practical ability, candor, unsentimentality, integrity, independence, learning, courage, love of privacy and nature and hygiene and health -- which Emerson, Irving, Cooper, James, Santayana, and other Americans found in the Englishman, what do they add up to but to a portrait of Thoreau himself? Emerson habitually referred to his friend Thoreau as *"the* man of Concord"; but he was, if anything, even more impressed by the "invincible stoutness" and the self-sufficiency -- as well as by the devotion to privacy, to hygiene and vitality, and to distinguished living -- that he observed everywhere in the English character:

> I find the Englishman to be him of all men who stands firmest in his shoes. They have in themselves what they value in their horses -- mettle and bottom . . . .
> They dare to displease, nay, they will let you break all the commandments, if you do it natively and with spirit. You must be somebody; then you may do this or that, as you will . . .
> Every man in this polished country consults only his convenience, as much as a solitary pioneer in Wisconsin . . . .
> Of absolute stoutness no nation has more or better examples. They are good at . . . any desperate service which has daylight and honor in it . . . .
> Their culture is not an outside varnish, but is thorough and secular in families and the race. They are oppressive with their temperament, and all the more that they are refined. I have sometimes seen them walk with my countrymen when I was forced to allow them every advantage, and their companions seemed bags of bones.[9]

Nor were Emerson's impressions unique. Irving, too, affirms that he does "not know of a finer race of men than the English gentlemen. Instead of the softness and effeminacy which characterize the men of rank in most countries, they exhibit a union of elegance and strength."[10] And Cooper finds that the Englishmen "are simple, masculine in manner and mind, and highly cultivated," that they "have the merits of courage, manliness, intelligence, and manners."[11]

In all, the American observers from Irving to Santayana were vividly impressed by the fact that what governs the Englishman is, in Santayana's words, "the love of a certain quality of life, to be maintained manfully."[12] The same, it hardly needs to be said, is pre-eminently true of Henry David Thoreau -- his aim in life always being to "have my immortality now, that it be in the *quality* of my daily life" (*J*, III, 351). But what, exactly, is meant by the "quality of life" which both Thoreau and the Englishman love and manfully maintain? For Thoreau, "Life consists with wildness. The most alive is the wildest" (*W*, V, 266); and after a meditation, in "Walking," on the American West, he abruptly announces that "The West of which I speak is but another name for the Wild; and what I have been preparing to say is, that in Wildness is the preservation of the World" (*W*, V, 244). ("Walking" itself was originally entitled "The Wild.") This is immensely important; for it reveals that the West became meaningful for Thoreau only when he spoke of it in terms of the Wild -- as a symbol, that is, for a disciplined, intense *way* of living. And *this* particular Wild West -- Thoreau's West -- was not to be found in the actual American West, but in England -- as Thoreau himself might have realized had he been a little less smugly parochial in his preference for Concord ("the most estimable place in all the world" [*J*, IX, 160]). For if the West of which Thoreau spoke is but another name for the Wild, it can also be shown that the Wild of which he spoke is but another name for the quality of life loved and maintained by the English gentleman. Of course, Thoreau did not refer, usually, to a literal wilderness or to a literal wildness when he spoke of the Wild any more than he referred to a geographic place when he spoke of the West (like his journey to the actual West, his journeys to an actual wilderness, to *The Maine Woods* and to Canada, were disappointing rather than fructifying experiences); nevertheless what he meant by wildness was something very definite indeed. Primarily, as I have indicated, Thoreau had in mind a particular, ideal stance toward life -- a stance devoted to such values as independence, originality, intensity, and vitality -- when he spoke of wildness. "It is in vain," he stressed, "to dream of a wildness distant from ourselves. There is none such . . . . A little more manhood or virtue will make the surface of the globe anywhere thrillingly novel and wild" (*J*, IX, 43). He also noted that "original and independent men are wild, -- not tamed and broken by society" (*J*, II, 448). As for himself, Thoreau wrote in his *Journal* in 1841 that "It does seem as if mine were a peculiarly wild nature, which so yearns toward all wildness. I know of no redeeming qualities in me but a sincere love for some things, and when I am reproved I have to fall back on to this ground" (*J*, I, 296). And by "a sincere love for some things" Thoreau meant his love for the world of nature as it presented itself to his senses -- a religious outlook, in fact ("Therein I am God-propped" [*J*, I, 296]), which stressed, always, the unspeakable importance of preserving health and vitality and of living "a *purely* sensuous life" (*W*, I, 408). In other words, Thoreau's mysticism was not at all Emersonian or Transcendental; rather, it was Oriental, a belief in the divinity of the immediate, sensuously and aesthetically apprehended world.[13] "Are we to be put off and amused in this life," he asked rhetorically and impatiently, "as it were with a mere allegory? Is not Nature, rightly read, that of which she is commonly taken to be the symbol merely? . . . What is it, then, to educate but to develop these divine germs called the senses?" (*W*, I, 408). Even more to the point, Thoreau was -- unlike, say, Emerson or Melville -- essentially uninterested in metaphysics, in God or in another world.[14] In his own life, from beginning to end, he compellingly displayed what Santayana came to love in the English: "contentment in finitude, fair outward ways, manly perfection and simplicity."[15] "One world at a time," he exclaimed in his famous deathbed remark; and in his first book he insisted that "Here or nowhere is our heaven" (*W*, I, 405). Thus, in the simplest terms, if the West equals the Wild, the Wild equals a love of the actual, natural world *and* a love of a certain quality of life which entails an unaffected, disciplined, intense, and vital living in the world. For Thoreau it is always the way one *lives* that counts; "To be a philosopher," as he cogently put it in *Walden*, "is not merely to have subtle thoughts . . . but so to love wisdom as to live according to its dictates, a life of simplicity, independence, magnanimity, and trust." And "it is admirable to profess because it was once admirable to live" (*W*, II, 16).

Thus it is that Thoreau's search for a real philosopher, for a real believer in the doctrine of wildness, for that ideal man whom he found neither in the frontier West nor in the civilized East, *should* have taken him to England. For what the American observers discovered in the English character -- energy, independence, freedom of action, manliness, refinement -- was precisely that cluster of attitudes, virtues, and values which Thoreau referred to as Wildness. Specifically, the observers found that what distinguished the Englishman above all things was, simply, the *way* he lived, what Santayana calls his

> distinction in the way of living. The Englishman does in a distinguished way the simple things that other men might slur over as unimportant or essentially gross or irremediable; he is distinguished -- he is disciplined, skilful, and calm -- in eating, in public gatherings, in hardship, in danger, in extremities. It is in physical and rudimentary behaviour that the Englishman is an artist.[16]

("To affect the quality of the day," said Thoreau, "that is the highest of arts. Every man is tasked to make his life, even in its details, worthy of the contemplation of his most elevated and critical hour" [*W*, II, 100].) (In *English Traits* Emerson states, categorically enough, that the English are "some ages ahead of the rest of the world in the art of living," while in his address at Thoreau's funeral he explained that Thoreau declined "any narrow craft or profession, aiming at a much more comprehensive calling, the art of living well."[17]) Consequently, too, the Englishman, like Thoreau, is resolutely this-worldly and *un*transcendental: it is this life that counts. ("Even here," said Thoreau in the "Sunday" chapter of his first book, "we have a sort of living to get . . . . There are various tough problems yet to solve, and we must make shift to live, betwixt spirit and matter, such a human life as we can" [*W*, V, 74].) This attitude is epitomized for Santayana in the "Death-Bed Manners" (how like Thoreau's own conduct during his last long illness![18]) of the English: their resolute refusal to make any fuss about death. "English manners are sensible and conducive to comfort even at a death-bed . . . . Death, it is felt, is not important. What matters is the part we have played in the world, or may still play there by our influence . . . . We have tried to do right here. If there is any Beyond, we shall try to do right there also."[19] "One world at a time," said Thoreau.

Finally, it should be stressed that the life to which both Thoreau and the Englishman are first and last devoted is, as I have indicated, necessarily a vital, healthy, robust life. This is of course evident in Thoreau's ever-present commitment to his doctrine of Wildness ("The whole duty of man," he declared early in his career, "may be expressed in one line, -- Make to yourself a perfect body" [*J*, I, 147]); as for the English, American observers from Irving to Santayana were simply awe-stricken by the energy and by the vitality of that people. Emerson, for example, was so conscious of the "impressive energy" of the English that in his lectures to them he "hesitated to read and threw out for its impertinence many a disparaging phrase which I had been accustomed to spin about poor, thin, unable mortals; so much had the fine physique and the personal vigor of this robust race worked on my imagination."[20]   Henry James, too, noted "the personal energy of the [English] people and their eagerness to take, in the way of exercise and adventure, whatever they can get," while Oliver Wendell Holmes granted, quite simply, that the English are "taller, stouter, lustier, ruddier, healthier"[21] than the people of New England. In spite of America's celebrated frontier tradition, that is to say, the prominent Americans who actually went to England were forced to concede that this country was, in Santayana's words, "a beautifully healthy England" ("domestic, sporting, gallant, boyish, of a sure and delicate heart") in a way that America was not. This means, in other words -- as Santayana explains and as Thoreau in his own life so indelibly illustrated -- that "The *man* is he who [whatever his geographic fortunes] lives and relies directly on nature, not on the needs or weaknesses of other people. [And] These self-sufficing Englishmen, in their reserve and decision, seemed to me truly men."[22]

Thoreau's achievement as a writer grew, essentially and crucially, from his original, creative use of the frontier metaphor and of the Western myth. If at times he tended toward chauvinism in asserting that "Adam in paradise was not so favorably situated on the whole as is the backwoodsman in America," he was more often tough-minded and to the point in remarking that it "remains to be seen how the western Adam in the wilderness will turn out" (*J*, II, 152-153). And in *Walden* he showed, classically, that this western Adam in the wilderness was not turning out so well after all; that Americans would have to return to first principles if they wished to realize the American dream of the West; that the West itself will remain illusive as long as it is identified with a geographic region rather than with a state of mind and with a disciplined, intense way of living. Yet as Wright Morris has pointed out,[23] Thoreau himself was an archetypal American in his preference for taking to the woods rather than for staying in the village -- in his insistence that the "*essential* facts of life" (emphasis mine) are to be found in the woods rather than in the village. In preferring the woods Thoreau was, as he said, only following the prevailing tendency of his countrymen to leave the city and to withdraw into the wilderness. But *why* do Americans have such an urge to flee the city? Because, as Morris explains, "Each of these cultural centers, each of these established towns, became a fragment of Europe and a past to get away from -- the prevailing tendency of Americans being what it was. Thoreau did not expose this tendency to examination -- he accepted it."[24]

All of which is to say that Thoreau's life and writings classically dramatize a central question inherent in any attempt to understand the American westering experience: what value and importance, comparatively, should be placed upon our frontier and upon our European -- especially our English -- traditions? Like most Americans, I am not at all unsympathetic to the Western myth, and it is obvious that no true account of America can ignore this myth. Yet the fact that Thoreau's ideal man was not, as he knew, the historic American westerner, a man who sought geographic rather than inner frontiers, but -- as he did *not* know -- the historic English gentleman, a man who stayed at home and sought to maintain a certain distinguished quality of life, is a striking reminder of the one-sidedness to which the Western myth can lead. And it reminds us, too, that Santayana may well have been right when he said that "English liberty" -- by which he meant the English belief that true freedom is created by responsibility, manliness, and respect for privacy -- "is the best heritage of America, richer than its virgin continents."[25] Perhaps more than any other American, Thoreau embodied the English view of life and of liberty. If his quest for wildness, for a truly westering experience, took him to the woods, it also took him, unknowingly, to England.

Chapter 2

Notes

1. Ralph Waldo Emerson, *The Complete Works of Ralph Waldo Emerson* (Boston: Houghton Mifflin, 1903), X, 459.
2. Along with Emerson, the following American observers in England offered, from 1820 to 1920, strikingly similar reports on the Englishman's vigor, independence, courage, manliness, and refinement: Washington Irving (*The Sketch Book*), James Fenimore Cooper (*Gleanings in Europe: England*), Nathaniel Hawthorne (*Our Old Home*), Oliver Wendell Holmes (*Our Hundred Days in Europe*), Henry James (*English Hours*), and George Santayana (*Soliloquies in England*).
3. Edwin Fussell, *Frontier: American Literature and the American West* (Princeton: Princeton University Press, 1965), pp. 175-231. See also Lawrence Willson, "The Transcendentalist View of the West," *The Western Humanities Review*, 14 (1960): 183-191; and C.A. Tillinghast, "The West of Thoreau's Imagination: The Development of a Symbol," *Thoth*, 6 (Winter, 1964): 42-50.
4. References to the first six volumes of the Walden Edition of *The Writings of Henry David Thoreau* (Boston: Houghton Mifflin, 1906) are indicated in my text by a "*W*" and followed by volume and page numbers. Volumes VII-XX of this edition are *The Journal of Henry David Thoreau*. References to the Journal are indicated by a "*J*," with the *Journal* volume and page numeration following.
5. Cf. Fussell, p. 189.
6. (New York: Scribner's, 1935), pp. 284-285.
7. Cf. Walter Harding, *A Thoreau Handbook* (New York: New York University Press, 1959), pp. 154-155; Roderick Nash, *Wilderness and the American Mind* (New Haven: Yale University Press, 1967), pp. 91-95; and Charles Roberts Anderson, *The Magic Circle of Walden* (New York: Holt, Rinehart and Winston, 1968), pp. 151-178, and *passim*.
8. George Santayana, *Soliloquies in England and Later Soliloquies* (Ann Arbor: The University of Michigan Press, 1967), pp. 37, 86.
9. Emerson, *Works*, V, 102-103, 105, 131, 304-305.
10. Washington Irving, *The Sketch Book of Geoffrey Crayon, Gent.* (New York: Dutton, 1963), p. 58.
11. James Fenimore Cooper, *Gleanings in Europe: England* (New York: Oxford University Press, 1930), pp. 238, 192.
12. Santayana, p. 31.
13. "In short, the Oriental uses the purely aesthetic to constitute the nature of the divine...instead of using the aesthetic merely as an analogical symbol to convey a divinity which is defined in some other way." F. S. C. Northrop, *The Meeting of East and West: An Inquiry Concerning World Understanding* (New York: Collier, 1966), p. 404. Cf., too, Stephen Railton, "Thoreau's 'Resurrection of Virtue!'," *American Quarterly*, 24 (May, 1972): 210-227, esp. 210-211.

14.   Cf. Jonathan Fairbanks, "Thoreau: Speaker for Wildness," *The South Atlantic Quarterly*, 70 (Autumn, 1971): 499.
15.   Santayana, p. 2.
16.   Santayana, p. 53.
17.   Emerson, *Works*, V, 101; and X, 452.
18.   See Walter Harding, *The Days of Henry Thoreau* (New York: Alfred A. Knopf, 1965), pp. 450-468.
19.   Santayana, pp. 91, 92.
20.   Emerson, *Works*, V, 106.
21.   Henry James, *English Hours* (New York: The Orion Press, 1960), p. 26; Oliver Wendell Holmes, *Our Hundred Days in Europe* (Boston: Houghton Mifflin, 1907), p. 294.
22.   Santayana, pp. 3, 5.
23.   Wright Morris, *The Territory Ahead: Critical Interpretations in American Literature* (New York: Atheneum, 1963), pp. 39-50, esp. p. 43.
24.   Morris, p. 42.
25.   George Santayana, "English Liberty in America," in Santayana, *Character and Opinion in the United States* (New York: Scribner's, 1921), p. 232.

CHAPTER 3

Hawthorne's Dream in the Forest

At the heart of America's Western myth lies a conflict between what Henry Nash Smith has called "Consciousness and Social Order."[1]

On the one hand, there is the belief, or, more correctly, the myth, that the West -- the free, natural world beyond the frontier -- represents the possibility of transcendence; that the European-American who crosses the frontier becomes a new, better, freer man; that he gains a capacity for perspective and perception, an Homeric kind of innocence, and a deep, intuitive sense of right and wrong -- and of reality itself -- which are simply unattainable within the old European and European-American social order. On the other hand, there is the conservative and, as I wish to stress in this chapter, essentially Puritan view that Social Order is, after all, an intrinsic human need; that we must seek salvation within community because, as Leslie A. Fiedler has put it in speaking of the "tragic Humanism" of Melville and Hawthorne, "our only protection from destructive self-deceit is the pressure and presence of others."[2] In speaking of this conflict between Consciousness and Social Order, Smith was referring to Fiedler's challenging assertion, in *The Return of the Vanishing American*, that the American West is, by definition, an "alteration of consciousness" -- that the "Western" as a literary form "represents a traditional and continuing dialogue between whatever old selves we transport out of whatever East, and the radically different other whom we confront in whatever West we attain." For Fiedler, "That other is the Indian still" -- the Indian who "in the language of archetype" stands "for alien perception." And certainly Fiedler has shown brilliantly and, I believe, conclusively that the most authentic American westering dream, the dream, at least, which characterizes our classic literature, is the dream of entering "the world of the Indian: the world not of an historical past, but of the eternally archaic one" -- the dream, that is, of falling "not merely out of Europe, but out of the Europeanized West, into an aboriginal and archaic America." Of course Fiedler has also argued that this indigenous dream-image of the West is a West for males only, that our classic writers have traditionally equated women with history, Europe, and Christianity, and that they have consequently and continually retold "the old, old fable of the White outcast and the noble Red Man joined together against home and mother, against the female world of civilization." Examining Thoreau's mythicized and paradigmatic description, in *A Week on the Concord and Merrimack Rivers*, of the friendship of Alexander Henry and Wawatam, Fiedler discovers "the real point at last. It is a *Pagan* Paradise Regained that Americans have dreamed of in the forests of the New World, a natural Eden lost when Christianity intervened -- which means when woman intervened."[3]

Yet while Fiedler is surely right in relating the myth of the West to consciousness itself, it is important to remember that this is just one side of the mythological coin of the West. As Fiedler himself has shown in his classic study of American fiction, *Love and Death in the American Novel*, the Western myth can be viewed within the context of the Faustian nightmare quite as easily as it can be viewed within the context of the American dream; for they hold "in common the hope [inherent in the Western myth] of breaking through all limits and restraints, of reaching a place of total freedom where one [can] with impunity deny the Fall, live as if innocence rather than guilt were the birthright of all men."[4] Thus the frontier itself is a metaphor for one of two things: salvation or damnation. When the European-American crosses the frontier, falls entirely out of his European heritage, does he emerge as Adam or as Faust? Is he reborn or damned? Is the real West, as Fiedler suggests in *The Return*, a "peculiar form of madness which dreams, and achieves"? Or is it, as he suggests in *Love and Death*, truly *madness*, "the [tragic, Faustian] dream of transcending one's humanity"?[5] Fiedler does not answer these questions for us, nor is there any reason that he should -- for they are contradictions not in *his* thought, but in the American mind itself. The important thing, after all, is surely to recognize that there *is* a deep-rooted ambivalence toward the West in our history and in our literature and to recognize, too, that this ambivalence stems from two opposing world-views -- Puritan and Romantic -- which are themselves deeply rooted in our history and our literature.

Pre-eminently, of course, it was Nathaniel Hawthorne who translated, dramatized, and raised to the level of tragedy the essential meaning of our Puritan heritage. Like the Puritans themselves, Hawthorne consistently defined the frontier metaphor as a *Faustian* metaphor,[6] and believed that total self-reliance was not (as Emerson claimed) God-reliance, but its opposite. Like the Puritans, too, he was not (as Winthrop and his followers proclaimed before leaving England) "of those that dream of perfection in this world";[7] and because he had no dream of human perfection, he, like the Puritans, realized (as Winthrop eloquently explained in mid-voyage)[8] that man can save himself only by humbly joining the human community, by subjecting himself, without illusions, "to earth's doom of care, and sorrow, and troubled joy" (IX, 58).[9] Still, we must guard against seeing Hawthorne as a latter-day Puritan so obsessed with the past and with what he felt were the dark truths of Puritanism that he was untouched by the buoyant, Westward-looking, and, for better or for worse, more typically "American" age in which he lived and wrote. He did, after all, live in the Age of Jackson (for whom, as a matter of fact, he had great admiration);[10] he was a friend of Emerson and Thoreau and was much more committed to democratic ideals than they ever were;[11] and while it is true that during his early life he lived for twelve years as a recluse, he emerged from those twelve years to take an active interest in the immediate concerns of his age -- including a participation ("essentially a day-dream, and yet a fact" [III, 2]) in the utopian colony at Brook Farm. Thus the drama which his life and writings yield is really the drama of an intense, unresolved conflict between the dream of freedom and rebirth embodied in America's Western myth and the Puritan belief that evil is irremediable, that sin is permanently warping,[12] and that the Way West is a Faustian temptation rather than a viable human possibility. Clearly to see this we need go no further than *The Scarlet Letter*, whose greatness lies precisely in the tragic conflict between the worlds of Hester and of Dimmesdale -- between, that is, an Emersonian world of freedom and self-creation and a Puritan world of sin, expiation, and social responsibility.

Moreover, while Hester is Hawthorne's single greatest embodiment of what Frederic I. Carpenter has called "the authentic American dream of freedom and independence in the new world,"[13] it is a striking fact that *women* are portrayed everywhere in Hawthorne's fiction as avatars of "a dream of happiness" (I, 222), as he called it in *The Scarlet Letter*, to which -- in spite of his stern, Puritan view that happiness is illusory, a vain hope of men too weak to recognize life's grim reality -- he was strongly attracted. For Hawthorne, in other words, the Western dream of freedom and self-renewal is represented by women. This is not to say that he was not deeply ambivalent toward women -- especially his independent and incomparably sexual Dark Ladies -- but it is to say that in his attitude toward women we have the key to an understanding of his attitude toward Puritanism and toward the West.[14]

A consideration of Hawthorne's attitude toward women and toward Puritanism should begin with his biographical sketch of "Mrs. Hutchinson" (1830), a sketch which the young would-be writer prefaces with a display of male chauvinism that could hardly have been surpassed by his Puritan ancestors. Noting that there are "changes gradually taking place in the habits and feelings of the gentle sex, which seem to threaten our posterity with many of those public women, whereof one was a burden too grievous for our fathers," Hawthorne adamantly declares that "Woman's intellect should never give the tone to that of man; and even her morality is not exactly the material for masculine virtue." And noting specifically that "The press . . . is now the medium through which feminine ambition chiefly manifests itself," he warns that it would be a mistake to encourage women writers out of "A false liberality, which mistakes the strong division-lines of Nature for arbitrary distinctions."[15] Thus do we find Hawthorne forthrightly endorsing the Puritan interpretation of the Fall in the Garden: woman (feeling, passion) represents a dangerous, subversive threat to the male intellect: "the strong division-lines of Nature" demand that men and reason rule in the affairs of the world and that the antinomian impulses of women be held in check. "We are not wont," declares John Endicott at the end of "The May-Pole of Merry Mount," "to show an idle courtesy to that sex, which requireth the stricter discipline" (IX, 65). It comes as no surprise, then, that when Hawthorne turns to Anne Hutchinson herself he exhibits no sympathy for her "strange and dangerous opinions"[16] but a great deal of sympathy for

John Winthrop, the Puritan leader who had to contend with such a strong-willed, free-thinking woman. For Anne Hutchinson is clearly an important historical prototype for those protagonists found everywhere in American fiction who -- like Leatherstocking or Huckleberry Finn or Isaac McCaslin -- are ready to follow private impulse and conscience in defiance of an entire social order. Just like the American Puritans, in other words, Hawthorne identified the antinomian Western dream of rebirth and freedom not with the lonely, chaste male but with the beautiful, passionate female. In the forest of the New World his imagination discovered not an American Adam, but an American Eve; and -- unlike his Puritan ancestors -- he was human enough and hopeful enough to be enchanted as well as frightened by his dream-image of women.

But, again, 1830 was quite a different matter. Hawthorne was surely aware that when the magistrates demanded of Anne Hutchinson "How she did know that it was God that did reveal these things to her, and not Satan," she did not go quite so far as to reply with Emerson that "if I am the Devil's child, I will live then from the Devil" -- but she did insist upon her capacity to know "by an immediate revelation."[17] This, as Hawthorne and his Puritan ancestors knew, was a belief, like Leatherstocking's, which placed individual conscience above society and the law, a belief which threatened both social and moral anarchy. In 1830 he was as ready as the Puritans to bid her to "go out from among them, and trouble the land no more."[18]

While Anne may have stopped troubling the Puritans, it is clear that she continued to trouble Hawthorne. His becoming an artist at all was, in fact, contingent upon his superseding the Puritans' simplistic, chauvinistic view of women and of Anne Hutchinson's antinomianism. Yet even for Hawthorne, as Larzer Ziff has shown, woman and what she represents -- "natural" values: freedom, beauty, vitality, sexuality, love -- remained at best an alter ego. "The figure of the dark lady fascinated because in her strong sexuality and her antinomian doctrines, she was like the creative impulses which had led him to writing. But in her denial of fallibility and her disregard for history, she was far too destructive."[19] To this dilemma Hawthorne found no solution. At the same time that he shared the Puritans' dark view of the human heart, he disapproved of their rigid, rational, logic-centered way of life precisely because it denied the claims of the heart.[20] How can one affirm the heart at the same time that he has a Calvinistic sense of its foulness? In answer to this question -- perhaps, for him, *the* essential life-question -- Hawthorne has given us his greatest characters; significantly, they are all women: Beatrice Rappacini, Hester Prynne, Zenobia, Miriam. Significantly, too, these characters are, as women, directly related to Nature, or, that is, to the West. The threshold of a fuller, freer, happier existence -- one important way, certainly, of defining the West -- is imaged by the beautiful, and pagan, woman in a natural setting. "What we did had a consecration of its own," Hester Prynne affirms, and believes. Thus the human heart -- so often to Hawthorne (as in "Earth's Holocaust") but a "foul cavern" -- was still what infinitely mattered, was central to his more hopeful Western imaginings. Describing (in "Main-street" [1849]) the first Puritan settlers at Salem, for example, he exclaims, "How sweet must it be for those who have an Eden in their hearts...to find a new world to project it into, as they have" (XI, 53). This Eden did not last, of course -- either in American history or in Hawthorne's imagination. But he became haunted by its possibility even as he was haunted by his ancestors' crimes. And this, too, is why the Puritan setting -- "a forest-bordered settlement of the western wilderness" (XI, 61) -- was the inevitable setting of Hawthorne's greatest work, for *here* the forest and its conflicting meanings had to be confronted, in dread or in hope. Even during the magnificent scene of Hester's forest-change, for example, Hawthorne still refers to nature as "that wild, heathen Nature of the forest, never subjugated by human law, nor illumined by higher truth" (I, 203). Hawthorne's ambivalence toward the forest and toward the American dream of the West was tragic, then, because it was total -- as total, at least, as the historic conflict between the Puritan emigrants and the Native Americans. He imagined, with Hester, that the forest offered freedom and rebirth; he feared, with Goodman Brown, that it led to damnation.

In "Young Goodman Brown" (1835), certainly, we have nothing less, according to Q. D. Leavis' fine definition, than "a dramatic poem of the Calvinist experience in New England."[21] Far from being, as Edwin Fussell claims,[22] an allegory of the American westering experience, young Goodman Brown's dream in the forest -- and, indeed, his very journey into the forest --

clearly allegorizes that sinister yielding of the imagination to visions of evil
which was so typical of the Puritan mind. And Hawthorne's main point, of
course, is that Brown's obsession with evil carries its own nemesis: it renders
his own life not evil, perhaps, but certainly joyless and loveless: "A stern, a
sad, a darkly meditative, a distrustful, if not a desperate man did he become
from the night of that fearful dream . . . . And when he had lived long, and
was borne to his grave . . . they carved no hopeful verse upon his tomb-stone;
for his dying hour was gloom" (V, 89-90). In opposition to the moral
desolation and inhumanity of Brown's Calvinistic Puritanism, stands his
young, newly wed wife, Faith. *She* could have saved Brown if he had had
faith in her, if he had loved her. But like so many of Hawthorne's
protagonists,[23] Brown is incapable of love; consequently, he is damned.
Quite significantly, then, Hawthorne's greatest Puritan tale renders what is
perhaps the strongest statement that he ever made *against* the Puritan
doctrine that woman is the agent of man's Fall into original sin. For if
Hawthorne was unable to answer his wife's question as to whether Beatrice
Rappaccini is "angel or devil,"[24] it is evident that he would have had no
trouble answering the same question about Faith Brown. As Daniel G.
Hoffman has pointed out, she alone, of all the Puritans, "has such faith in
man that she can transcend the revelation that he is fallen."[25] As for Brown,
the point is that he did not *have* to journey into the forest and to indulge in
doubts of Faith or in visions of universal, orgiastic evil. Faced with the
choice of loving his wife or believing in his religion, he chose, disastrously for
him, to do the latter.

Far happier than Goodman Brown's dream of witches and wickedness
is the dream of innocence, beauty, and love in "The May-Pole of Merry
Mount" (1836); for the Lord and the Lady of the May (and their merry
cohorts) are not burdened with the Puritans' dark view of the human
condition. In fact, their lives at Merry Mount are a pagan celebration of
those very areas of human experience which the Puritans distrusted and
consciously repressed: aesthetic, sensuous impressions of the beauty of the
natural world and of the human body. Quite unknown to the Lord and the
Lady of the May is the guilt-ridden, sinister Puritan view of sex which was

objectified in young Goodman Brown's forest-dream: instead of dreaming about a Satanic witches' orgy, the revelers at Merry Mount venerate the Maypole, which, as Harry Levin has said, is "the most primitive archetype of sexuality."[26]

In this story Hawthorne celebrates the rich, natural, passionate love of Edgar and Edith in much the same way, for example, that he celebrates the rich beauty and the natural, passionate love of Hester Prynne. "The May-Pole of Merry Mount" would seem, in other words, *almost* to affirm Hester's belief that a genuine, passionate love has "a consecration of its own" (I, 195) and needs no other form of sanctification. "Almost" because there is, in the final analysis, irreducible opposition between Hester's and Hawthorne's points of view: whereas Hester believed that she *could* realize her dream of a rebirth of love and happiness by fleeing the Puritan community -- a *westward* flight, as she passionately urges Dimmesdale during their final meeting in the forest, deeper and deeper into the American wilderness -- Hawthorne, in "The May-Pole of Merry Mount" no less than in *The Scarlet Letter*, insists that love must be subject to and sanctioned by the laws of society and religion. Endicott is hardly an appealing figure, but the Puritan view which he personifies -- the view that life is burdensome, evil-threatened, and care-ridden; that it must, consequently, be made subject to restraint and to law -- is the view that Hawthorne finally, albeit unconvincingly, affirms. No story of Hawthorne's is, in its clear-cut contrast between paganism and Puritanism, more like *The Scarlet Letter* than "The May-Pole of Merry Mount"; and the fact that Hawthorne tries unsuccessfully in this story, as in *The Scarlet Letter*, to resolve the conflict between the romantic forest-dream of Merry Mount and the Puritan vision of life's harsh limitations and realities proves all the more clearly just how unresolvable he found this conflict to be. Just as Hester is the most compelling character in *The Scarlet Letter* in spite of Hawthorne's disclaimers about her "sin" and her "shame," so too is Merry Mount's dream of love and of a rich, fecund harmony between man and the natural world intrinsically far more compelling, in spite of Hawthorne's final disclaimer about "the vanities of Merry Mount" (IX, 67), than the "branding and cropping of ears" found in the Puritans' own "well-ordered settlements" (IX, 64). Nor is the reader especially gratified by Endicott's prediction that

Edgar can be made "valiant to fight" (IX, 66) when it is recalled that Hawthorne earlier characterized the Puritans as fanatical zealots whose "weapons were always at hand, to shoot down the straggling savage" (IX, 60). Thus when Hawthorne attempts to end his tale with his lovers being wisely, if sadly, initiated into the Puritan community, the reader only senses that, as Richard Harter Fogle has put it, "their fate is a surrender to values imperfect and incomplete."[27] It is a feeling akin, perhaps, to the disappointment and the dismay experienced by many readers when, at the end of *The Scarlet Letter*, they are presented with a penitent Hester Prynne who no longer "vainly imagined that she herself might be the destined prophetess" of a "new truth" -- the truth that "love should make us happy" (I, 263).

The Scarlet Letter is the most fully developed, intense, and sustained dramatization of the conflict between private, human values and social, religious values which lies at the heart of Hawthorne's ambivalence toward women, toward Puritanism, and toward the American myth of the West. Hester, of course, with her tall, statuesque figure "of perfect elegance," her "dark and abundant hair" (I, 53), her "impulsive and passionate nature" (I, 57), and her "rich, voluptuous, Oriental" (I, 83) temperament, is nothing less than a prototype of womanhood. She embodies the value of earthly, human love -- and, not least, she embodies the American dream of a new, free, happy life in the New World. "Hester," as Edwin Fussell has said, "is the wilderness, Dimmesdale the settlements"[28] -- and in no work did Hawthorne have a more anguished experience deciding between the two, between, that is, our traditional American westering dream of complete natural freedom and the Puritan doctrine of civil freedom.[29] Moreover, the fact that Hester stands for the claims of the *heart*, that *love* is the reality-principle of her life,[30] left Hawthorne with a dilemma which, it seems to me, has been much overlooked. We know that for Hawthorne the single greatest sin is, without question, the *Unpardonable Sin* of violating the human heart, yet no one has pointed to the fact that Arthur Dimmesdale commits this sin.[31] Like all of Hawthorne's violators of the heart -- like Ethan Brand or Aylmer or Hollingsworth; like Richard Digby and young Goodman Brown and the rest of Hawthorne's Puritan characters -- he is the victim of a monomania (in this case, an obsession with theological concepts) which destroys -- or, more correctly, which he *allows* to destroy -- his capacity for a fully *human* responsiveness to his emotions. How ironic, then, that it is Dimmesdale himself who, in the forest scene, accuses Chillingworth of being the only one to have "violated . . . the sanctity of a human heart" (I, 195)! Of course, it is easier to sympathize with Dimmesdale than with, say, young Goodman Brown or with any of Hawthorne's other Unpardonable Sinners; but we should not blink at the fact that, quite as much as these others, he is guilty of submitting to an obsession which leads to a rejection of love: he rejects Hester just as Richard Digby rejects Mary Goffe or young Goodman Brown rejects Faith or Hollingsworth rejects Zenobia. If, then, Hawthorne could expressly condemn Catherine in "The Gentle Boy" (1831) for denying the claims "of natural affection" and martyring her *human* love to an other-worldly religious commitment (IX, 87), we can, I think, legitimately wonder why Dimmesdale does not receive the same judgement.[32]

Of course we need not wonder for very long. Saying that Dimmesdale was wrong, identifying him for the Unpardonable Sinner that he actually is, would have been tantamount to saying that Hester was right -- and Hester, standing at the very "threshold" of American history,[33] personifies the American westering dream of individualism, of freedom, and of rebirth into a new, fuller, happier life: personifies, that is to say, a dream which Hawthorne could never bring himself wholly to affirm. As a matter of fact, what is astonishing about *The Scarlet Letter* is not that Hawthorne is inclined toward Dimmesdale's Puritanism, but that he makes the anti-Puritan, characteristically *American* point of view, embodied by Hester, so compelling and cogent. As we know, though, it is only in the crucial scene in the *forest* that Hester's values can be fully and freely expressed. And Hester does *not* try to impose her values of freedom and of love upon Dimmesdale;[34] in fact, she begins by praising the life that he has been living for the previous seven years. It is only after she has been convinced of the utter hopelessness of Dimmesdale's present life, and only after he has begged her to "Advise me what to do" (I, 196), that she is emboldened to present her own view of "all these iron [Puritan] men, and their opinions" (I, 197); to urge Dimmesdale westward into the American forest ("There thou art free!") or, at least, eastward to Europe; to suggest, in any case, that both of them flee New England, live together, and love each other. When Dimmesdale agrees, when he exclaims that "This is already the better life!" and when he calls Hester his "better angel" (I, 201), the case for love and for romantic individualism and freedom -- for, that is to say, Nathaniel Hawthorne's dream of the American West -- is complete. Hester is reborn: "There played around her mouth, and beamed out of her eyes, a radiant and tender smile, that seemed gushing from the very heart of womanhood . . . . Her sex, her youth, and the whole richness of her beauty, came back from what men call the irrevocable past, and clustered themselves, with her maiden hope, and a happiness before unknown, within the magic circle of this hour" (I, 202). But the dream of freedom, happiness, and love which Hester embodies -- and which is *briefly* realized in the forest -- is not affirmed by Hawthorne's romance as a whole. Hester must put the Letter back on and confine her hair under her cap; Dimmesdale must return to the Puritan community, preach his Election Sermon, and confess on the platform where Hester stood seven years earlier. Yet no reader of *The Scarlet Letter* can forget that this is an ending which *Hester*, at least, regards as nothing less than a betrayal of love, and against which she raises a passionate protest -- a protest which cuts to the very heart of Hawthorne's own agonized ambivalence toward a religion which recognized the reality of human sin but not the redemptive power of human love.

> "Is not this better," murmured he, "than what we dreamed of in the forest?"
> "I know not! I know not!" she hurriedly replied [I, 254].

In 1830 Hawthorne complacently approved of Anne Hutchinson's banishment from the Puritan community while at the same time he sentimentally hoped "that, in the stillness of Nature, her heart was stilled."[35] But he was never again able to dismiss so easily the complex social, moral, and religious issues embodied in Anne's banishment. Never again could he be *completely* certain that the antinomian American westering dream is a false and self-destructive dream, that the New World forest imaged a Faustian temptation rather than a viable human possibility for rebirth and for transcendence. His uncertainty about these issues was never resolved but was, instead, finally brought to a point of tragic tension in his greatest work. The simplistic and unsympathetic portrait of "Mrs. Hutchinson" was more than redeemed when, twenty years later, Hawthorne created a Hester Prynne who followed Anne's footsteps. In the stillness of Nature, Hester's heart was not stilled. For in the forest her -- and America's -- dream of freedom and of happiness was born.

Chapter 3

Notes

1. "Consciousness and Social Order: The Theme of Transcendence in the Leatherstocking Tales," *Western American Literature*, 5 (Fall, 1970): 177-194.
2. *Love and Death in the American Novel*, 2nd ed. (New York: Dell, 1966), p. 432.
3. *The Return of the Vanishing American* (New York: Stein and Day, 1968), pp. 175, 186, 178, 25, 175, 177, 115-116.
4. *Love and Death*, p. 143.
5. *The Return*, "Preface"; *Love and Death*, p. 443.
6. Edwin Fussell's *Frontier: American Literature and the American West* (Princeton: Princeton University Press, 1965) is an important but uneven study of the use of the frontier metaphor by six major pre-Civil-War writers. His treatment of Hawthorne is limited and one-sided precisely because he ignores the Faustian dimension in Hawthorne's view of the frontier and of the West.
7. Quoted in Edmund S. Morgan, *The Puritan Dilemma: The Story of John Winthrop* (Boston: Little, Brown, 1958), pp. 52-53.
8. John Winthrop, "A Modell of Christian Charity," in Loren Baritz, ed., *Sources of the American Mind: A Collection of Documents and Texts in American Intellectual History*, 2 vols. (New York: John Wiley & Sons, 1966), I, 2-11.
9. Numbers within parentheses following quotations from Hawthorne indicate volume and page in *The Centenary Edition of the Works of Nathaniel Hawthorne*, ed. William Charvat, Roy Harvey Pearce, Claude M. Simpson, Fredson Bowers, and Matthew J. Bruccoli (Columbus: Ohio State University Press, 1962).
This quotation is taken from Hawthorne's description, in "The May-Pole of Merry Mount," of Edgar's and Edith's presentiment of the life-fate awaiting them once they had truly loved.
10. See Arthur M. Schlesinger, Jr., *The Age of Jackson* (Boston: Little, Brown, 1945), p. 42.
11. Cf., for example, *Our Old Home* (1863) in which Hawthorne responds quite unfavorably, and even chauvinistically, to the English class system and to the English aristocracy. In sharp contrast to Hawthorne, Emerson, in *English Traits* (1856), is strongly affirmative about the English aristocracy and -- because of his favorable impressions of the aristocracy -- refuses to condemn the class system which supports it.
12. Cf. Charles Child Walcutt, "*The Scarlet Letter* and Its Modern Critics," *Nineteenth Century Fiction*, 7 (1953): 264.
13. *American Literature and the Dream* (New York: Philosophical Library, 1955), p. 71.
14. J. Golden Taylor's monograph on *Hawthorne's Ambivalence Toward Puritanism* (Logan: Utah State University Press, 1965) is the best and

the most complete study of Hawthorne's attitude toward Puritanism. See also Barriss Mills, "Hawthorne and Puritanism," *New England Quarterly*, 21, (1948): 78-102; Joseph Schwartz, "Three Aspects of Hawthorne's Puritanism," *New England Quarterly*, 36 (1963): 192-208; and Larzer Ziff, "The Artist and Puritanism," in *Hawthorne Centenary Essays*, ed. Roy Harvey Pearce (Columbus: Ohio State University Press, 1964), pp. 245-269.
Insightful analyses of Hawthorne's attitude toward women may be found in Frederic I. Carpenter, "Puritans Preferred Blondes: The Heroines of Melville and Hawthorne," *New England Quarterly*, 9 (June, 1936): 253-272; Morton Corin, "Hawthorne on Romantic Love and the Status of Women," *PMLA*, 69 (1954): 89-98; Gloria Chasson Erlich, "Deadly Innocence: Hawthorne's Dark Women," *New England Quarterly*, 41 (June, 1968): 163-179; Fiedler, *Love and Death*, pp. 222-241; Philip Rahv, "The Dark Lady of Salem," *Partisan Review*, 8 (1941): 362-381; and Ziff, "The Artist and Puritanism."
Fussell's *Frontier* contains the only critical study of Hawthorne's attitude toward the American West.

15.   *The Works of Nathaniel Hawthorne*, ed. George Parsons Lathrop, 15 vols. (Boston: Standard Library, 1882-83), XII, 217, 217-218, 218. Hereafter cited as *Works*.

16.   *Ibid.*, p. 219.

17.   The Emerson quotation is from his essay on "Self-Reliance"; the quotations from Anne Hutchinson's trial are taken from Morgan, *The Puritan Dilemma*, p. 152.

18.   *Works*, XII, 224.

19.   Ziff, "The Artist and Puritanism," in *Hawthorne Centenary Essays*, ed. Pearce, p. 268.

20.   "Hawthorne differed most from the Puritans in his emphasis on the heart." Taylor, *Hawthorne's Ambivalence Toward Puritanism*, p. 57. "The Puritans, it would seem, placed too much trust in the intellect and too little in the heart." Mills, "Hawthorne and Puritanism," p. 92.The place and importance of the heart in Hawthorne's psychology is discussed perceptively in the following articles: Nina Baym, "The Head, the Heart, and the Unpardonable Sin," *New England Quarterly*, 40 (1967): 31-47; James E. Miller, Jr., "Hawthorne and Melville: The Unpardonable Sin," *PMLA*, 70 (1955): 91-114; and Donald A. Ringe, "Hawthorne's Psychology of the Head and the Heart," *PMLA*, 65 (1950): 120-132.

21.   "Hawthorne as Poet," *Sewanee Review*, 59 (1951), 197.

22.   *Frontier*, pp. 82-84.

23.   Other examples: Aylmer, Ethan Brand, Giovanni, Parson Hooper, Hollingsworth.

24.   See Julian Hawthorne, *Nathaniel Hawthorne and His Wife*, 2 vols. (Boston: Houghton, Mifflin, 1884), I, 360.

25.   *Form and Fable in American Fiction* (New York: Oxford University Press, 1961), p. 168.

26.   *The Power of Blackness: Hawthorne, Poe, Melville* (New York: Random House, 1958), p. 54.

27.   *Hawthorne's Fiction: The Light and the Dark*, 2nd ed. (Norman: University of Oklahoma Press, 1964), p. 64.

28. *Frontier*, p. 64.
29. For the importance of Hawthorne's use of the distinction between natural freedom and civil freedom in *The Scarlet Letter*, see Chester E. Eisinger, "Pearl and the Puritan Heritage," *College English*, 12 (1951): 323-329.
30. See Seymour L. Gross, "'Solitude, and Love, and Anguish': The Tragic Design of *The Scarlet Letter*," *College Language Association Journal*, 3 (March, 1960): 154-165; and Ernest Sandeen, "*The Scarlet Letter* as a Love Story," *PMLA*, 77 (1962): 425-435.
31. Donald A. Ringe has interestingly noted that it is only after Chillingworth has totally rejected the values of the heart that he returns (in Chapter XIV) to a belief in Calvinism; thus "he becomes, perhaps, representative of the [Puritan] society in its worst form." "Hawthorne's Psychology of the Head and Heart," p. 125. Insightful as Ringe's point is, it needs to be taken one crucial step further: for wherein, essentially, does Dimmesdale differ from Chillingworth? This question does not readily suggest itself because Hawthorne has, I believe -- and this quite probably was unconsciously, as psychic-defense -- gone to extremes in his portrayal of Chillingworth's blackness in order to evade the issue of Dimmesdale's own Unpardonable Sin against the heart.
32. At another point in "The Gentle Boy" Hawthorne states that Catherine "had...violated the duties of the present life and the future, by fixing her attention wholly on the latter" (IX, 85). It seems to me that this indictment applies with equal validity to Arthur Dimmesdale.
33. Cf. Fussell, pp. 99-100.
34. Cf. Gross, pp. 161-163.
35. *Works*, XII, 225.

CHAPTER 4

Hawthorne's Parricidal Vision of the American Revolution:
"My Kinsman, Major Molineux"

Not only do Nathaniel Hawthorne's life and writings dramatize his New Englander's tragic ambivalence toward America's antinomian dream of the West: one of his earliest, unquestionably one of his greatest, stories -- "My Kinsman, Major Molineux" -- also dramatizes his New Englander's sense of the guilt and of the tragedy inhering in America's dream of separation from England: from, as this story and as the title of his later book on England make clear, *Our Old Home*. For "My Kinsman, Major Molineux" is indeed, as Q. D. Leavis has pointed out, "a dramatic precipitation of, or prophetic forecast of, the rejection of England that was to occur in fact much later."[1] Tellingly, too, Hawthorne's dramatization of the tragedy inhering in America's rejection of England yields at the same time a dramatization of the shallowness and the inadequacy of America's Midwestern myth of the self-made man. For surely in this story of Robin Molineux' "rise" Hawthorne has, as we shall see, written an anti-American success story, a New Englander's penetrating inversion of the American -- which is to say, the Midwestern -- myth of success.

Robin Molineux, "barely eighteen years," with "well-shaped features, and bright, cheerful eyes" (p. 617),[2] and -- thinking "it high time to begin in the world" (p. 634) -- "upon his first visit to town" (p. 617) does, indeed, as Leavis has said, represent young, pre-Revolutionary America. The youth, the vigor, the too-callow optimism, the Yankee assertiveness and practical-mindedness are all there. Nothing, in fact, could be clearer or more self-evident: Robin, with his strength, his cudgel, his "shrewdness," and with the patronage of his prominent kinsman, is certain to "rise in the world" (p. 641), to have the brightest of futures. And no one, to be sure, is more certain of this bright future than Robin himself -- at least not until, having stepped off the ferry and having entered the city of night, "it occurred to him that he knew not whither to direct his steps" (p. 618).

This, of course, is by way of saying that "My Kinsman, Major Molineux" *is*, as I have mentioned, a subtle inversion of America's Midwestern myth of success. For in this story Robin's "shrewdness" serves but to lead him into greater and greater confusion, perplexity, and, indeed, terror. It is suggestive, therefore, that much of the plot of "My Kinsman" is, as Julian Smith has demonstrated, based upon "that seminal study of young America coming of age, *The Autobiography of Benjamin Franklin*."[3] In his article Smith points out such provocative facts as that Hawthorne had been reading Franklin's *Autobiography* at the time he wrote "My Kinsman"; that "Franklin's early career in Philadelphia and Robin's adventures in 'the little metropolis of a New England colony' take place at roughly the same time in American history"; that "Ben and Robin are shrewd, manly youths who are the same age"; and that both youths misguidedly "rely on the material bounty of older men." Mr. Smith then argues that Hawthorne's story of Robin and Franklin's story of his own mythic, metamorphic self both dramatize "that major requirement of the American Dream -- the necessity of change, of moving away from one's father's home, of advancing in the world on one's own merits and shrewdness."[4]

What is most telling, most meaningful in Hawthorne's story of young Robin and in Franklin's story of young Benjamin is not, however, the surface similarities: it is the essential contrasts. For if it is true that Robin's experiences in a New England town basically parallel Franklin's experiences in Philadelphia, it is hardly true that the *results* of these experiences are comparable. Franklin's youthful adventures in Philadelphia are, in Franklin's own view, a triumphant demonstration of the viability of Yankee "shrewdness" -- of common sense, self-reliance, industriousness, and practicality -- as a reliable and, indeed, as an ultimate guide for life. Such "errata" as one may occasionally commit are not to be viewed as disturbing evidences of evil in man's nature -- certainly not as anything like Original Sin or Innate Depravity -- but only as "errors" which everyone makes now and then and which should not be brooded over. And, indeed, if one so wishes, it is altogether possible to succeed at "the bold and arduous Project of arriving at moral Perfection."[5] In short, as D. H. Lawrence's bitter essay reminds us, it would be difficult to conceive of a moral complacency greater than that which Franklin exhibits in his *Autobiography*; and, conversely, it would be difficult to conceive of a writer *less* morally complacent than Nathaniel Hawthorne. This warns us that to note certain parallels in the lives of young Robin Molineux and of young Benjamin Franklin is to note only half, or less than half, of the truth: unlike Franklin in his *Autobiography*, Robin is totally abused of the naive notion that American practical-minded, success-oriented "shrewdness" is an adequate stance toward life's challenges and toward life's problems.

If, then, Robin is not a young Ben Franklin, what is he? What does he represent within the social-historical context of the story? What he is and what he represents, I suggest, is a young pre-Revolutionary, self-satisfied, success-minded America that in Hawthorne's view badly needs to relearn a few lessons from an older and, in its understanding of man's moral nature, wiser Puritan America. For if Robin begins his journey into the town as a young Ben Franklin, he ends that journey as something very much like a young Goodman Brown. Robin, like Brown, discovers that evil is ineradicable in man's nature. There is, in fact, no more illuminating way to approach Hawthorne's story of Robin Molineux and the Young America that he represents than by noting the similarities between the experiences of young Robin and of young Goodman Brown. Both "My Kinsman" and "Young Goodman Brown" are masterfully controlled allegories of psychological struggle, and both stories are vivified by dream-imagery, by Hawthorne's creation of a dreamlike state and sequence, that renders the horror of "The Haunted Mind." In both stories the psychological struggle is objectified by the archetypal motif of the journey (but, again, a journey that is as much dream as reality). Notable, too, is the fact that both stories are, to borrow Hawthorne's adjective for *The Scarlet Letter*, "hell-fired": both take place at night, and in each story the climactic scene, the Recognition Scene, is illuminated by blazing torches. Finally, both stories dramatize not just the discovery of evil but the *experience* of evil: both Robin and Brown are left with a devastating awareness of their own complicity in the evil that surrounds them.

But, we want to say, young Goodman Brown was a Puritan, and not only a Puritan but an archetypal Puritan whose perversely dark and Calvinistic view of man's moral nature led him to reject even a young and devoted wife -- a man who represents the extreme antithesis of the young, hopeful, forward-looking, pre-Revolutionary America that Hawthorne symbolizes in Robin Molineux. Surely Hawthorne is not suggesting that there are hidden affinities between the dark and treacherous world of the Puritans and the bright and confident world of the American Revolution? In fact, however, he is doing just that. "My Kinsman" dramatizes the discovery -- and of course it is not just Robin's discovery but the reader's, too -- that evil and guilt are an ineradicable part of the *American* past, even of the American Revolutionary past that most Americans proudly point to as an unqualified good.[6]   In other words, Hawthorne's story is *not*, as Harry Levin has suggested, a "lesson of modernity" in which Robin learns that if he "wants to rise in the world, he must rely upon his own efforts and not upon family connections; that an independent race of men must stand on its own feet, rejecting the past while forging the future."[7]   As a matter of fact, there is every reason to believe that Robin *could* have relied upon his family; upon his English heritage; upon his kinsman, Major Molineux. That this does not happen is Robin's fault -- and the New England colony's fault: it is in no way the fault of his well-meaning and kindhearted kinsman. What Robin really learns, then, upon not only witnessing but also participating in the destruction of his kinsman is that he -- as well as his savagely merry "friends" -- can *never* forget, and therefore (try as he may) can never fully reject the past: his English family, his English heritage. "Guilt" (as Roy Harvey Pearce has said) "is the price which Hawthorne makes Robin pay for his freedom."[8] And guilt, too, Hawthorne implies -- for the mad, savage mob (the whole town in fact) is obviously as guilty as Robin -- is the price that America has had to pay for her freedom. Like Irving in "Rip Van Winkle" -- but with a "power of blackness," an awareness of evil and of guilt far beyond Irving's grasp -- Hawthorne is suggesting that Robin, and all of America with him, would perhaps have been better off sleeping through the Revolution, that America's wholehearted and callow rejection of the past, along with her adolescent commitment to Progress, did not create a more attractive or a more admirable society.

It is, however, the precise nature of the guilt -- the guilt of parricide -- which Robin and the colony incur that the story's critics have overlooked, and this has hindered a grasp of the story's total meaning. We need, of course, go no further than the story's title to guess that *kinship* is at least one theme of the story; and in the story itself we are explicitly told that Robin's father and the Major "were brothers' children" (p. 634) -- meaning, as Leavis has noted, that "one brother had stayed in England and the other had left to colonize New England";[9] that the families had kept on friendly terms; and that the Major, having "acquired civil and military rank" and "being childless himself," had generously offered to help in the "future establishment" (p. 634) of one of his American cousin's sons. So it is clear that Robin's participation in the destruction of his kinsman is nothing short, as he himself senses ("I have at last met my kinsman, and he will scarce desire to see my face again" [p.641]), of a parricidal act. And what is true for Robin is equally true for the town and (as Hawthorne clearly suggests in his ironic prefatory paragraph) for *all* of pre-Revolutionary America. Everyone, it seems, has noted that the Major represents *British* rule without examining the immense cultural and psychological implications of this fact. For in rejecting and in diabolically destroying the Major, the townspeople are not repudiating some mere abstract Order, Tradition, and Authority: they are repudiating a specifically English order, tradition, and authority -- the heritage of their Old Home. Culturally, this is parricidal: the townspeople are as guilty as Robin, and for the same reason. So if there is (and, clearly, there is) a depth-psychological dimension to Robin's rejection of his kinsman, we might as well face the fact that there is a depth-psychological dimension to the American Revolution -- to the very origin, or essence, of American history. "Somewhere deep in every American heart" -- an Englishman, D. H. Lawrence, sensed -- "lies a rebellion against the old parenthood of Europe."[10] The dark, unconscious terror and ambivalence and tragedy of this rebellion receive their classic dramatization in Hawthorne's story.

This is to say, further, that Hawthorne's story is *gothic* in the strictest sense of that word: a dreamlike, symbolic projection of unconscious desires in which the darker impulses of man's soul are starkly revealed. (During his "evening of ambiguity and weariness" Robin soon begins to wonder if he is awake or dreaming, and immediately after the Recognition Scene the kindly stranger inquires, "Well, Robin, are you dreaming?" [p. 640].) Hawthorne uses Satanic imagery to render this hell within man's unconscious; it is, in fact, Satan himself[11] who presides over, and leads, the mob in the tar-and-feathering of Major Molineux. And even the colonists who do not actively participate in the violence are "applauding spectators" (p. 638). We have, in short, under the auspices of Satan himself, a midnight vision of evil entirely like -- but, I think, more realistically rendered and therefore more compelling and more terrifying than -- the witches' meeting at which young Goodman Brown discovered the diabolic nature of all his townsmen: "On they went, like fiends that throng in mockery around some dead potentate, mighty no more, but majestic still in his agony. On they went, in counterfeited pomp, in senseless uproar, in frenzied merriment, trampling all on an old man's heart" (p. 640).

Perhaps the most terrifying aspect of this vision of evil is the fact that the old man whose heart is trampled on is, from all that we can gather, utterly undeserving of such cruelty. "He was an elderly man, of large and majestic person, and strong square features, betokening a steady soul" -- a man whose head had "grown gray in honor" (pp. 638, 639). Why then do Robin and his "friends" reject, why do they torment this man? And why is Robin's shout "the loudest there" (p. 640)? As Simon O. Lesser has made clear,[12] we can answer this question only psychoanalytically: the destruction of a father-image. But, again, this destruction, this parricide, is *social* as well as personal (witness the immense irony in Robin's reference to his "friends"). The story's psychoanalytical meaning can not be separated from its historical meaning, and indeed the historical meaning *is* psychoanalytical. Personally, the Major is Robin's relative; socially and politically, he is a representative of *Our Old Home* and a symbol of governmental authority. Robin joins the town in rejecting this symbol of authority; but it is a rejection which -- because the authority, as embodied in the Major, was, after all, honorable, and because the Major was, after all, his kinsman -- leaves Robin, as the final scene of the story clearly shows, with a profound sense of parricidal guilt,[13] a sense of guilt that the whole town, the whole colony, will, perhaps, come to share once it realizes what it has done.

We are left finally with the question of whether Hawthorne's art-vision of America's newly emergent, nationally independent society is in any way hopeful, whether it in any way accords with the American dream. And it is clear that the answer must be negative. For in Robin's and in the town's parricidal act we see, as Pearce has said, that "Something like Original Sin becomes the prime fact of our political and social history. Adam's Fall and the Idea of Progress become not two myths but one."[14] Within Hawthorne's own world-view, there is, of course, a qualified hopefulness implicit in the fact that Robin *does* "fall,"[15] that he recognizes both his complicity in evil and the inescapableness of evil. But this is another way of saying that Hawthorne -- as an ancestral, as an archetypal New Englander -- could not endorse the American (Midwestern) dream of innocent progress: of a guiltless escape from, or a guiltless repudiation of, the past. Surely there is in our literature no more forceful dramatization than "My Kinsman, Major Molineux" of what Leslie A. Fiedler has pointed to as one of the "obsessive concerns of our national life": "the guilt of the revolutionist who feels himself a parricide."[16] Hawthorne's rendering of this intrinsically American -- and, above all, New Englander's -- guilt is tragic in the classic sense of that word: when his eyes met the eyes of his kinsman -- brutally humiliated but still embodying, still upholding, even in his humiliation, the manly, aristocratic values and traditions of our Old Home -- "Robin's knees shook, and his hair bristled, with a mixture of pity and terror" (p. 639).

Chapter 4

Notes

1.   Q. D. Leavis, "Hawthorne as Poet," *The Sewanee Review*, 59 (Spring, 1951): 199.

2.   All page references within the text are to *The Works of Nathaniel Hawthorne*, ed. George Parsons Lathrop, 15 vols. (Boston: Standard Library Edition, 1882-83), III.

3.   Julian Smith, "Coming of Age in America: Young Ben Franklin and Robin Molineux," *American Quarterly*, 17 (1965): 550-558.

4.   *Ibid.*, pp. 550, 551, 555, 558.

5.   *The Autobiography of Benjamin Franklin*, ed. Leonard W. Larabee et al. (New Haven: Yale University Press, 1964), p. 148.

6.   Cf. Roy Harvey Pearce, "Hawthorne and the Sense of the Past: Or, the Immortality of Major Molineux," *ELH*, 21 (Dec., 1954), 327-349; and Roy Harvey Pearce, "Robin Molineux on the Analyst's Couch: A Note on the Limits of Psychoanalytic Criticism," *Criticism*, 1 (Spring, 1959): 83-90.

7.   Harry Levin, *The Power of Blackness: Hawthorne, Poe, Melville* (New York: Random House, 1958), pp. 52, 179.

8.   Pearce, "Robin Molineux on the Analyst's Couch," p. 87.

9.   Leavis, p. 199.

10.   D. H. Lawrence, *Studies in Classic American Literature* (Garden City, N. Y.: Doubleday, 1951), p. 15.

11.   Cf. Hawthorne's description of the "unprecedented physiognomy" of the stranger who tells Robin that Major Molineux will "pass by" in an hour: "The forehead with its double prominence, the broad hooked nose, the shaggy eyebrows, and fiery eyes were those which [Robin] had noticed at the inn, but the man's complexion had undergone a singular, or more properly, a twofold change. One side of the face blazed an intense red, while the other was as black as midnight....The effect was as if two individual devils, a fiend of fire and a fiend of darkness, had united themselves to form this infernal visage" (*Works*, III, 629).

12.   Simon O. Lesser, "The Image of the Father: A Reading of 'My Kinsman, Major Molineux' and 'I Want to Know Why,'" *Partisan Review*, 22 (Summer, 1955): 372-390.

13.   It is pertinent here to recall Hawthorne's lifelong obsession with the story of Dr. Johnson's public penance in the Uttoxeter market-place for disobeying his father. Clearly, Robin's guilt in rejecting his kinsman is not something that Hawthorne took lightly. See Hawthorne's account of his "pilgrimage" to Uttoxeter in *Our Old Home* (*Works*, VII, 148-168).

14.   Pearce, "Hawthorne and the Sense of the Past," p. 330.

15.   Cf. Melvin W. Askew, "Hawthorne, the Fall, and the Psychology of Maturity," *American Literature*, 34 (Nov., 1962): 335-343.

16.   Leslie A. Fiedler, *Love and Death in the American Novel*, 2nd ed. (New York: Dell, 1966), p. 27.

CHAPTER 5

Henry Adams and The American Dream

So many myths, and so many place-myths, inhere in the American experience and in the American dream that studying a particular American writer's relation to the American dream simply means identifying the myths that, in the case of this writer at least, can be subsumed under the rubric "American dream." In the case of Henry Adams, I find that his life and his writings are related significantly to three American myths: the Jeffersonian, westering myth of a perfect, new-world, history-freed, progressive democracy; the New England place-myth of an ideal, pre-Liberal, Puritan, eighteenth-century (Quincy) past; and the Bostonian-Midwestern place-myth of material success as the sole passage to maturity or worthiness or identity in American (Bostonian State-Street) society.

With regard to the Jeffersonian myth of a new history-freed, progressive American democracy, one notes immediately that two of Adams's works, the novel *Democracy* and the classic *History of the United States of America During the Administrations of Jefferson and Madison*, were written with hardly any other purpose than to show the falsity, not to mention the tragedy, of the Jeffersonian new-world democratic experiment, the Jeffersonian myth. In *Democracy*, for example, Adams's heroine, Madeleine Lee, is determined to discover whether the American democratic experiment is a success or a failure. "'There is only one thing in life,' she went on, laughing, 'that I must and will have before I die. I must know whether America is right or wrong. Just now this question is a very practical one, for I really want to know whether to believe in Mr. Ratcliffe. If I throw him overboard, everything must go, for he is only a specimen.'"[1] Needless to say, Madeleine *does* finally throw Ratcliffe overboard -- and with him any belief in the rightness or feasibility of the American, Jeffersonian dream of a new socially, intellectually, culturally, morally progressive democracy. "The bitterest part of all this horrid story" -- as Madeleine writes to Carrington after rejecting Ratcliffe and, with him, America itself -- "is that nine out of

ten of our countrymen would say I had made a mistake."[2] So much, then, for
any faith in the discrimination, tastes, intelligence, or moral standards of the
American democratic citizenry! Like Huckleberry Finn, Madeleine "lights
out" at the end -- for Egypt. "Democracy has shaken my nerves to pieces.
Oh, what rest it would be to live in the Great Pyramid and look out forever at
the polar star!"[3]

Democracy shook Henry Adams's nerves to pieces, too, and drove
him, like Madeleine Lee, to the simple, overpowering urge to escape -- to
Cuba, to the Rocky Mountains, to the South Seas, to medieval France. Yet
he always came back -- usually to Washington, which, as Adams almost
despairingly reiterates in the later chapters of *The Education*, was "home."
Unlike Madeleine Lee, that is to say, Adams was not content just to discover
whether America was right or wrong: knowing that it was wrong, he was
driven all his adult life to trying to understand *why* it was wrong. One result
of this effort was, of course, his great *History* -- a work which Jay Martin
correctly defines as "the history of national failure," as an effort "to discover
the germ of decay inherent in the beginnings of American culture."[4] And the
conclusion to which the *History* inexorably leads is that the American,
Jeffersonian dream of a socially and intellectually liberating, culturally and
morally progressive new-world democracy was -- given the moral and the
spiritual needs and realities of human nature -- hopelessly naive and
predestined, or doomed, to failure. This is not to say that Adams was
unmoved by the Jeffersonian dream, or vision, or that he did not sympathize
with Jefferson's urgent wish to build a liberated, progressive, democratic
republic that would rise above, would not repeat, the misery and the
corruption and the evil of the past, of Europe.[5] Indeed, as Walter Allen has
pointed out, Adams's *History* is, for one thing, the first American book to
have applied "the analogy of the dream . . . to the American experiment."[6]
This analogy is presented in the brilliant chapter on "American Ideals" where
Adams scolds critics, like Wordsworth or Dickens, of early nineteenth-
century America for failing to perceive the idealism inhering in Jefferson's
democratic experiment, for failing to appreciate

> the force or the scope of an emotion which caused the poorest
> peasant in Europe to see what was invisible to poet and

philosopher -- the dim outline of a mountain-summit across the
ocean, rising high above the mist and mud of American
democracy. As though to call attention to some such difficulty
[to a failure to understand American idealism], European and
American critics, while affirming that Americans were a race
without illusions or enlarged ideas, declared in the same breath
that Jefferson was a visionary whose theories would cause the
heavens to fall upon them . . . . Every foreigner and Federalist
agreed that he was a man of illusions, dangerous to society and
unbounded in power of evil; but if this view of his character
was right, the same visionary qualities seemed also to be a
national trait, for everyone admitted that Jefferson's opinions,
in one form or another, were shared by a majority of the
American people . . . . [In short, as Adams goes on to conclude]
the hard, practical, money-getting American democrat . . . was
in truth *living in a world of dream* [emphasis mine], and acting a
drama more instinct with poetry than all the avatars of the East
. . . , in ambition already ruling the world and guiding Nature
with a kinder and wiser hand than had ever yet been felt in
human history . . . . [E]verywhere, in the White House at
Washington and in log-cabins beyond the Alleghenies, except
for a few Federalists, every American, from Jefferson and
Gallatin down to the poorest squatter, seemed to nourish an
idea that he was doing what he could to overthrow the tyranny
which the past had fastened on the human mind.[7]

Not easily would one find a more eloquent description than the above
of American new-world, westering, *democratic* idealism. Clearly, Adams was
sympathetic to Jefferson's dream of building a revolutionary progressive
democracy that would "lift the average man upon an intellectual and social
level with the most favored" (p. 115). Yet at the same time his awareness of
history and of his own archetypally *New Englander's* life-experience, or
consciousness, forced him -- from the perspective of his true home: his
eighteenth-century Quincy -- to take a tough-minded, conservative, Puritan
stance toward "this doubtful and even improbable principle" (p. 115). The
looming problem, the tragedy, inhering in Jefferson's history-defying
democratic experiment was that it overlooked the moral realities and
imperatives of man's life.

In the early days of colonization [as Adams points out] every
new settlement represented an idea and proclaimed a mission .
. . . The Pilgrims of Plymouth, the Puritans of Boston, the
Quakers of Pennsylvania, all avowed a moral purpose, and
began by making institutions that consciously reflected a moral
idea . . . . No such character belonged to the colonization of

> 1800 . . . . Greed for wealth, lust for power, yearning for the
> blank void of savage freedom . . . -- these were the fires that
> flamed under the caldron of American society, in which, as
> conservatives [Henry Adams, for one] believed, the old, well-
> proven, conservative crust of religion, government, family, and
> even common respect for age, education, and experience was
> rapidly melting away [pp. 128-129].

Not only is this passage a valid, important description and criticism of American society and of the American Westward Movement in 1800: it also clearly reveals Adams's preference for a pre-Liberal, Puritan, New England past[8] -- for the kind of moral idealism that, in *The Education*, he defines as his eighteenth century *Quincy* inheritance.   For Adams saw Jefferson's visionary liberating, progressive democratic experiment, however well intentioned, as operating *in reality* as a negative ideal, serving -- among westering American democrats -- but to stimulate "greed for wealth, lust for power, yearning for the blank void of savage freedom." The positive ideal -- for Henry Adams, for New England -- is a society like the Puritans', or like the America visioned by Adams's own grandfather-President and great-grandfather-President, that "avows a moral purpose" and in which the individual finds his fulfillment and his freedom *through* his commitment to that purpose.   Adams's *History* stands, that is to say, as a massive documentation of the validity of his own ancestral New Englander's, Puritan view of human nature and of man's absolute need for *civil*, as opposed to merely democratic or natural, freedom. "The most unfree souls go west," was D. H. Lawrence's Englishman's challenge to Americans, one century after the beginning of Jefferson's new-world experiment, "and shout of freedom."[9] Adams's account of the failures of Jefferson's Administration, especially his account of the failure of the embargo, overwhelmingly demonstrates that the American dream of total, natural freedom and of spontaneous, self-made material, social, intellectual, moral progress -- of an apostasy, an escape from history and from "the institutions of church, aristocracy, family, army, and political intervention" (p. 115) -- was indeed a delusory dream: an illusion engendered by an unrealistic and naive view of human needs and of human nature.   At the end (1815) of the *History*, American nationality has triumphed, the American character -- confident, complacent, sanguine, intellectually quick (or shrewd), practical-minded, energetic, forward (which is to say, Westward)-looking -- has been fixed; and the only remaining question is whether or not this conclusion to Jefferson's and Madison's Administrations is, culturally and morally, a triumph in any real sense. "What interests were to vivify a society so vast and uniform? What ideals were to ennoble it? What object, besides physical content, must a democratic continent aspire to attain? For the treatment of such questions, history required another century of experience" (p. 417). That century of experience is provided in *The Education of Henry Adams*, which besides being Adams' greatest work is also the most revealing, penetrating, and dramatic account of his relation to the American dream.

While the failure of American democracy is self-evident throughout *The Education*, this work goes beyond the failure of the Jeffersonian new-world democratic vision, or myth, to examine and to dramatize at least two other central American myths. These, as I have indicated, are the myths of success and of an ideal eighteenth-century New England, or Quincy, past. And in *The Education* these myths are tested and dramatized by the life-experience, the education ("seventy years of it"), of one Henry Adams -- which is another way of saying, too, that *The Education* is a work of literature quite as much as, say, *Walden* or *The Scarlet Letter*. This, of course, is not to say that the events in *The Education* did not actually occur -- only that, as a literary artist must, Adams is selecting and organizing the events he relates, and raising them to the level of symbols. As William C. Spengemann and L. R. Lundquist have pointed out, the subject of an autobiography inevitably becomes a literary character, a persona, rather than an exact duplicate of the person who writes the autobiography. For "no man maintains the same stance throughout his life, nor does he usually take the same attitude toward all problems at any one time in his life. His journals and his letters may show him taking on a number of . . . personae over time. But when he comes to write his autobiography . . . he must adopt some consistent, overriding view of himself and his past."[10] And this is especially true of an autobiography that is told in the *third person* and in which the central character, as Adams tells us in his "Preface," is not "the Ego" but "a manikin on which the toilet of education is to be draped in order to show the fit or misfit of the clothes." In fact, Adams affirms, "The object of study [in *The Education*] is the garment, not the figure. The tailor adapts the manikin as well as the clothes to his patron's wants."[11] If this means anything at all, it means, quite clearly, that we are to regard *The Education* as a literary work in which "Henry Adams" is a character created to serve the author's purpose.

That purpose is, for one thing, to treat a theme that one encounters everywhere in American literature: the moral (and, for "Henry Adams" at least, the severely practical) problem of success in American society. It is no accident that Adams refers in his "Preface" to Benjamin Franklin as the only "model...of self-teaching" in American literature, or that he refers to his own draping of the toilet of education upon the manikin "Henry Adams" as an effort "to fit young men, in universities or elsewhere, to be men of the world, equipped for any emergency" (pp. ix, x). Quite as much as Franklin, that is to say, Adams is writing in the tradition of the American success story: he wants to show young men *how* to succeed. Unlike Franklin, though, Adams will instruct by negative examples, examples of failure: "the garment [of education] offered to them [young men] is meant to show the faults of the patchwork fitted on their fathers" (p. x).

There is, however, another respect in which Adams differed from Franklin: he was an ironist. Any reader of *The Education* quickly ceases to take very seriously Adams's reiteration of his innumerable failures. If anything, Adams takes pride in his failures: they are examples of the low marketability of Adams's New Englander's moral idealism in modernist, materialistic, democratic America. So far, then, from showing young men "the faults of the patchwork fitted on their fathers," *The Education* actually shows them the faults of an egalitarian, progressive American society in which the eighteenth-century New England idealism of their fathers is neither respected nor rewarded. Quite as penetratingly, in short, as his fellow ancestral New Englander Hawthorne in "My Kinsman, Major Molineux," Adams is in *The Education* inverting Benjamin Franklin's morally complacent American success-story. For in its final import *The Education* is related not at all to Franklin's *Autobiography* but to the entire Romance tradition in American fiction: a tradition, as Chapter 12 argues, that focuses upon the consciousness, the starkly individual, starkly isolated experience, of lonely protagonist-heroes *outside* society: men -- or boys -- on the run who repudiate the American dream of success, who refuse novitiate into America's prevailing society of (solely) self-made men. Our classic fictionists have, quite simply, been unable to believe in a progressive, egalitarian, competitive society that provides its members with but one measure of worthiness: success. The truly *westering* success -- spiritual change and rebirth ("a success unexpected in common hours") -- that Thoreau achieved and celebrated in *Walden* is, as Thoreau himself well knew, unacknowledged and unrecognized by the prevailing American society: by the commercial, progressive society that Henry Adams, even as a ten-year-old boy, saw inhering in and emanating from the State-Street heart of Boston itself. What *is* recognized and socially rewarded is the totally secular (economic, practical, scientific, political) success epitomized -- and, indeed, mythicized -- by Benjamin Franklin.

As Daniel G. Hoffman has shown, the psychologically disintegrative, the *self*-destructive effect of the American dream of success as mythicized by Benjamin Franklin derives from its "set[ting] its exemplars in linear motion through" a series of metamorphoses (Adams is forever beginning a "new" education) that are essentially profane, that have no meaning beyond the sheerly secular and pragmatic.[12] Certainly Adams was aware of this. His insistence, throughout *The Education*, upon failure has nothing to do with failure in its Ben Franklin, or Bostonian State-Street, or Midwestern, mythical meaning, but is based, instead, upon his anguished awareness of modernist America's repudiation of the moral idealism which informed "that eighteenth-century [New England, Puritan] inheritance which he took with his name" (p. 7) -- and of the consequent inevitable (social, practical) failure of any attempt (such as his own) to live in accordance with the standards of that idealism. Thus, for example, Adams's description of his stark, inescapable economic situation upon his return to America after the Civil War: "He was for sale, in the open market. So were many of his friends. All the world knew it, and knew too that they were cheap; to be bought at the price of a mechanic. There was no concealment, no delicacy, and no illusion about it" (p. 240). And as for the result -- both personal and national -- of

America's single-minded commitment to egalitarian democracy and to economic individualism: years later,

> in 1892, neither Hay, King, nor Adams knew whether they had attained success, or how to estimate it, or what to call it; and the American people seemed to have no clearer idea than they. Indeed, the American people had no idea at all .... They had lost the sense of worship; for the idea that they worshipped money seemed a delusion .... The American mind had less respect for money than the European or Asiatic mind, and bore its loss more easily; but it had been deflected by its pursuit till it could turn in no other direction. It shunned, distrusted, disliked, the dangerous attraction of ideals, and stood alone in history for its ignorance of the past [p. 328].

How could Henry Adams, "a citizen of Quincy" (p. 500), be truly successful in a modern, morally directionless, Quincy-abandoned, history-defiant, history-ignorant society that "shunned, distrusted, disliked, the dangerous attraction of ideals"? He could not, of course. Yet the "Henry Adams" of *The Education* tried. Exactly this effort, or search, for success -- when added to his other traits, his other values -- renders "Henry Adams" one of the most complex, symbolically rich, and important characters in American literature. Quite as much as Ishmael or Huckleberry Finn is he a wanderer and an outcast; quite as much as Thoreau or Isaac McCaslin is he in quest of spiritual fulfillment; yet at the same time he is also, like Benjamin Franklin, fully on the make, intent upon making his mark, gaining power and prestige -- if he can. He is, to borrow Whitman's words, "both in and out of the game" -- but never, like Whitman, above it. Rather, he is an example of what Richard Lehan has called "the Nowhere Hero" in American fiction[13] -- a hero who tries to realize, to achieve, moral and spiritual ideals in a society that recognizes no ideals other than the sheerly economic and pragmatic, and who consequently ends up nowhere and with nothing. What one inevitably asks, then, is *why* Henry Adams persisted in his humiliating, almost quixotic attempts to follow the mythic pattern of success in America -- why he did not, like most protagonist-heroes in classic American literature, simply repudiate the American dream of success.

The answer lies, I think, in Adams's relation to "that eighteenth-century inheritance which he took with his name." We have seen Adams' emphatic observation in his *History* that the westering, colonizing American society after 1800 no longer "avowed a moral purpose" or "reflected a moral idea"; yet Henry Adams was acutely aware of the fact that in his own *New England* heritage, at least, moral idealism -- as epitomized in the life and the character of John Quincy Adams -- *had* lived beyond 1800. And, more than this, he clearly felt the need to prove himself worthy of his New England, Quincy heritage -- with full understanding that the eighteenth-century values and principles which he inherited with his name were "colonial, revolutionary, almost Cromwellian" (p. 7) as to the emphasis they placed on the *moral* improvement of society. "Resistance to something was the law of New England nature; the boy [Henry Adams] looked out on the world with the instinct of resistance; for numberless generations his predecessors had viewed the world chiefly as a thing to be reformed, filled with evil forces to be abolished, and they saw no reason to suppose that they had wholly succeeded in the abolition; the duty was unchanged" (p. 7). This, clearly, is a Puritan-like *social* ideal: the world must be reformed; evil forces must be abolished; the individual must contribute to that reformation and to that abolition. There is, however, a vital assumption underlying this ideal: the assumption that the society *as a whole* is committed to moral improvement. And, as Adams forcefully shows in his *History*, this was not true of American westering, democratic society after 1800. The classic example, in fact, is Adams's own grandfather, John Quincy Adams -- who for Henry Adams was nothing less than "the eighteenth century, as an actual and living companion" (p. 20). Nowhere more clearly than in the career of John Quincy Adams does one see that the eighteenth-century values of duty, discipline, truth, morality, and restraint were becoming increasingly ignored and disrespected in the aggressive and progressive America of Jackson and of Polk. Had he not been humiliatingly defeated by Jackson on the grounds of his being too "aristocratic"?

Yet John Quincy Adams's dream of an America committed to resistance to State Street; to truth, duty, and freedom (p. 22); to *moral* as well as to material progress (a dream that was given classic statement, for example, in his first Annual Message as President) was Henry Adams's dream, too: implicit in the very tone and attitude of the opening chapters of

The Education; fully explicit, later on in *The Education*, when Adams describes America's 1893 "submission to capitalism" (under "the creation of a single gold standard") as among those "disagreeable certainties -- like age, senility, and death -- against which one made what little resistance one could" and when he claims, proudly, to have "stood up for his eighteenth century, his Constitution of 1789, his George Washington, his Harvard College, his Quincy, his Plymouth Pilgrims, as long as any one would stand up with him" (pp, 344, 343).   Like his grandfather-President, moreover, Henry Adams believed that the true vision, or dream, of America must be earned: Freedom can be won, can be achieved, only *through* Resistance, Truth, Duty (p. 22). The individual must serve society and, in turn, be served by it.[14]   To have achieved *this* end would, for Henry Adams, have been true success. And to no other end (in an episode [pp. 12-14] that R. P. Blackmur has rightly pointed to as one of the most crucial and most symbolic in the entire book[15]) is the six-year-old Henry Adams's "boy's will" broken by the seventy-six-year-old President who leads him off to school: to the end that Henry Adams may carry on the Adams tradition of resistance, of discipline, of duty, and of winning freedom *through* service.   There is, however, a world of significance in the fact that John Quincy Adams's mind was probably "troubling itself little about his grandson's iniquities, and much about the iniquities of President Polk," (p. 13) at the very moment that he initiated his grandson -- at Quincy -- into the Adams tradition of duty and of service. For such a tradition was being, just then, increasingly, relentlessly challenged and, ultimately, overthrown by the ruthlessly pragmatic, acquisitive, morally visionless America epitomized in President Polk. And only four years after having been led to school, at the same grandfather-President's Eulogy in Boston, the ten-year-old boy already fully knew ("for knowledge was beginning to come fast") that what his Adams, his Quincy, heritage *really* required was resistance to Boston and to State Street. "Quincy had always been right, for Quincy represented a moral principle -- the principle of resistance to Boston. His Adams ancestors must have been right, since they were always hostile to State Street. If State Street was wrong, Quincy must be right [pp. 21-22]!"

Given the difficulty, and finally the impossibility, of his attaining true success as defined by his inherited Adams tradition--that tradition itself being symbolized by the ancestral Adams home: Quincy -- it is not surprising that Henry Adams dwells so lovingly upon his childhood in the opening "Quincy" chapter, unquestionably one of the strongest chapters of *The Education*. And in so doing Adams becomes obsessed with another central myth of American culture: the myth of an ideal, paradisal past -- which, as I have mentioned, in the case of Henry Adams happens to be an eighteenth-century, pre-Liberal, Puritan, New England, Quincy-centered past. ("[F]or some remote reason, [Henry Adams] was born an eighteenth-century child. The old house at Quincy was eighteenth century" [p. 11].) Like Jay Gatsby, Adams dreams of repeating, of preserving -- for himself and for America -- his eighteenth-century, Quincy past; but, unlike Gatsby, he *knows* that the past can not be repeated. This is his despair, as it has been the despair of many of our classic writers, including Cooper, Twain, Fitzgerald, and Faulkner. In *The Education*, that is to say, Adams is developing a theme, pervasive in our literature, that growing up in America is a special kind of Fall from which there is no recovery. Only in his childhood, only at Quincy, could Adams be free of any "doubt whether a system of society which had lasted since Adam would outlast one Adams more" ("to him, that there should be a doubt of his being President was a new idea"!) (p. 16). Mythically, Adams is lamenting a Lost America,[16] a pristine, natural, preindustrial, precapitalistic, idyllic past. Like Mark Twain, Adams grew up in a still relatively simple America, reached his maturity precisely at the Civil War, and lived on to witness the complexities and the corruptions of the Gilded Age. That Twain's and Adams' pasts were vastly different is, mythologically, finally irrelevant: both turned intently to their childhoods and invested them with all the ideals that were glaringly betrayed by post-Civil-War America.[17] Of course Adams, at least, was fully aware that he was working with myth: pre-Civil-War America was far from idyllic, as John Quincy Adams knew from bitter personal experience and as Henry Adams' own *History* abundantly shows. Yet this is, in itself, one form, one function, of myth: wish-fulfillment, the expression of dreams, of ideals, rather than the depiction of realities. Moreover, as to Quincy -- his own home, his own heritage, his own childhood -- this myth, this

ideal past, *was* for Henry Adams deeply real.   As real as Walden to
Henry Thoreau, was Quincy to Henry Adams.   Quincy was country: "the
endless delight of mere sense impressions given by nature for nothing, and
breathed by boys without knowing it" (p. 8).   Quincy was home: the inherited
Adams tradition of New England, Puritan moral standards embodied in a
living grandfather-President.   Both were real.

If, however, *The Education* is a dream of the past, it is also a
nightmare vision of the future.   In this, too, it is an intrinsically *American*
book, and "Henry Adams" is an archetypal American literary hero who sees
his childhood paradise destroyed, who spends his life wandering through
chaos and disaster, and who desperately searches for some form of certainty
and of unity -- for some escape from the wreckage of time, of history.
Throughout *The Education*, as Kenneth MacLean has shown,[18] there is a
sharp, tragic tension between mechanical time (clock-time, calendar-time)
and imaginative, or mythical, time.   Like many American protagonists -- like
the "I" of *Walden*, like Isaac McCaslin, like Quentin Compson, or like Jay
Gatsby -- "Henry Adams" dreams of transcending mechanical, historical time:
dreams of finding an absolute, unchanging, pure, Edenic time.   "One's
instinct abhors time" (p. 228).   Yet of course both the *History* and *The
Education* overwhelmingly tell that there can be no escape from time, from
history -- for "Henry Adams" or for America.   Indeed, it would be difficult to
name another American book (unless it be Faulkner's *The Sound and the
Fury*) that is so despairingly obsessed with the tragic passage of time, with
the anguish of change, with the wreckage of history.   Even at Quincy the ten-
year-old boy "felt that something was wrong" ("but he concluded that it must
be Boston") (p. 21).   When that boy, now a young man, returns to America
after the Civil War, he sees American society as "a long straggling caravan,
stretching loosely towards the prairies" -- as a society that was "trying, almost
as blindly as an earthworm, to realize and understand itself; to catch up with
its own head, and to twist about in search of its tail" (p. 237).   And when that
young man, now an old man, returns once again, he fronts a society whose
change and whose movement toward chaos and toward anarchy is "more
striking than ever -- wonderful -- unlike anything man had ever seen -- and
like nothing he had ever much cared to see" (p. 499).

At this point -- as "Henry Adams" returns, in the last chapter of *The Education*, to New York City (November 5, 1904) and as the "two-thousand-years failure of Christianity roar[s] upward from Broadway" (p. 500) -- all dreams have been lost. Jefferson's dream of a new-world democracy yielding newly independent, socially and intellectually liberated American citizens has, in one century, given way to appalling mediocrity, corruption, mindless commercialism, and confusion. America's dream of repudiating the past, of overthrowing the tyranny of the past, of escaping history, has left her floundering and directionless and entrapped by vast mechanical historical forces beyond her control or her comprehension. Adams's own dream-vision of an eternal eighteenth-century Quincy -- a heritage, a social ideal, a moral absolute, that had begun to vanish even with his boy's life -- has everywhere been denied by and violated by his adult experience in America. His ever-frustrated effort, through effective education, to achieve the American dream of success has only demonstrated the shallowness and the elusiveness of that dream -- has shown, indeed, that Americans have lost even a definition for success. Like so many truly *American* books, *The Education* ends, as it begins, with a deep sense of betrayal. This, too, is an American myth. As Philip Young has movingly put it, the myth that our youth and our promise have been betrayed, that we, as a nation, "*would* have been, . . . *could* have been" much better, much wholer, much happier than we actually are had we not been "crippled before we were grown by the world we were given to grow in" is "as deep, and as great and beautiful, as any myth we have."[19] Henry Adams put it somewhat differently, but no less movingly, when, in the last sentence of *The Education*, he voiced the hope that he and Hay and King might, on the occasion of their centenary, "be allowed to return together for a holiday . . . and [that] perhaps then, for the first time since man began his education among the carnivores, they would find a world that sensitive and timid natures could regard without a shudder." The whole of *The Education* belies such a hope, of course. But the dream of a better world still lives.

Chapter 5

Notes

1.   Henry Adams, *Democracy: An American Novel* (New York: Arimont, 1968), p. 45.
2.   *Ibid.*, p. 190.
3.   *Ibid.*, p. 188.
4.   Jay Martin, *Harvests of Change: American Literature 1865-1914* (Englewood Cliffs, N.J.: Prentice-Hall, 1967), p. 300.
5.   Cf. Merrill D. Peterson, "Henry Adams on Jefferson the President," *The Virginia Quarterly Review*, 39 (Spring, 1963): 187-201.
6.   Walter Allen, *The Urgent West: The American Dream and Modern Man* (New York: Dutton, 1969), p. 227.
7.   Henry Adams, *History of the United States of America during the Administrations of Jefferson and Madison*, ed. Ernest Samuels (Chicago: The University of Chicago Press, 1967), pp. 124, 125, 127. Hereafter all page references for the *History* will be to this edition and will be included within the text.
8.   Cf. Elisha Greifer, "The Conservative Pose in America: The Adamses' Search for a Pre-Liberal Past," *Western Political Quarterly*, 15 (March, 1962): 5-16.
9.   D. H. Lawrence, *Studies in Classic American Literature* (Garden City, New York: Doubleday, 1951), p. 17.
10.   William C. Spengemann and L. R. Lundquist, "Autobiography and the American Myth," *American Quarterly*, 17 (Fall, 1965): 514.
11.   Henry Adams, *The Education of Henry Adams* (New York: The Modern Library, 1931), p. x. Hereafter all page references for *The Education* will be to this edition and will be included within the text.
12.   Daniel G. Hoffman, "The American Hero: His Masquerade," in *His Form and Fable in American Fiction* (New York: Oxford University Press, 1965), pp. 38-82. Esp. pp. 79-81.
13.   Richard Lehan, "Focus on F. Scott Fitzgerald's *The Great Gatsby*: The Nowhere Hero," in *American Dreams, American Nightmares*, ed. David Madden (Carbondale: Southern Illinois University Press, 1970), pp. 106-114.
14.   "He had a notion that the individual could live well only when he made some sort of contribution to the whole, and was generously served by that whole, too." Elizabeth Stevenson, *Henry Adams: A Biography* (New York: Macmillan, 1956), p. 350.
15.   R. P. Blackmur, "Adams Goes to School," *Kenyon Review*, 17 (Autumn, 1955): 597-623.
16.   Cf. Tony Tanner, "The Lost America -- The Despair of Henry Adams and Mark Twain," *Modern Age*, 5 (Summer, 1961): 299-310.
17.   Cf. Tony Tanner's remark that "The Civil War was a fall -- *the* fall for those who experienced it, and consequently youth, for those who had spent it before the war, took on a paradisaical, mythical glow." *The Reign of Wonder: Naivety and Reality in American Literature* (Cambridge: Cambridge University Press, 1965), p. 148.
18.   Kenneth MacLean, "Window and Cross in Henry Adams' *Education*," *University of Toronto Quarterly*, 28 (July, 1959): 332-344.

19.   Philip Young, "The World and an American Myth," in his *Ernest Hemingway: A Reconsideration* (University Park: Pennsylvania State University Press, 1966), pp. 259, 260.

SECTION II

THE MIDWEST AND THE WESTWARD MOVEMENT:

FREDERICK JACKSON TURNER, FULTON COUNTY SETTLERS

CHAPTER 6

The Turner Thesis, the Historic Westerner,
And the Mythic West:
Suggestions for a New Historiography of the Westward Movement

The importance of the frontier in American history, culture, and literature is clear and essentially beyond debate. What historians, literary critics, and sociologists continue to debate and to investigate is the precise "significance" -- as Frederick Jackson Turner called it in his famous essay -- of America's frontier heritage. Happily, we have now passed the period of heated and often wrongheaded argument over the validity of Turner's own thesis about the cultural implications of the American westering experience. Scholars, especially historians, are displaying a new humility about the abiding importance of Turner's ideas to our understanding of American history and American culture. For the point is not that Turner's ideas are always "right," but that they are enormously challenging, suggestive, and seminal. Few theories have led to as many insights into the nature of American culture and the American character as Turner's. In this chapter, then, I wish to show the need for a new historiography of the Westward Movement -- one which does not abandon Turner but uses him as a starting point, usually qualifies and sometimes denies his ideas, incorporates knowledge from fields -- especially from literature -- which Turner chose not to consider, but always acknowledges his influence.

In an important article on the Turner thesis, Jackson K. Putnam reminds us that Turner was interested in the frontier primarily as a process rather than as a place.[1] This of course is one aspect of Turner's thesis that needs modification: he seems to have been unaware of, or at least unconcerned with, what is commonly called "a sense of place" -- with cultural geography or with cultural landscapes. Nevertheless, what Turner says about the pioneering process (and the heart of this process, for him, was the first settlement by farmers) is still immensely valuable; in some respects -- as with the democratizing effect of the frontier experience[2] -- it seems, for certain regions at least, to have been historically true. Where the thesis is not true, it prods us to seek the truth. How valid, for example, is Turner's claim that those traits which are intrinsically American were born on the frontier? In my view this is the single most important aspect of his thesis, and a rich field for study. "The forest clearings," Turner insisted, "have been the seed plots of American character." "In the crucible of the frontier the immigrants were Americanized, liberated, and fused into a mixed race, English in neither nationality nor characteristics." And the key American traits which Turner attributed to the frontier experience are listed in the 1893 essay: coarseness, strength, inquisitiveness, practicality, restless energy, individualism, buoyancy, exuberance -- these, he said, "are traits of the frontier, or traits called out elsewhere because of the existence of the frontier."[3] It has yet to be shown that Turner was not on to something here: certain of the traits which he identifies with either the experience or simply the existence of the frontier *are* recognizably American. In the following study of the westering experience in the Midwestern county where I grew up and where, since 1979, I have been a self-employed businessman -- Fulton County, Indiana -- I find the traits which Turner enumerates to be fairly representative of the original settlers in the area -- though I do *not* find evidence that these traits were evoked by the Fulton County frontier. Rather, I find that these traits were *brought* to the frontier by the settlers themselves, and that, once on the frontier, these particular homesteaders, at least, stubbornly resisted the "forest-change" that Turner so fondly attributed to them. But even the evidence that a Turnerian forest-change was strongly resisted is important, I like to think, to our understanding of the history and the culture of one fairly representative Midwestern county -- which is to say, again, that Turner's thesis can serve, and often *should* serve, as an important focus for American studies.

Few scholars will argue, I think, that Turner is "usable" in the ways that I have been describing. The question is, how can we make him even more usable? How can we achieve a more comprehensive historiography of the American Westward Movement? This can be done by taking careful note of some limitations in Turner's views. For example, my reading of Turner is one which finds him much less "romantic" and "mythic" about the

American westering experience than he is commonly thought to be. Even the famous passage in the 1893 essay celebrates traits which I, at least, do not see as wholly positive. (In a phrase especially worth meditating, Turner himself sees American individualism "working for good and for evil.") Elsewhere Turner is much more explicit about his viewing the pioneering experience strictly in terms of economic "opportunity" ("The West was another name for opportunity") and about his belief that the hero in the settlement drama was an old American standby, the self-made man. "The self-made man was the Western man's ideal, was the kind of man that all men might become. Out of his wilderness experience, out of the freedom of his opportunities, he fashioned a formula for social regeneration,--the freedom of the individual to seek his own."[4] It is difficult to see how the freedom of the individual to seek his own is a good formula for social regeneration, but Turner seems to have been sincere about this. Unlike major American writers throughout the nineteenth and twentieth centuries, in other words, he seems not to have worried much about the cultural limitations of the self-made man or about the spiritual barrenness of democratic individualism. This, frankly, is a serious failure not only in his understanding of American society but also in his understanding of the American frontier. For, to the American imagination at least, and as other chapters of this book -- especially the chapters on Stephen Crane -- aim to show, the frontier has often represented an escape from the very social conditions that Turner celebrates. In other words, the frontier is central to the American experience not simply as fact, but as myth. Why else did Thoreau self-consciously build a hut at Walden at the very time that his countrymen were frantically pushing westward?

It is the mythic West for which the Turner thesis offers no account, but for which an adequate historiography must account. As Henry Nash Smith, R. W. B. Lewis, Leslie A. Fiedler, and Edwin Fussell, among others, have shown, the mythic West is as much a *fact* of American history and of American culture as is the Westward Movement itself.[5] This is to say that besides researching the actual history of the frontier -- discovering whether or not the classic Turnerian traits were in fact developed on, or by, actual American frontiers -- we need to keep in mind the fact that Americans, especially American writers, have traditionally *imaged* the West in ways that often have nothing to do with our actual history. In the following study of narratives by Fulton County, Indiana, pioneers, for example, I do not find the "buoyancy and exuberance" which are among the traits which Turner celebrates as "traits of the frontier." As I have aimed to show in Chapter 2, however, I *do* find such traits in Thoreau, who deliberately chose ("I went to the woods because I wished to live deliberately, to front only the essential facts of life") to be a symbolic rather than an actual frontiersman -- or, as he would have put it, the only *true* frontiersman. In Thoreau we have a classic example of the fact that the mythic West can be more *real* than the historic West. The Fulton County settlers experienced no Turnerian rebirth, no forest-change; Thoreau did.   Moreover, Thoreau carefully set about developing in himself traits appropriate for his concept of the ideal frontiersman -- a man uniting wildness *and* refinement -- such as could be found on no actual American frontier. He cultivated the positive Turnerian frontier traits, vigorously repudiated all the others, and, as my earlier chapter argues, added essential ones that (unknown to him) were actually the *English Traits* insightfully observed and described by his friend Emerson. Of course the stance of Thoreau is not unique to our literature. It is clear that our classic literature, especially fiction, celebrates westering heroes who seek to transcend, to go *beyond*, the (symbolic or literal) frontier, to opt out of society entirely. This needs to be accounted for, as I believe that it can if we focus upon, but also go *beyond*, a subject that was so central and so crucial for Turner himself: American democracy.

As I have suggested in my chapter on Henry Adams, and as a later chapter will argue more extensively, the entire Romance tradition in American fiction -- and its concomitant search for a mythic West -- is directly related to our fictionists' dissatisfaction with American democracy. For our purposes, here, this can perhaps be seen most strikingly by looking at the writer who is widely believed to have begun the Romance tradition in American fiction: James Fenimore Cooper. Two things can be said immediately: 1) Cooper's Leatherstocking Tales are a major literary treatment of the American Westward Movement; 2) Cooper's Leatherstocking Tales make almost no sense at all if we try to read them in

Turnerian terms. Why this contradiction? The answer, as I have indicated, lies in Cooper's attitude toward American democracy. As D. H. Lawrence so clearly perceived, and as any reader of Cooper's travel writings -- especially, as my last chapter will illustrate, his book on England -- can plainly see, Cooper deplored the cultural effects of American democracy. So the Leatherstocking Tales embody, and were created out of, what Lawrence has famously called "a wish-fulfillment vision, a kind of yearning myth."[6] From Lawrence's point of view, which I accept, a Turnerian birth of democracy on the frontier is the least of Cooper's interests or concerns. As Lawrence was the first to point out, the silliest thing we can do with Cooper is to try and read him in realistic terms. The action of *The Prairie*, to take a specific example, is totally improbable; and there is no Turnerian settlement process. Indeed, there is no settlement at all. "Except for Leatherstocking," as Edwin Fussell has noted, "all the white characters are in the end, by Cooper's dispensation, backtrailers."[7] Many things are involved here, the most important probably being that the Westward Movement was for Cooper a tragic story as of course it never was for Turner. This Romance, then, the most "Western" of all the Romances in the Leatherstocking Saga, is Cooper's least sympathetic treatment of the American Westward Movement. The harsh high-plains landscape itself is hostile to intruders, and Cooper seems to delight in this. Much more importantly, there is the archetypal American westering hero, Leatherstocking, who stands outside of -- and utterly opposed to -- "the waste and wickedness of the settlements." Herein, as Roy Harvey Pearce has noted, lies the tragedy: Cooper "could see that westward expansion and progress in crushing such a man as Bumppo would crush something heroic in American life."[8] "When I am gone," says Natty, "there will be an end of my race." Although critics have wondered endlessly about the precise meaning of this averment, one thing is very clear: it has nothing to do with Turner's busy, buoyant, triumphant pioneers. As for the actual pioneers of the Romance -- the Bush family -- there is nothing very cheerful, optimistic, or buoyant about them, either. It is true that the Bush family -- or at least Ishmael -- does undergo an important change on the prairie, but it is important to note that this change has nothing to do with Turner's classic settlement process. This change, the humanization of Ishmael -- his development of a sense of justice *and* forgiveness -- occurs outside any settlement.

Where does all this leave us in the historiography of the Westward Movement? It suggests, I believe, that Turner's ideas need to be retained but also modified and expanded in at least three ways. Most obviously, we need to remember that -- since Fenimore Cooper, at least -- there have always been a mythic West and a mythic Western hero *beyond* the frontier. Turner chose not to try to account for this vision of the West as "territory" -- as an escape from, or a transcendence of, civilization itself[9] -- even though it was in his own day already a central tradition in American literature. Then we need to examine the relationships between the mythic West and Turner's West. Central here, as I have indicated, is the matter of American democracy itself. As Leatherstocking, and even Ishmael Bush, were aware, democracy, with its emphasis upon economic individualism and upon land ownership, militates against what Max Westbrook has usefully termed the "sacrality" of space and place.[10] In other words, the mythic West can be seen as a response to -- as a wish, that is, to transcend or, minimally, to escape from -- the secularizing tendency of American democracy. Finally, we need to continue to research the actual motives and experiences of historic westerners. Were they really Turner's independent, self-assured, self-made men? Or did "that restless, nervous energy" which Turner rightly ascribes to them derive instead, as Jackson K. Putnam has suggested, from their being driven by conflicting motives ("to be free and . . . to be rich") which produced "intolerable irritants deep in their psyches"?[11] In either case, we are, as the following chapter aims to show, still living with their legacy.

Chapter 6

Notes

1.   "The Turner Thesis and the Westward Movement: A Reappraisal," *Western Historical Quarterly*, 7 (October, 1976): 377-404.

2.   See Merle Curti, *The Making of an American Community: A Case Study of Democracy in a Frontier Country* (Stanford, Calif.: Stanford University Press, 1959).

3.   *Frontier and Section: Selected Essays of Frederick Jackson Turner* (Englewood Cliffs, N.J.: Prentice Hall, 1961), pp. 64, 52, 61.

4.   *Ibid.*, p. 69.

5.   Smith, *Virgin Land: The American West as Symbol and Myth* (New York: Random House, 1950); Lewis, *The American Adam: Innocence, Tragedy, and Tradition in the Nineteenth Century* (Chicago: The University of Chicago Press, 1955); Fiedler, *The Return of the Vanishing American* (New York: Stein and Day, 1968); Fussell, *Frontier: American Literature and the American West* (Princeton: Princeton University Press, 1965).

6.   *Studies in Classic American Literature* (Garden City, New York: Doubleday, 1951), p. 60.

7.   *Frontier*, p. 48.

8.   "The Leatherstocking Tales Reexamined," *South Atlantic Quarterly*, 46 (1947): 527.

9.   See Henry Nash Smith, "Consciousness and Social Order: The Theme of Transcendence in the Leatherstocking Tales," *Western American Literature*, 5 (November, 1970): 177-194; and see John Cawelti, "God's Country, Las Vegas, and the Gunfighter: Differing Visions of the West," *Western American Literature*, 9 (February, 1975): 273-283.

10.   *Walter Van Tilburg Clark* (New York: Twayne, 1969), pp. 12, 23-24, 32-33, and *passim*.

11.   *Frontier and Section*, p. 61; "The Turner Thesis and the Westward Movement," p. 403.

The Westering Experience in Fulton County, Indiana:
A Historical Study in Midwestern American Culture
And the American Character

Fulton County and the Westering Experience

There are two major sources for the study of the cultural history of Fulton County, Indiana. In 1909 a newspaper editor, Marguerite L. Miller, of Rochester, Indiana, was inspired to collect personal narratives by Fulton County pioneers. She then printed these narratives in a two-volume book which she titled *Home Folks: A Series of Stories by Old Settlers of Fulton County, Indiana.* One other personal narrative by an original settler, Benjamin C. Wilson, was printed in the Rochester *Union Spy* in 1875, and has been reprinted by the Fulton County Historical Society. In addition to these stories by early settlers, the student of Fulton County's cultural history has a volume of sixty-six family histories titled *Fulton County Folks*, published in 1974 and written, for the most part, by members of the various families.[1] While the material in these two books is not as extensive as one might wish, it *does* provide the essential story of Fulton County from its first white settlement in the 1830s; and, placing the books side by side, what one really has are two sets of memories: memories of nineteenth-century Fulton County and memories of twentieth-century Fulton County. To study the memories recorded in these two books, and to compare the two books, is, as I hope to show, one effective way of discovering some of the root-values in Midwestern American culture and of gaining a sense of the quality of life, past and present, in a fairly typical Midwestern county.

As I have said in Chapter 1, I find the place-myth of the Midwest to be the thinnest, the most secular, the least fructifying of American myths of place. I believe that Warren French is right when he describes the Midwest as "a culture that has always piously overprompted itself and produced little that creates any sense of the central role of sacrality [of a Thoreauvian, a *Western*, belief in the sacredness of the primordial, natural world and in the sacredness, also, of 'a *purely* sensuous life'] in expanding human experience."[2] And I have found nothing in *Home Folks* or in *Fulton County Folks* to abuse me of this view. In both books the stories told and the sensibilities revealed are, with rare exceptions, startlingly devoid of truly humanist, of truly cultural, of truly sacral values. I mean that there is no evidence in either book that Fulton County "folks" ever formed a meaningful -- which is to say, a sacred -- relation either to the land that they sought or to one another as members of an organic, purposeful, *believing* community. The evidence is quite the opposite. As such, what these books actually attest to is the failure of Midwestern culture -- or, at least, the cultural failure of one Midwestern county.

That failure began with westering, with the American westering dream of building a new, better, freer life in a virgin land. The westering experience in Fulton County is of course recorded in *Home Folks*. There is, however, a significant, unintentional irony in the very title of this book -- for most of the Fulton County settlers were *not* home folks in any truly westering way. As Max Westbrook has pointed out, the founding of a home is potentially, ideally a sacral act -- and in my view it also is, or should be, one intrinsic, one defining act of true American westering. "A home," as Westbrook explains,

> . . . represents for the sacred man the ordering of one's family under God; and the founding of the home is comparable to God's original act of bringing order out of chaos. To the profane man, a home may represent [solely] a financial investment. . . . To found a home in a sacred way is to tap primordial energies -- within one's self and within the universe -- and to relate the home to the real. To consider a home an investment is to serve profane values, to divide one's self from regenerative contact with the original.[3]

Coming into a new country, building log cabins in the virgin wilderness, the Fulton County westerners were of course fronting a historical chance to found their homes and to relate to the land in a truly westering, a truly sacral way. At the very same point in American history, an archetypal American frontiersman, Henry David Thoreau, was doing exactly so at Walden Pond. And at least one highly principled, truly humanist, truly westering Fulton

County family, the William Rannells family -- a family that fled Virginia because it found slavery intolerable -- was also doing so. "[F]reeing his slaves and pushing out into a new country, 'The Great Republic of the West,' as he was wont to call it," William Rannells built a "house of logs, such as was generally found in the far west in those days [1838]." By 1842 a new "house was finished -- large, substantial, and the counterpart, as far as possible, of the old home in Virginia."[4] The story of the Rannells family -- which contains vivid and affectionate memories of a daughter and also of a grandson of William Rannells -- makes it clear that westering for *this* family was indeed meaningful. They founded in Fulton County a *Southernlike*, family-centered, genial, truly humanist, truly cultured way of living -- *minus* the slavery that they had repudiated. The Rannells family's history, as narrated in *Home Folks*, clearly reveals, indeed, that the family members' devotion to their home and to their home-life rivalled even the *English* devotion to domesticity that is described in this book's last chapter.

With the exception of the history of the Virginia-bred Rannells family, though -- significantly enough, I believe, the *only* ancestrally *Southern* family in *Home Folks* -- the homesteading recorded in *Home Folks* was darkly willful and grasping -- profane rather than sacred. Most of the Old Settlers' stories show them viewing their new homes and the new land solely from the perspective of economic aggrandizement. As Henry Adams described so forcefully in his *History*, a goading pressure, or greed, for economic, material success was inherent in America's early nineteenth-century bold, naive, new-world, westering experiment in democracy. So it is not surprising that the Fulton County settlers were less conscious of the spiritual possibilities of westering than the man who -- unknown to them -- was just then building a hut at Walden. But I *am* surprised, and disappointed, by the absence of *any* sense of novelty or excitement or exuberance in their accounts of their westering experience. "The country was new," says Job V. Pownall; "therefore a wilderness and swamps. We therefore contracted ague, and had it to our satisfaction."[5] This seems to be the extent of the Old Settlers' thoughts about the newness of the country. And the references to the actual homesteading experience -- clearing the land, building log cabins -- are equally vapid. William A. Ward, for example, does not find the experience even worth writing about: "To go into the details of constructing a home, clearing land and the many privations sustained by my people, would lengthen this effort too much."[6] Benjamin C. Wilson does describe the homesteading process, noting very matter-of-factly that "We settled right in the woods; not one foot of land was cleared on our claims prior to our coming." But all that he really cares to emphasize about this experience is how *hard* it was: "I want to say just here to those of the present time [1875] who are complaining about hard times and the hardships they are enduring in order to get a start in the world, that you have not yet taken one lessen [sic] in hard labor or experienced any such thing as hard times."[7] Again, I have no wish to deny that homesteading *was* hard, but it seems to me that, with only a little imagination, it could have been something more, too. Clearly, Fulton County settlers did not, like Thoreau, go to the woods because they "wished to live deliberately, to front only the essential facts of life"; and clearly, too, they did not, living in the woods, experience the "forest-change" that Frederick Jackson Turner so fondly argued as the essential characteristic of American frontier-life. They knew what they wanted -- land ownership, economic aggrandizement -- long before they reached the Fulton County frontier, and they never wavered in their single-minded dedication to this exclusive goal. The constant theme -- the fundamental value -- in *Home Folks* and in *Fulton County Folks* is "Progress." As such, both books abundantly illustrate the truth in John Ditsky's reminder that "we have created this our culture almost exclusively out of the matter of male intellectuality, a raw and rugged assertion of will like the firearm over the fireplace."[8]

Westering in this sense, as an assertion of will merely, leaves no room for transcendence -- for the impulse toward spiritual rebirth that lies at the heart of our most vibrant, our most authentic American westering dream -- or, as the second part of this chapter aims to show, for the creating of a cultural landscape, a vivid, living sense of place. None of the settlers seem seriously to have wondered about themselves *in relation* to the new, virgin land: they wanted simply to make the land productive and themselves prosperous. Although he was "not quite six years of age,"

George Perschbacher "walked every step of the way from York county, Penn., to Indiana." Eventually his father "bought eighty acres north of [the] Tippecanoe river . . . . It was a dense forest, covered with tall timber of beach, walnut, oak, [and] ash." When George, his older brothers, and his father finally reach their new home (1845), the essential reason for their long journey is suddenly and starkly revealed: "We were well pleased[,] for it was the first foot of real estate [that] we [had] ever owned."[9] Like most of the pioneer-narrators in *Home Folks*, Perschbacher speaks in his story from the self-satisfied, sharply limited point of view of one who has Made It, successfully homesteaded, in a new country. There is, no doubt, something to be said for a fierce determination to survive and to prosper -- but successful homesteading alone can not, and did not, create either an admirable culture or a cultural landscape. Take, for example, the settlers' attitude -- often inimical, rarely more than indifferent -- toward the wildlife in "what [according to Perschbacher] was then called Tippecanoe country." "I have seen from two to three deer in a drove," says Perschbacher -- "but as there were no hunters in our family, they were of little use to us."[10] Or: riding horseback, Jonas Myers's father discovered a black bear -- even then (1839) a rare sight in Fulton County. "He called a dog which chased the bear up a tree. Securing a club, Father climbed the tree and struck the bear on the head, and when it fell to the ground, the dog killed it."[11] No mysticism, no mythology in Fulton County about Old Ben or about the spirit of the wilderness!

I see the historical Fulton County westering problem, or failure, as the one that Max Westbrook has analyzed in his stimulating book on Walter Van Tilburg Clark: American democracy, with its "awesome demands" for personal responsibility and for personal success, places the socially and religiously free individual "in a profane rather than a sacred relation to his world."[12] This was clearly the case in the settlers' stance -- their *Midwestern* stance -- toward their new home, the new land, the new landscape. It was even more clearly the case in their stance toward the original inhabitants -- the Potawatomi Indians -- of Fulton County. For the evidence is strong that as earnest and as earnestly progressive American westering democrats --

the settlers were compelled, blindly compelled, to transform Fulton County into an image of the prosperous agricultural Garden that they remembered having left in New York or Pennsylvania or Ohio. And this meant that the closer-to-home image of The Old Northwest as "territory," Indian territory, had to be changed. Quickly, efficiently, violently, it was.

> I shall never forget [says William A. Ward] with what deep regret I witnessed my red brethren bunched together and driven like cattle from their native land, to a place selected for them by the Government, beyond the "Father of Waters." Among them were my boyhood playmates and staunch friends, whom I regarded with brotherly affection, and who held a friendship for me equal to kinship. Out of their kindly disposed feeling for me, they had offered me gold and enough land to make me a wealthy man, had I taken advantage of them, which I am glad to say I refused to do, notwithstanding that I was repeatedly urged to accept their generous offers. They were gathered together, -- the chief [Menominee, who had been bound hand and foot and thrown into a log jail atop a wagon], braves, squaws and old men -- some walking, some on ponies, some in wagons because [they were] too old to walk, and started westward on their long journey. For more than a mile I followed them out of town [Rochester] fully determined that I would go with them, my mother following and as much determined that I should return home.[13]

Ward's regret is genuine, causing his writing suddenly to gain impressive strength; but his sorrow could neither appease the disgraceful, tragic event nor alter its tragic cultural consequences for Fulton County. The event -- which Ward witnessed as a nine-year-old boy -- was, after all, the infamous Trail of Death (1838) during which the last of the Potawatomi in Marshall and Fulton counties were driven single-file through the small frontier town of Rochester, and all the way to Kansas. Ostensibly, this forced march West was in accordance with a legitimate treaty -- one that Chief Menominee had not signed in the first place; in tragic fact, it was a consequence of the settlers' insatiable greed for land.[14]   More tragically still, it was a consequence of the settlers' profane -- *willfully* profane -- stance not simply toward the new land but also toward a different people, a different culture, a different consciousness, a different ontology. *This* is where Fulton County westering failed; where a potentially true, or a *far*, West was vigorously, violently rejected in favor of a success-bent, self-satisfied, morally complacent *mid*-West; where a potentially new human relation, new human culture, new human consciousness was denied in favor of the utilitarian, democratic, progressive culture and the shrewd, practical, sensible consciousness that the settlers had transported from the East. The image of the Potawatomi being marched through the frontier settlement stands, then, at the threshold and at the heart of Fulton County's history -- an image that haunts Fulton County "folks" to this day; an image that residents with roots in this county's past, myself included, would like to forget, and can not forget. Even as this book is being prepared for press, the Fulton County Historical Society is preparing for various observances of the One Hundred Fiftieth Anniversary (1988) of the Trail of Death -- observances that will include a retracing of the actual Trail from Twin Lakes in Marshall County, through Rochester, and all the way, six hundred miles, to Paola, Kansas. Without necessarily accepting the ontology of D. H. Lawrence's assertion that "the unappeased ghosts of the dead Indians act within the unconscious or under-conscious soul of the white American, causing . . . the Orestes-like frenzy of restlessness in the Yankee soul, the inner malaise which amounts almost to madness, sometimes," or that the American landscape "is full of grinning, unappeased aboriginal demons,"[15] one can see clearly that the removal of the Potawatomi is *the* crucial event, a watershed, in the history -- social, economic, cultural, and even religious -- of Fulton County. I mean that the Indian removal left the settlers alone and free to pursue, with utter singleness of purpose, the commitment to cash-crop farming, to business, to wealth, and to Progress that was their foremost reason for moving West in the first place. Their powerful urge to transform the "territory" could now be gratified without resistance; a profane, and inherently Midwestern, attitude toward land -- agriculture as business -- would be permanently established.

Indian removal achieved, westering -- such as it was for these Midwestern pioneers -- ended, there is not much more to be said about Fulton County. What we have, again, is the poverty of a culture with no impulse toward transcendence, toward, that is, a truly westering experience. Thoreau went to the woods "to transact some private business" related to "the importance of a man's soul and of to-day"; but the Fulton County pioneers went to the woods *for business*, indeed. Not surprisingly, then, in 1875 the oldest living settler, Benjamin C. Wilson, gave a pep-talk to the fellow citizens of his county, assuring them that "It is progress and improvement that makes wealth" and that "There is . . . a future for Fulton county that we know not of, in which the coming generation will far excel the present in wealth and personal enterprise." Indeed,

> If we could have even at this late day a through-line railroad,
> Rochester would soon hum with manufactories and general
> industry, the population would be doubled in a remarkably
> short time and citizens who are now worth hundreds of dollars
> could count their wealth by thousands. The farmer would find
> a direct market for all his produce, and for his wheat, corn,
> oats, potatoes, etc., he would receive the same prices paid at
> other county towns. Not only this but his farm and timber land
> would be increased in value from 25 to 50 per cent.[16]

Wilson's dream-image of Fulton County as a wealthy, progressive agricultural *and* industrial -- as opposed to a truly agrarian -- society is, historically, a central myth of Midwestern American culture, a myth that he dwells upon lovingly. For only "Those who have had the experience" -- he claims -- can "comprehend the change that [Fulton County] has passed through from a howling wilderness, possessed almost exclusively by savage Indians, who practiced all manner of barbarities, to a fertile county, inhabited by a moral, intelligent, wealthy and progressive people."[17] True enough, perhaps -- but Wilson's astonishing lack of insight into the moral and cultural realities of the very history that he helped to make does not speak well for the quality of the westering experience in Fulton County.

And we are living with the legacy of this experience -- a bitter heritage. Perhaps our present vapid, secularized, atomized, strictly-business society can not be traced solely to the failures of our first settlers; but they did begin a tradition of cash-crop farming and of economic individualism which, in the American Midwest, has yet to be changed. The record of this impoverished heritage, for Fulton County, is *Fulton County Folks*. Here are the up-to-date stories of the most prominent Fulton County families, and there is simply very little in all of these stories of any real interest or importance: no fresh experience to be related, few lives of a quality that compels or inspires. How can there be when the values by which a people lives are still those which Benjamin C. Wilson urged them to pursue: business, progress, wealth? *Home Folks* has the intrinsic interest of having been written out of the actual westering experience; *Fulton County Folks* is only, as I have said, the record of the failure of this experience. One thing that *Fulton County Folks* does, though, is to illustrate Frederick Jackson Turner's insight into one aspect of the American "wilderness experience": it bred the ideal, the myth, of the self-made man.[18] *This* is what, on the evidence, still moves, still motivates the people of Fulton County. Everywhere in *Fulton County Folks* there are proud references to certain self-made men -- farmers, merchants, businessmen, doctors -- and indeed some of these stories are, in themselves, quite remarkable. But we have long been aware of the cultural limitations of the self-made man, and of a society committed exclusively to this ideal. It is pertinent, here, to remember Santayana's point that a truly attractive culture--for Santayana, and for the other famous observers studied in Chapter 13, this was of course *English* culture--must be based upon a people's "love of a certain quality of life, to be maintained manfully," and upon a people's understanding that "the prize of life [is] worth winning, but not worth snatching."[19] It is this humanistic priority of the *quality* of life that most of the first settlers forgot when -- seeking land ownership more than they sought a new landscape or a new life -- they came into Fulton County; and this is what most of the people of Fulton County, trapped in the Midwest's myth of progress and of economic success, seem still to forget.

If we are going to talk seriously about the culture or about the cultural heritage of the Midwest, it seems to me that we are going to have to get back to the quality of individual lives. For the people of Fulton County this would mean remembering that at least one pioneer, William Rannells, did not come to the county solely for land; or that Col. Isaac Washington Brown dedicated his life to working and speaking for the saving of birds; or that a struggling doctor, Winfield Scott Shafer, not only envisioned but actually founded Rochester College; or that Marguerite L. Miller single-handedly preserved their early history by compiling and printing *Home Folks*. "It is this life of the individual, as it may be lived in a given nation, that determines the whole value of that nation," as Santayana said; "and America will not be a success, if every American is a failure."[20] This is true, too, of the American Midwest.

Fulton County and the "Sense of Place" in the Midwest

In speaking of a "sense of place" I have in mind what Lawrence J. Evers has termed a "cultural landscape." "By imagining," as Evers says, "who and what they are in relation to particular landscapes, cultures and individual members of cultures form a close relation to those landscapes."[21] Henry David Thoreau, for example, serves once again as a vibrant, classic illustration not only of a truly westering experience but also of a true sense of place: the entire topography of *Walden* is symbolic, the pond itself an image of Thoreau's ideal, renewed, reborn self. While reading the stories of *Home Folks*, I was curious not only as to whether the original Fulton County settlers seemed to have experienced a true, or Thoreauvian, sense of westering but also as to whether they seemed to have experienced a true, or Thoreauvian, sense of place. For the two experiences -- westering and creating a sense of place -- are not necessarily interdependent. It can be argued, indeed, that these experiences tend, if anything, to be antithetical: that those cultures with the strongest *sense* of place -- England, New England, the American South -- are also strongly backward-looking rather than forward-looking, or westering, cultures. A vibrant sense of place may well depend upon a vibrant sense of the past -- upon vivid, loving memories, as with Henry Adams and Quincy, of an intensely meaningful past intensely lived in a particular place. So John Crowe Ransom is, I believe, right that a true, a living sense of place will not grow in those American regions -- the Midwest, for one -- that insist upon being progressive, upon pioneering, ceaselessly, on principle. And as for the original Fulton County pioneers, they were, as we have seen, devotedly, blindly progressive: there is startlingly little nostalgia -- evocative of any real sense of place -- in their stories. One exception, along with the earlier-mentioned Rannells family, is Nelson B. Waymire, who remembers that "Our home was like those of other settlers, a log cabin," and that "like all other children we climbed a ladder to bed, slept between feather bedspreads, ate bread that mother baked in the fire place, and crowded more real happiness into each hour, than children of the present time have in a day."[22] Similarly, one of Fulton County's early newspaper editors, Michael L. Essick, is genuinely nostalgic as to the scenes of pioneer-days:

> Indiana was then a beautiful state . . . . Let us look at her as I have seen her, as well as other old settlers now living . . . .This was a dense timbered country. It had neither little streams or rivers, but run water the whole year round. All her lakes, rivers and small streams were alive with and filled with fish. The woods were alive with bear, wolves, deer, antelope, gazelles, turkeys, squirrels, beaver, otter and nearly every fur animal. You could stand on the banks of the Tippecanoe, Eel or Wabash rivers and see the poplar, walnut, ash, sugar, beech, sycamore, the monarchs of the forest, some bending over the water. Could see the deer come down to the stream to drink. In the near distance you could see the green sward, the smoking tepee of the Indians. If you visited their camp you found the tepee covered with skins, robes of fur on the floor, and clothes of fur to keep them warm. In this land of his, before he was disturbed by white men, he was happy and independent . . . . Now he is gone with the timbered wood lands. Fine bridges, beautiful collonades, magnificent palaces, towns and farms take their places, but nature always has [excelled] and always will excel art in grandeur. Don't you wish you had lived then?[23]

This is a vivid picture, expressive of a sensibility and of a sense of place otherwise essentially absent in the two volumes of *Home Folks*. Essick appears, indeed, to have been a wholly remarkable Old Settler. In the same sketch he speaks, approvingly enough, of "those glorious days of this early people" when "They had plenty of whiskey, made ten years old in ten days, brewed with dog-leg tobacco, apple cores, copperas and other filth, called forty-rod whiskey"; but he bitterly condemns "the teachings of the cranky old bachelor Paul" -- which teachings, he says, "The fathers of that day would quote to their wives . . . and the blessed, meek mother would obey, never thinking that those teachings of Paul had enslaved her sex for more than 1800 years."[24]

Had the other settlers shared Essick's appreciation of the landscape and of the Indian's culture -- or simply his enlightened, humanistic attitude toward women -- westering in Fulton County unquestionably would have been more promising. Such was not the case, as we have seen. And the willful, acquisitive, male-dominated, chauvinistic, profane westering that *was* the case had -- along with the ruinous historical and cultural consequences already mentioned -- a ruinous effect, also, upon the creation of any true sense of place. For in improvement, in prosperity, in progress -- in continuous, ever-accelerating pioneering on principle -- there is, I believe, less and less of any living sense of place. The Removal of the Indians and the abandonment of their mill at Lake Manitou, near Rochester, may have "left the field clear," as Charles A. Mitchell remarks, "for profitable investment in the building of another grist mill"[25] -- it did not, culturally and humanistically speaking, leave the field clear for anything else.

Not terribly concerned about cultural consequences, however, the settlers were, as I have said, intent upon changing the Territory. They were also chauvinistically secure in their conviction that the Territory *should* be changed. Even William A. Ward -- who remembers so painfully his witnessing of the Indians' removal -- complacently begins his sketch by remarking that "it has been my good fortune to see this part of Indiana change from unbroken forest, filled with wild game and inhabited by Indians, to a highly civilized land of cities, fertile farms and comfortable homes."[26] The point of course is that the Fulton County westerners were single-mindedly pursuing Thomas Jefferson's new-world, democratic American dream of Progress, of building God's country in the American wilderness: they were immune to other imaginings about the West, incapable of creating any other vision of place. When Ward contrasts the "unbroken forest, filled with wild game and inhabited by Indians," to the "highly civilized [1909] land of cities" and of "fertile farms," there is little doubt -- in spite of his inviolable memories of boyhood Indian "playmates and staunch friends" -- as to where his *final* sympathies lie. In the final paragraph of his sketch, Ward falls, indeed, from the honest, vivid, strong, moving writing that characterized his description of the Trail of Death into vapid, false, popular, *Midwestern*, self-satisfied and self-deceiving assertions about his having helped to "make 'the desert blossom as the rose'" and about his having lived "out of the semi-savage state" to enjoy "the pursuit of business" and "the blessings of refined civilization."[27]   Benjamin C. Wilson, as we have seen, also approvingly, proudly remarks that "Fulton county of to-day [1875] can hardly be realized as the same territory we inhabited forty years ago. [Only] [t]hose who have had the experience can . . . comprehend the change that it has passed through from a howling wilderness, possessed almost exclusively by savage Indians, who practiced all manner of barbarities, to a fertile county, inhabited by a moral, intelligent, wealthy and progressive people."[28] The recollections not only of "Uncle Ben" Wilson but also of nearly all of the Old Settlers who appear in *Home Folks* evidence that it was *this* vision, this idea, of the new-world West as God's country -- as the site for a new, industrious, productive, *prosperous* community -- that prevailed in Fulton County. In his last newspaper sketch (11 June 1875), Wilson affirms that although Fulton County has not "become as wealthy as we desire to be, we are not without progress and comparative wealth . . . . I notice many who formerly rode to town in their old farm wagons, now ride in fine spring wagons and fine carri[a]ges, drawn by large fat horses, the harness[es] of which glitter in the sunlight as you pass." And he predicts "a future for Fulton county . . . in which the coming generation will far excel the present in wealth and personal enterprise."[29]

It is true that Fulton County developed much as Benjamin C. Wilson and the other original settlers hoped it would. And this alone -- this obsessive, compulsive, exclusive emphasis upon "progress," upon "wealth and personal enterprise" -- stopped, totally stopped, any creation of a true sense of place. As really imaginative westerners, as truly *westering* pioneers, these settlers failed: they did not wonder about or truly *relate* to the new land and to the new landscape; they did not consider that the "West" to which they came *could* have been something different from the East which they had left.

Chapter 7

Notes

1. Marguerite L. Miller correctly predicted in a letter (September 16, 1940) to the editor of the Rochester *News-Sentinel* that "in years to come *Home Folks* will grow in greater and still greater value as history." She not only collected the personal narratives contained in the book but also set the type and bound the pages. Happily, the Fulton County Historical Society has sponsored a hardcover reprint (Marceline, Mo.: Walsworth, n.d.) of both volumes of this book. My references are to this hardcover edition, hereafter cited as *Home Folks*. *Fulton County Folks* is edited by Shirley Willard, President of the Fulton County Historical Society, and published by Walsworth.
2. Warren French, book review in *The Old Northwest*, 3 (June, 1977): 200; Henry David Thoreau, *A Week on the Concord and Merrimack Rivers* (New York: The New American Library, 1961), p. 324.
3. Westbrook, *Walter Van Tilburg Clark* (New York: Twayne, 1969), p. 12.
4. *Home Folks*, II, pp. 89-90, 91.
5. *Home Folks*, I, p. 128.
6. *Ibid.*, p. 2.
7. Wilson, "Fulton County -- What I know about its early settlements," *Fulton County Historical Society Quarterly*, 10 (August, 1974), 7-8. First printed in 1875 in the Rochester *Union Spy*.
8. "'Directionality': The Compass in the Heart," *The Westering Experience in American Literature: Bicentennial Essays*, ed. Merrill Lewis and L.L. Lee (Bellingham: Western Washington University Press, 1977), p. 219.
9. *Home Folks*, I, pp. 105, 106, 107.
10. *Ibid.*, pp. 106, 108.
11. *Ibid.*, p. 94.
12. Westbrook, pp. 12-13.
13. *Home Folks*, I, p. 6.
14. See Otho Winger, *The Potawatomi Indians* (Elgin, Ill.: The Elgin Press, 1939), pp. 33-53.
15. *Studies in Classic American Literature* (Garden City, New York: Doubleday, 1951), pp. 44, 60.
16. Wilson, pp. 23, 24.
17. *Ibid.*, p. 5.
18. Turner develops this idea in his essay titled "The Problem of the West," *Atlantic Monthly*, 78 (September, 1896): 289-297.
19. Santayana, *Solilquies in England and Later Solilquies* (Ann Arbor: The University of Michigan Press, 1967), pp. 31, 37.
20. *Ibid.*, p. 64.
21. Lawrence J. Evers, "Words and Place: A Reading of *House Made of Dawn*," *Western American Literature*, 11 (February, 1977): 297, 298.
22. *Home Folks*, I, p. 77.
23. *Ibid.*, pp. 58-59.
24. *Ibid.*, pp. 59-60, 61.
25. *Ibid.*, p. 67.

26.   *Ibid.*, p. 1.
27.   *Ibid.*, p. 7.
28.   Wilson, p. 5.
29.   *Ibid.*, pp. 23-24.

SECTION III

THE FAR WEST:
STEPHEN CRANE

CHAPTER 8

Stephen Crane and the Western Myth

When one considers the immense importance of the myth of the West in American history and culture and literature, it is surprising to note that one of our major writers, Stephen Crane, has not been adequately studied from the point of view of the Western myth -- even though in his life and in his writings he added a fascinating chapter to the history of this myth. Neither of the classic studies by Henry Nash Smith and by R. W. B. Lewis mentions Crane's relationship to the Western myth. And even Leslie A. Fiedler, comprehensive as he usually is, does not mention Crane in his provocative analysis of "that peculiar form of madness which dreams, and achieves, and *is* the true West." David W. Noble does discuss Crane in his *The Eternal Adam and the New World Garden*, but his treatment of Crane's relationship to the Western myth is cursory and misleading: he argues that Crane repudiated the myth of the West, but he bases his argument upon discussions of *Maggie, George's Mother,* and *The Red Badge of Courage.* Crane's Western stories and sketches, and his letters, are simply ignored. Joseph Katz's "Introduction" to his edition of Crane's Western sketches does make the point that the Western trip was a crucial experience for Crane, but it does not examine either the trip or the sketches from the point of view of the Western myth.[1] Those who *have* written about Crane and the West have also -- with the important exceptions of Crane's first two biographers, Thomas Beer and John Berryman -- generally assumed that Crane wrote about the West only to laugh at it, that he never took the Western myth seriously. Even Edwin H. Cady, whose suggestive article on "Stephen Crane and the Strenuous Life" is the truest statement we have of the great attraction which "Rooseveltian neo-romanticism" held for Crane, makes the vastly oversimplified assertion that "'The Bride Comes to Yellow Sky' is a hilariously funny parody of neo-romantic lamentations over 'The Passing of the West.'"[2]

In this chapter and in the two which follow, I want to suggest that a careful examination of Crane's Western writings *and* of his own Western experience will support the contention that his attitude toward the American Western myth is far more serious than has yet been recognized. Crane was, perhaps, not as obsessed with the consequences of the vanishing of the American frontier and the American wilderness as were Cooper or Twain or Faulkner; but his writings show that he did have an intense awareness of the American myth of the West and that his essential attitude toward "The Passing of the West" was not parodic, not satiric -- but serious, sympathetic, and even tragic. Moreover, the West profoundly changed Crane's outlook on life by teaching him to believe in man's potential for courage, and this, in turn, profoundly changed the kind of literature that he began to produce after his Western experience.

It is important, first of all, to place Crane's Western writings within the historical context of the time in which he lived and wrote. For Edwin Cady is surely right in insisting that "Crane died a Seeker" and that "his critics have paid too little attention to the forces and attractions of the American society through which he sought."[3] Quite obviously, one of the strongest of these "forces and attractions" was what Cady calls "Rooseveltian neo-romanticism": the frantic, laughable, touching attempt -- epitomized by T. R. -- of many prominent Americans in the last decades of the nineteenth century to recover and to relive frontier virtues in defiance of reality -- in defiance of the passing of the frontier itself. For, as Frederick Jackson Turner announced in 1893, the frontier *had* passed; and Turner, for one, could not be overly hopeful about the future of a nation suddenly deprived of what was in his view the most vivifying and the most regenerative influence upon its historical development. In other words, the 1890's -- the single decade of Stephen Crane's creative life -- witnessed a decisive and an irrevocable change in American life and in American society: the passing of the frontier and the ascendancy of a centralized, progressive, capitalistic system. Any hope for any other kind of society could be expressed only in the form of myth -- which is why the Western myth has, to this day, such a tenacious hold upon the American imagination. For at this point it is important to remember that the "Western myth" in its peculiar form of cowboys, saloons, and shoot-outs is only the last chapter in the American myth of the West (the Adamic myth of freedom and of rebirth in a pristine natural world) which, as Henry Nash Smith and R. W. B. Lewis have shown, was a major reality of nineteenth-century America. The cowboys, and especially the heroic marshals, are all, to borrow Smith's words, "Sons of Leatherstocking."[4] Thus, the reason for the immense popularity of Western dime novels at the end of the nineteenth century is not far to seek: they satisfied an urgent American need to mythicize the frontier hero in the only American *place* where a frontier at least seemed still to exist. It was the last stand of the American Adam in his flight from civilization.

When Stephen Crane left for the West in 1895, he was of course aware of the Western myth;[5] and he was aware, too, as his Western sketches show, of the basic cultural conditions which gave rise to the myth. But much more important than this is the fact that he himself became, so to speak, a figure in the myth: the more he was in the West (especially the Southwest), the more he liked the West, the more seriously did he take the myth that Westerners *were* different and better,[6] and the more clearly did he realize that he himself was in fact changed by his Western experiences. Indeed, "The consequence of these six months [in the West and Mexico] to his art can," as John Berryman notes, "barely be measured"; for "henceforth Crane could be an heroic writer."[7] That is, in the West Crane discovered, in himself and in others, a capacity for courage and for heroism which he had earlier (as in *The Red Badge of Courage*) treated either satirically or, at best, skeptically. Thus it was not, as Ford Madox Ford thought, simply whim or posturing which led Crane to wear "cowboy breeches and no coat" while living in his English villa at Oxted.[8] And much less a matter of whim was his hopeless dream, upon leaving Havana and the Spanish-American war, of buying a ranch in Texas.[9] For Crane, the myth of the West became a reality: only in the West could he live the kind of masculine, free, unaffected life which he urgently wanted to live. The proof of this lies, of course, in Crane's own Western stories and sketches. Except for "The Blue Hotel" and "The Bride Comes to Yellow Sky," they have been strangely neglected -- and, as we shall see, this neglect has led to the false view that Crane did not take the myth of the West seriously.

Any one of Crane's Western sketches, for example, serves in some way to illustrate his deep attraction to the Western myth. The first, and probably the best, of Crane's Western sketches was "Nebraskans' Bitter Fight for Life" -- a sketch which shows how profoundly he was impressed by the courage and stoicism of the Nebraskan farmers. "They were strong, fine, sturdy men, not bended like the Eastern farmer, but erect and agile" (p. 11).[10] "They are a fearless folk, completely American . . . . They summoned their strength for a long war with cold and hunger . . . . It was a supreme battle to which to look forward. It required the profound and dogged courage of the American peoples who have come into the west to carve farms, railroads, towns, cities, in the heart of a world fortified by enormous distances" (p. 5). There is even a hint, here, of Crane's endorsing (unknowingly) Turner's thesis that frontier-life generated the greatest and the most *American* traits of the American people. And, in any case, it is striking enough simply to note that Crane's attitude toward these Western farmers is genuinely sympathetic. Clearly, the West was changing Crane. Seeing a group of people "depend upon their endurance, their capacity to help each other, and their steadfast and unyielding courage" (p. 14) was a sobering and an encouraging experience for one whose view of life and of human nature had, till then, tended toward bitterness and cynicism.

But, as Johnnie and the scandalized cowboy exclaim in "The Blue Hotel," Nebraska is not *out West*. The trouble with Nebraska, as Crane noted in his sketch of "Galveston, Texas, in 1895," was that "For years the farmers [had] been driving the cattlemen back, back toward the mountains and into Kansas, and Nebraska [had] come to an almost universal condition of yellow trolly-cars with clanging gongs and whirring wheels" (p. 31). Obviously, however much Crane respected the Nebraskan farmers, he was displeased with their role as the forerunners of a civilized, commercialized, urban society. In other words, for Crane -- as for Americans generally -- the Western heroes were of course not the domestic, settlement-oriented farmers but "the cattlemen" who were ceaselessly being driven "back, back toward the mountains" and deeper and deeper into the realm of myth. In the Galveston sketch Crane pretends to ridicule the obsessive American desire to discover "radical differences between Eastern and Western life" (p. 31), but it is all too obvious that he himself was almost childishly obsessed with this desire. This is seen not only in his lamenting Nebraska's capitulation to Eastern trolley cars but also in his scarcely veiled disgust that Galveston itself "does not represent Texas" (p. 35). In fact, Galveston presents one with "a thousand details . . . which are thoroughly typical of any American city. The square brick business blocks, the mazes of telegraph wires, the trolly-cars clamoring up and down the streets, . . . all disappoint the traveller" (p. 31). The point is that Crane *was* trying to find something different; like Leatherstocking or any of the sons of Leatherstocking, he wanted to escape "the great and elemental facts of American life" (p. 31); he wanted to find a true West. At San Antonio he almost did.

As Thomas Beer tells us, "when [Crane] reached San Antonio, he fell in love with that maligned city and with Texas . . . . All the adolescence in him frothed to a head. His letters from San Antonio are almost childish."[11] Yet even San Antonio was ultimately no true West, no real escape from civilization: it, too, was being modernized and Americanized, and Crane's reaction to this fact was nothing short of outrage. Clear proof of this is Crane's highly revealing sketch of San Antonio titled "Patriot Shrine of Texas" -- a sketch that is crucial to our understanding of Crane's relation to the American myth of the West because it is informed with an intense bitterness toward the triumphant march of modern American civilization. The early paragraphs of this sketch are a forthright statement of disgust at the "totally modern aspect" which has resulted from the progress-mad Anglo-saxon's invasion of "the holy place of legends":

> The principal streets are lanes between rows of handsome business blocks and upon them proceeds with important uproar the terrible and almighty trolley car. The prevailing type of citizen is not seated in the sun; on the contrary he is making his way with the speed and intentness of one who competes in a community that is commercially in earnest . . . .
> The serene Anglo-Saxon erects business blocks upon the dreams of transient monks; he strings telegraph wires across the face of their sky of hope and over the energy, the efforts, the accomplishments of these pious fathers of the early church passes the wheel, the hoof, the heel...Here and there...one finds

in the main part of the town little old buildings yellow with age, solemn and severe in outline, that have escaped . . . the whirl of the modern life . . . . [B]ut despite the tenderness which San Antonio feels for these monuments, the unprotected mass of them must get trampled into [the] shapeless dust which lies always behind the march of this terrible century [p. 36].

Here, surely, we have an outrage at the culturally and spiritually destructive effects of America's mindlessly aggressive, prevailing capitalistic system that is entirely equivalent to the feelings which led Thoreau to renounce "this restless, nervous, bustling, trivial Nineteenth Century."[12] Even in Texas, even in San Antonio, Crane could not *finally* escape modern American civilization; but the very fact that he was trying to do so shows how deeply he was influenced and motivated by the myth of the West. Moreover, he *did* love San Antonio -- he loved every aspect of it that was not American. As John Berryman says, Crane's Western trip was "the happiest time perhaps he was to know -- an idyl";[13] and San Antonio was at the heart of that idyl. Why else his intense bitterness at the fact that Progress was relentlessly impinging upon this idyl?

While historical, cultural, and biographical evidence is of great importance, an analysis of Stephen Crane's relation to the American Western myth must of course be supported finally by the literature that grew out of his Western experience. And the most immediate evidence for Crane's being changed by the West lies in the kind of fiction that he began to write *after* his Western trip. For while Crane's important early works -- *Maggie, George's Mother, The Red Badge of Courage* -- render an essentially deterministic view of life, it cannot be emphasized too strongly that his writings after his Western trip *do* affirm man's free will and his potential for courage and for heroism. Crane's Western stories, as we shall see, nearly all dramatize a code of courage and of manliness as embodied in the Western myth. A similar code -- as Chapter 10 aims to show -- is clearly evident in "The Open Boat" and in Crane's later war stories. And while Crane's shipwreck experience and his war experiences no doubt contributed to the change from a sardonic to an affirmative attitude toward human nature as rendered in his later writings, it should be noted that this change really began in 1895 with his trip to the West and Mexico. Before his shipwreck on New Year's Day, 1897, Crane had already written three fine Western stories -- "One Dash -- Horses," "The Five White Mice," and "A Man and Some Others" -- each one of which dramatizes and affirms the code of courage that is central to the Western myth.

It might be asked at this point whether or not Crane's attraction to the West was rooted in his interest in violence. In my opinion this interest can easily be exaggerated and distorted. As John Berryman has said, Crane went West because he "needed danger. Privation was interesting and he had enjoyed a good deal of this; but danger was something else, which after imagining it for a masterpiece he needed to feel, and to see what he would do with it."[14] What really fascinated Crane, then, was not violence but danger -- the chance, that is, to discover courage. Thus I think it is no accident that the only Western story in which raw violence supersedes a study of fear, or courage, or historical change, is the slight melodrama "Twelve O'Clock" -- a story which, as John Berryman notes, was written when Crane's "mind was blazing with death" and when his imagination was "parodying itself, without meaning."[15] In the other Western stories violence is clearly secondary to Crane's dramatization of the Western code of manliness and of courage -- with the exception of "The Blue Hotel," which, as we shall see, dramatizes not frontier courage but civilized cowardice. In short, Crane's Western stories are essentially studies of courage from the point of view of an American myth which sees this virtue as existing only on the frontier, outside civilization. The subject of courage was of course hardly new for a young man who had already written *The Red Badge of Courage*, but what is entirely new is Crane's sympathetic, unskeptical, unironic treatment of this subject.

We can begin by noting that two of Crane's earliest Western stories, "One Dash -- Horses" and "The Five White Mice," contain protagonists who are clearly surrogates for Crane himself and that each of these stories affirms a code of self-reliant courage. It should be noted, too, that these stories are, strictly speaking, not Western but Mexican stories. This in itself seems to me to be highly significant, for it shows quite clearly that in 1895 the only West that Crane could find *was* Mexico. Only in Mexico could he experience a mad dash-for-life across the plains; only in Mexico could he really believe that one's life depended upon one's courage to make a quick draw. Thus in "The Five White Mice" the New York Kid, faced with imminent death, first found his mind filling with memories and with images which "were perfectly stereopticon," but at the same time

> He suddenly knew that it was possible to draw his revolver, and by a swift manoeuver face down all three Mexicans . . . . It was a new game . . . .
> He thought of the weight and size of his revolver, and dismay pierced him. He feared that in his hands it would be as unwieldy as a sewing-machine for his quick work . . . . Some of the eels of despair lay wet and cold against his back.
> But at the supreme moment the revolver came forth as if it were greased and it rose like a feather . . . .
> Perhaps in this one series of movements the kid had unconsciously used nervous force sufficient to raise a bale of hay . . . . The revolver gleamed in the darkness with a fine silver light [pp. 49-50].[16]

Thus the Kid's discovery of his capacity for courage. It hardly needs to be added that in this story Crane uses a familiar stereotype of the Western myth -- drawing the revolver -- and makes it work. Not for a moment does Crane allow us to stand outside the situation, to view it either comically or ironically. We identify with the Kid and participate in his change in consciousness.

Like "The Five White Mice," "One Dash -- Horses" is a story which clearly celebrates Crane's discovery of his own capacity for courage. We know that this story is a direct transcript of Crane's ride for his life while under the pursuit of a bandit, one Ramon Colorado, and that, in Beer's words, "This business was delicious to Crane." Delicious because, as Beer puts it in his justly famous insight, "the mistress of this boy's mind was fear. His search in aesthetic was governed by terror as that of tamer men is governed by the desire of women."[17] Thus before the dash-for-life in this story, Crane's surrogate, Richardson ("the American"), confronts death and, like the New York Kid, discovers his capacity to confront it courageously: "The American did not move. He was staring at the fat Mexican with a strange fixedness of gaze, not fearful, not dauntless, not anything that could be interpreted. He simply stared . . . . Ah, well, sirs, here was a mystery. At the approach of their [the fat Mexican has several companions] menacing company, why did not this American cry out and turn pale, or run, or pray them mercy?" (p. 16). The mystery here is the "mystery of manliness" which, as Edwin Cady has well said, Crane "pursued . . . into the West as far as Mexico, on to the filibuster *Commodore*, to Greece, and at last to Cuba."[18] The important point is that Crane's Western experience taught him that manliness really was not such a mystery after all. As John Berryman puts it, "Crane found that he was able to feel terror and act as if he did not feel terror and *so* survive. This discovery somewhat improved his view of human nature."[19]

While Crane's first two Western stories dramatize his discovery of courage through a protagonist who is clearly a surrogate for Crane himself, his third story, "A Man and Some Others," presents the theme of courage and self-reliance by use of a protagonist who, instead of being a Crane-surrogate, an Easterner learning Western values, is himself an embodiment of the virtues of the legendary Western hero. The Crane-surrogate in this story is not the protagonist, Bill, but the "young man . . . of a far, black Northern city" (p. 58) who just happens to ride into Bill's camp on the immense plains of southwest Texas and who learns from Bill and from the Western landscape "the inconsequence of human tragedy" (p. 62) as well as the great consequence of human courage. Conrad rightly called this story "an amazing bit of biography."[20] It is the story of what happens to Bill *in the West*. This is why Crane devotes the entire second part of his story to a detailed account of Bill's past life -- an account in which we learn very clearly that Bill has been no saint. In the West, though, Bill knows that "I've got rights, and I suppose if I don't see 'em through, no one is likely to give me a good hand and help me lick you fellers, since I'm the only white man in half a day's ride" (p. 54). Moreover, while Bill is ready to defend his rights against any and all odds, he has learned too the cowboy code of honor which forbids the involving of outsiders in one's personal troubles: "while I might like a man's company all right, I couldn't let him in for no such game when he ain't got nothin' to do with the trouble" (p. 59).

Bill, then, is ready to die, alone and unknown, for his rights. Moreover, he refuses to take the situation tragically or even seriously. This is the code of the legendary cowboy. As David Brion Davis says, "the cowboy hero stood out on the lonely prairie, dependent on neither man nor God. He was willing to take whatever risks lay along his road and would gladly make fun of any man who took life too seriously."[21] This is hilariously shown in Crane's story by Bill's bursting into a violent passion upon his discovery that the Mexicans destroyed his frying pan -- this at the same moment that the Eastern stranger is benumbed and nearly fainting because of his glimpse of a dead face (pp. 62-63). Like Crane before his Western trip, the stranger has not really understood "the message of the inconsequence of human tragedy" (p. 62) which inheres in the vast, indifferent Western landscape; and he has not yet learned that, given the indifference of nature, whatever value a man's life has must be supplied by his fidelity to his own code of courage. Before the story is over, though, the stranger, the Eastern dude, has gained a new point of view: "he suddenly felt for Bill, this grimy sheep-herder, some deep form of idolatry. Bill was dying, and the dignity of last defeat, the superiority of him who stands in his grave, was in the pose of the lost sheep-herder" (pp. 66-67).

None of Crane's earlier Western stories presents the theme of nostalgia, the lament of the coming of modern civilization, which is so important an aspect of the American Western myth and which is, as we have seen, a central theme in Crane's own newspaper sketches of the West. In Crane's later Western stories -- "The Bride Comes to Yellow Sky," "The Blue Hotel," and "Moonlight on the Snow" -- this theme is, however, quite clearly and quite forcefully presented, and in each case it is directly linked to the theme of courage which we have seen in the earlier stories.

In "Moonlight on the Snow," for example, Crane clearly admires and pointedly dramatizes the self-reliant, defiant, sardonic courage of one man, the gambler Larpent, who is himself the intended victim of War Post's capitulation to respectability and to real-estate profits. Unlike the quiet, well-mannered gambler in "The Blue Hotel," this gambler has not joined the forces of civilization; he does not lead "an exemplary home life" with "a real wife and two real children in a neat cottage in a suburb" (p. 167). In fact,

War Post, unlike Fort Romper, does not yet have suburbs; but, as Larpent understands and jeeringly points out, the suddenly virtuous, social-conscious, capitalist-bent citizens are clamoring to get them: this, in his view -- and I think in Crane's too -- is what has turned them into a pack of snivelling cowards. And the fact that Jack Potter ("a famous town marshal of Yellow Sky, but now sheriff of the county" [p. 188]) and Scratchy Wilson ("once a no less famous desperado" [p. 188]) intervene at the end of the story to relieve War Post of its embarrassing problem of trying to deal with Larpent serves but to illustrate the disconcerting paradox of the legendary cowboy who, in the words of David Brion Davis, "fights for justice, risks his life to make the dismal little cowtown safe for law-abiding, respectable citizens, but in so doing . . . destroys the very environment which made him a heroic figure."[22] War Post is going the way of Fort Romper; Jack Potter is helping out, relieving the newly respectable town of the responsibility of dealing with a man who -- like Bill in "A Man and Some Others" -- exhibits a remarkable courage and nonchalance in the face of death. It is not difficult, I think, to see that Crane is lamenting the approach of civilization and that he equates this approach with the disappearance of virtues inhering in the Western myth: courage, honesty, openness, self-confidence, unselfishness.

These are of course precisely the virtues which are *not* to be found in "The Blue Hotel." And that, for our purposes, is just the point: "The Blue Hotel" is not really a Western story. We can see this, for example, by recalling Crane's complaint in his "Galveston, Texas" sketch that "Nebraska has come to an almost universal condition of yellow trolly-cars," and comparing this complaint to Scully's enthusiastic outburst to the Swede: "Why, man, we're goin' to have a line of ilictric street-cars in this town next spring" (p. 149). As Johnnie says, Fort Romper simply is not *out West*: it is civilization, the East. This is immensely important in relation to the Western myth because only by recognizing that Fort Romper is *not* the West can we recognize that the hellishness -- the cowardice, the fear, the cheating, the hypocrisy, the greed, the violence -- of this story is the product not of the West but of the civilization of which Scully is so enthusiastic a proponent. As Jay Martin has pointed out, "it is not the Western myth, but the essentially savage character of man himself that is revealed" by this story.[23] In fact, none of the characters in this story, with the one exception of the cowboy, is really a Westerner; and although Crane emphasizes the obtuseness of this particular cowboy, one can at least venture the suggestion that had *he* known that Johnnie was cheating he would have stood up and said so.

If Fort Romper has already been civilized, has become in effect the East, Yellow Sky is of course poised at the precise moment of transition from the frontier West to the civilized East. All the critics of this story take note of this major fact, but most have erroneously assumed that Crane is treating the passing of the West comically and parodically. Only two critics, Robert Barnes and Kenneth Bernard,[24] have cut through the comic surface of this story and have identified the very serious elegy which is its essence. It is true of course that the story is funny, at times hilarious; that in fact is the point. As Bernard points out, it is too funny, painfully funny. There is, after all, a pathetic side to Scratchy's attempt to perform "a ritual in celebration of the old West"[25] while wearing "a maroon-colored flannel shirt, which had been . . . made principally by some Jewish women on the East Side of New York," and boots which "had red tops with gilded imprints, of the kind beloved in winter by little sledding boys on the hillsides of New England" (pp. 116-117). And far more pathetic is Jack's cringing before the subtle, vaguely sinister forces of civilization while he is on the train. It is clear enough, I think, that Crane is sympathizing with the plight of the once-heroic marshal suddenly thrust into a new environment in which he can no longer *be* heroic. Certainly this is shown in the story's final scene in which, again, the comic trappings are not so humorous as they first seem to be; for in this scene Jack displays a very real courage ("His heels had not moved an inch backward" [p. 119]) which Crane treats entirely without irony. This of course is in direct contrast to Jack's behaviour while on the train. The tragedy, then, is that the train, figuratively speaking, has won. Like the trains in Thoreau's *Walden* or in Faulkner's "The Bear," it presses on inexorably -- muddying Walden Pond, driving Old Ben from the wilderness, and robbing Western cowboys of their freedom and of their independence. "The great Pullman was whirling onward with such dignity of motion that a glance from the window seemed simply to prove that the plains of Texas were pouring eastward. Vast flats of green grass, dull-hued spaces of mesquite and cactus, little groups of frame houses, woods of light and tender trees, all were sweeping into the east, sweeping over the horizon, a precipice" (p. 109).

Is it going too far, in conclusion, to suggest that Crane envisioned his ideal self as a Jack Potter? We know, at least, that he wore cowboy breeches in England and that he wanted to buy a ranch in Texas. Like Jack Potter, Crane would have been happiest on some new frontier, outside civilization; and although there were no frontiers left, one wishes that he had at least been able to buy that ranch.

Chapter 8

Notes

1. Henry Nash Smith, *Virgin Land: The American West as Symbol and Myth* (New York: Random House, 1950); R.W.B. Lewis, *The American Adam: Innocence, Tragedy, and Tradition in the Nineteenth Century* (Chicago: The University of Chicago Press, 1955); Leslie A. Fiedler, *The Return of the Vanishing American* (New York: Stein and Day, 1968); David W. Noble, *The Eternal Adam and the New World Garden: The Central Myth in the American Novel Since 1830* (New York: George Braziller, 1968); Joseph Katz, "Introduction," in *Stephen Crane in the West and Mexico*, ed. Katz (Kent, Ohio: The Kent State University Press, 1970).
2. Edwin H. Cady, "Stephen Crane and the Strenuous Life," *ELH*, 28 (Dec., 1961): 279, 382.
3. *Ibid.*, p. 378.
4. See Book 2 of Smith, *Virgin Land*. See also Henry Bamford Parkes, "Metamorphoses of Leatherstocking," in *Literature in America*, ed. Philip Rahv (New York: Meridian Books, 1957), pp. 431-445.
5. "The passion felt by most American boys, until the West was improved, had been inflamed in this one by the revolver he had had since a lost Wyoming cowboy gave it to him on the Jersey shore, by Frederic Remington's pictures, by the stories of Garland and John Hilliard and a cowboy artist of 23rd Street who went crazy and died." John Berryman, *Stephen Crane* (New York: William Sloane Associates, 1950), p. 97.
6. Cf., for example, the letter which Crane wrote to Willis Brooks Hawkins in November of 1895, part of which reads as follows:

    "I have always believed the western people to be much truer than the eastern people. We in the east are overcome a good deal by a detestable superficial culture which I think is the real barbarism. . . . Damn the east! I fell in love with the straight out-and-out, sometimes-hideous, often-braggart westerners because I thought them to be the truer men."

    Stephen Crane: Letters, ed. R.W. Stallman and Lillian Gilkes (New York: New York University, 1960), pp. 69, 70. Hereafter cited as *Letters*.
7. Berryman, pp. 98, 107.
8. "I can see him sitting in the singularly ugly drawing room of the singularly hideous villa he lived in for a time at Oxted. Then he wore -- I dare say to shock me -- cowboy breeches and no coat, and all the time he was talking he wagged in his hand an immense thing that he called a gun and we would call a revolver. . . . Crane in those days . . . was in the habit of posing as an almost fabulous Billy the Kid."

    Ford Madox Ford, *New York Herald Tribune Books*, January 2, 1927, p. 1. Reprinted in *Letters*, p. 154, n. 127.
9. Berryman, p. 232; *Letters*, p. 198, n. 77.

10. All the page references to Crane's Western sketches are to *Stephen Crane in the West and Mexico*, ed. Joseph Katz.
11. Thomas Beer, *Stephen Crane: A Study in American Letters* (New York: Alfred A. Knopf, 1923), p. 114.
12. Henry David Thoreau, *The Variorum Walden and the Variorum Civil Disobedience*, ed. Walter Harding (New York: Washington Square Press, 1968), p. 249.
13. Berryman, p. 97.
14. *Ibid.*, p. 97.
15. *Ibid.*, p. 248.
16. All the page references to Crane's Western stories are to *The University of Virginia Edition of the Works of Stephen Crane*, ed. Fredson Bowers (Charlottesville: The University Press of Virginia, 1970), V.
17. Beer, p. 117.
18. Cady, p. 380.
19. Berryman, p. 107.
20. *Letters*, p. 154.
21. David Brion Davis, "Ten-Gallon Hero," *American Quarterly*, 6 (Summer, 1954): 121.
22. *Ibid.*, p. 113.
23. Jay Martin, *Harvests of Change: American Literature, 1865-1914* (Englewood Cliffs, N.J.: Prentice-Hall, 1967), p. 67.
24. Robert Barnes, *The Explicator* (April, 1958), Item 39; Kenneth Bernard, "'The Bride Comes to Yellow Sky': History as Elegy," *English Record*, 17 (April, 1967): 17-20.
25. Bernard, p. 18.

CHAPTER 9

Remarks on the Western Stance of Stephen Crane

Writing about his friend "Stevie" in 1927, Ford Madox Ford gave us the following vivid image of the Stephen Crane who for nearly ten months (July, 1897 to April, 1898) had lived in Ravensbrook Villa at Oxted, Surrey:

> I can see him sitting in the singularly ugly drawing room of the singularly hideous villa he lived in for a time at Oxted. Then he wore -- I dare say to shock me -- cowboy breeches and no coat, and all the time he was talking he wagged in his hand an immense thing that he called a gun and that we should call a revolver. From time to time he would attempt to slay with the bead-sight of this Colt such flies as settled on the table, and a good deal of his conversation would be taken up with fantastic boasts about what can be done with these lethal instruments. I don't know that he celebrated his own prowess, but he boasted about what heroes in the Far West were capable of . . . . Crane in those days . . . was in the habit of posing as an almost fabulous Billy the Kid.[1]

This portrait, taken alone, is striking enough -- but, as a matter of fact, both Crane's life and his writings are rich with incidents of Western role-playing and with images of the West. As a boy not yet in his teens, he "had been devouring Western paper-backs, becoming ingenious -- as his health improved -- in gang games based on them."[2] And when he was sixteen, "Stephen begged five dollars from his mother to start a lost cowboy back to Wyoming and the man gave him a real revolver alleged to have slain six Indians."[3] At Lafayette College two years later (in September, 1890), a band of hazing sophomores was stopped short upon breaking down the door of Crane's room. A witness of the scene relates that "Steve was petrified with fear and stood in a grotesque nightgown in one corner of the room with a revolver in his hand. His usual sallow complexion seemed to me a ghastly green. Whether he ever pointed the revolver or not, I do not know, but when I saw him, both arms were limp and the revolver was pointed to the floor."[4] Perhaps Crane was green with fear; it is more likely, as Edwin H. Cady has said, that he was green with the "shock proceeding from the realization that he had nearly murdered somebody." In any case, "Crane was hazed no more."[5]   It can be added that Ford's portrait of Crane in England is supported by at least one other Ravensbrook-visitor who records that "Mr. Crane [shot] with his revolver after lunch and he is a very fine shot."[6] Then, as he quarreled with Harold Frederic over *The Monster*, we find "Crane swarming up and down beating his revolver-butt on the furniture."[7] Crane made a point, too, of decorating his den at Ravensbrook with a Mexican blanket and with a set of silver spurs which he had collected from a ranch near the Nevada border.[8]

While the previous chapter has already argued that an understanding of Stephen Crane's relation to the American myth of the West is central to an understanding of his sensibility and of his art, I wish in this chapter to analyze that relation even more fully and to offer further evidence for my view of its life-changing importance. My point, as before, will be that Stephen Crane's life-long fascination with Western images and with Western traits -- along with the self-conscious Western role-playing which became prominent after his 1895 Western trip -- cannot with any fairness be relegated to the mere posturing that Ford and nearly all of Crane's critics[9] have claimed. For one thing, as Richard Harding Davis knew from vivid experience, "to Crane, anything that savored of a pose was hateful."[10] Still more important is the basic fact that in playing a Western role Crane was also taking a Western stance: he was affirming -- dramatizing in himself -- the legendary Western traits of masculinity, self-reliance, courage, independence, and magnanimity which, never having seen them before, he began to celebrate only during and after his travels in the West. The Ford portrait is, for example, quite significantly different from Willa Cather's portrait of the "stranded reporter" who was just then (February, 1895) on the threshold of his Western journey:

> Only a very youthful enthusiasm and a large propensity
> for hero worship could have found anything impressive in the
> young man who stood before the managing editor's desk. He
> was thin to emaciation, his face was gaunt and unshaven . . . .
> His grey clothes were much the worse for wear and fitted him
> so badly it seemed unlikely he had ever been measured for
> them. He wore a flannel shirt and a slovenly apology for a

necktie, and his shoes were dusty and worn grey about the toes and were badly run over at the heel.[11]

Not surprisingly, Cather's portrait of Crane in Lincoln, Nebraska, is strikingly like Corwin Knapp Linson's January, 1895 drawing titled "Mr. S. Crane starts WEST on a journalistic tare."[12] The point, though, is that this trip -- the forty-five-mile ride, for example, through the drought- and blizzard-stricken country around Eddyville, Nebraska -- quickly became something more than a "tare" and that Crane's Western journey was, in fact, inspiriting, fructifying, transformative: it changed his life-vision; it evoked in him a traditionally Western life-stance; it inspired him to affirm thereafter a Western code of endurance, stoicism, and courage. As I have mentioned elsewhere,[13] though, there is still what amounts to a tradition in Crane studies[14] to deny or to ignore the importance of Stephen Crane's Western experience and to claim that his attitude toward the West was parodic or satiric or -- at best -- ironic. Jamie Robertson, for example, has argued that Crane deliberately retained an Eastern outsider's, or tourist's, stance toward the West -- especially in his "use of the West as an artistic source."[15] The evidence is, I believe, just the opposite: Crane loved the West as he experienced it during his 1895 trip;[16] he talked with unaccustomed animation and excitement about the trip upon his return to the East;[17] he always fondly remembered the West and hoped against hope that he could somehow return to Texas to live and to restore his health;[18] and he drew upon his Western experience to enrich permanently his literature.[19]

I am convinced, in short, that Stephen Crane himself became, as I said in Chapter 8, a figure in the American myth of the West and that, for him, the myth became a reality: in a brief life of what Edwin H. Cady has accurately called "restless, desperate seeking,"[20] Crane came more and more to realize -- or at least to believe -- that his dream-vision of a free, masculine, unaffected life lay in the West. Thomas Beer reports that at the turn of the century, near death and trapped at Brede, "Crane spoke of Texas to James Pinker. He had been very well down there."[21] He had indeed been very well down there: he had touched the real, found an essential West, discovered in himself and in others a capacity for the manly Western virtues of courage, tenacity, endurance, generosity, self-confidence, and self-reliance. Crane was, in truth, the very last thing from a tourist in the American West. His letters alone make this clear. At San Antonio, for example, Crane "emptied his pocket to feed and start back home a lad of sixteen from Chicago who had invested a birthday gift of sixty dollars in a cowboy career and was sobbing on the Alamo Plaza penniless."[22] An uncle returned the money by telegraph, whereupon Crane sent (in March, 1895) the following letter to "Deadeye Dick":

> Thanks for sending back my money so fast. The hotel run me out, as my friends of the Bowery say and I was living in the Mex diggings with a push of sheep men till my boss in New York wired me money. Now, old man, take some advice from a tough jay from back East. You say your family is all right and nobody bothers you. Well, it struck me that you are too young a kid and too handsome to be free and easy around where a lot of bad boys and girls will take your pennies. So better stay home and grow a mustache before you rush out into the red universe any more.[23]

A good example, here, in Crane himself, of the openness and the generosity which he came to associate with the Western type. Equally important, I think, is Crane's empathy toward this young would-be cowboy -- a lad not unlike the sixteen-year-old Stephen who helped start a lost cowboy back to Wyoming. Now, of course, Crane describes himself, at twenty-three, as "a tough jay from back East" and advises the Chicago boy to wait a while for Western adventures. But he clearly sympathizes with the boy's impulse. Indeed, he was just then -- with increasing delight and excitement -- following the same impulse. And already, at the time of this letter, the impulse had proven itself sound.

Having recently fronted a blizzard to report the pain, the endurance, and the courage of Nebraskan farmers, Crane could with good reason, and proudly, call himself "a tough jay from back East." I think that this is indicative of a stance which Crane was already beginning to adopt: originally, geographically, an Easterner, yes, but -- like the New York Kid of his Western stories -- a "tough jay": in certain essential ways a Westerner. The sardonic young author of *Maggie* and of "An Experiment in Misery" who had "tried to make plain that the root of Bowery life is a sort of cowardice," a willingness to "be knocked flat and accept the licking," and who -- after his return to the East -- would soon be telling Nellie Crouse that he found the Eastern social world to be mainly "lies" was in search of a tougher, a more vital, and a more honest stance toward the world.[24] He found it in what Wallace Stegner has called "stiff-upper-lip country."[25] "How did you get along?" Crane asked one of the blizzard- and famine-stricken Nebraskan farmers. "Don't git along, stranger. Who the hell told you I did get along?" (VIII, 418).[26] Throughout his Western trip I see Crane testing himself, quite literally, in a way which Stegner has justly complained that we do now "only in fantasy and by standards we no longer think applicable to our real lives."[27] At a saloon in Lincoln, for instance, Crane risked a beating by trying to stop an unequal fight (actually a "local custom") between a big man and a smaller one.[28] Quite as much as Wallace Stegner, the westering Stephen Crane was beginning to recognize the disintegrative, emasculating effect of *Eastern* overcivilization -- and to respond. Shortly after his Western journey, we find him writing (in November, 1895) to Willis Brooks Hawkins that

> I have always believed the western people to be much truer than the eastern people. We in the east are overcome a good deal by a detestable superficial culture which I think is the real barbarism. Culture in it's [sic] true sense, I take it, is a comprehension of the man at one's shoulder. It has nothing to do with an adoration for effete jugs and old kettles. This latter is merely an amusement and we live for amusement in the east. Damn the east! I fell in love with the straight out-and-out, sometimes-hideous, often-braggart westerners because I thought them to be the truer men.[29]

What Stephen Crane came to hate more than anything else, and what he increasingly came to identify with the American East, was false, jaded, effete "overcivilization" -- living for amusement: he wanted really to live, to touch the real. In Nebraskan farmers and in Mexican Indians, in cowboys and in bandits, in the music of the Apache scalp-dance,[30] in bar-rooms and blizzards and deserts and mountains, Crane did indeed touch the real -- a reality that was neither romantic nor naturalistic, but *Western*: which is to say, rough, elemental, vital, honest, heroic. He was more than half-serious when (in July, 1896) he inscribed a copy of *George's Mother* "To Hamlin Garland of the great honest West, from Stephen Crane of the false East."[31] And his desperate, compulsive Western role-playing in England meant more to him emotionally than anyone has been willing to admit.

Interestingly enough, at the time of Crane's Western trip -- while he was soaking up impressions of new peoples and new landscapes, confronting new experiences that would permanently change his vision and his art -- he was also in love. Crane met Nellie Crouse earlier in the same month (January, 1895) that he left for the West; it may be true -- at least he claimed it was[32] -- that the sight of an American girl resembling Miss Crouse brought him back to New York City. It is unquestionably true that the love letters (seven in all, dating from 31 December 1895 to 18 March 1896) which Crane wrote to Miss Crouse after his Western journey are crucial documents for any study of this writer's sensibility. Other critics -- notably Edwin H. Cady and Marston LaFrance[33] -- have stressed the importance of these letters, but no one has carefully related them to Crane's Western trip or to the Western stance which that trip evoked.[34] The fact that the Nellie Crouse letters *are* importantly related to Crane's Western experience is shown, first of all, by his own remark that "in some semi-conscious manner, you [Miss Crouse] stood forth very distinctly in my memory" all during his journey -- up until he sighted the "American girl [resembling Miss Crouse] in a new spring gown [who] nearly caused me to drop dead." ("I ran to the railroad office. I cried: 'What is the shortest route to New York.' I left Mexico.")[35] Ultimately, though, these letters are related to Crane's Western experience in ways which are essentially moral and philosophical -- which concern the fundamental question of how one should live, and which reveal a Western-change in Crane's own attitude toward life. His newly adopted Western stance is, in fact, presented to Miss Crouse in the very first letter: "The lives of some people are one long apology. Mine was, once, but not now. I go through the world unexplained, I suppose." ("You have no idea" -- he was later to add -- "how it simplifies matters.")[36] And the following letters make clear that this was a stance which Crane would not change and which Miss Crouse could not appreciate. Much, that is, as Crane appears to have loved Nellie Crouse, as deliberately and as determinedly as he courted her in his earlier letters, the two of them obviously clashed -- and quickly fell out -- when they came to a discussion of the ideal man and the ideal way of living. Fresh from rough and elemental encounters throughout the West and Mexico -- his face gradually turning "the color of a brick side-walk," "nothing American about [him] save a large Smith and Wesson revolver"[37] -- Crane must have been considerably piqued by Miss Crouse's confession that "in her heart" she liked "the man of fashion more than . . . some other kinds of men."[38] It is true that Crane had naively -- or was it deliberately? -- set himself up for this challenge when (5 February 1896) he wrote to acknowledge receipt of Miss Crouse's photograph. Looking at her photograph, he had rushed to announce that "you have awed me. Yes, indeed, I am awed. There is something in your face which tells that there are many things which you perfectly understand which perhaps I don't understand at all . . . . I think it means that I am a savage. Of course I am admittedly a savage. I have been known as docile from time to time but only under great social pressure. I am by inclination a wild shaggy barbarian."[39] Such an averment -- even in play, and here it was not entirely in play -- could not have made a positive impression on a stylish, society-orientated, Eastward-yearning young woman from Akron, Ohio. Crane surely knew this. Perhaps, though, Miss Crouse's response to his "straight out-and-out," socially unpretentious Western stance was more severe than Crane had anticipated. (As Nellie Crouse's letters in reply to Crane's are lost, we are forced to guess.) His following letter (11 February 1896) is an effort to put matters straight; it is also the next-to-last, and the last really serious, letter that he ever wrote to Miss Crouse. I think he sensed that Nellie Crouse -- unlike the less proper, more individualistic Cora Taylor who would soon be his "wife" -- could never accept the Western view of life and of culture which Crane had endorsed so strongly in his November, 1895 letter to Willis Brooks Hawkins. Nevertheless, Crane -- rather heatedly -- tried to explain. He even tried to pretend that "I can stand the society man, if he don't interfere with me." But Miss Crouse should understand that the real "barbarians, savages" are the very "society leaders" who "lie" for the sake of "form." "Form really is truth, simplicity."[40] And that is why Crane told Hawkins that he had fallen in love with Westerners -- with Westerners more even than with Miss Crouse. "[W]hat I contend for" -- he had stressed to Hawkins -- "is the atmosphere of the west which really is frank and honest."[41] Still, not entirely wishing, one senses, to destroy his relation with Miss

Crouse, Crane began his letter by asserting that her preference for "the man of fashion . . . came nearer to my own view than perhaps you expected." But this is only wishful thinking: it becomes evident in his letter that he detests men of "fashion" or "society." "For my part, I like the man who dresses correctly and does the right thing invariably, but, oh, he must be more than that, a great deal more." Like Crane's own Jack Potter, he must, for one thing, "know how to stand steady" when he sees "cocked revolvers and death comes down and sits on the back of a chair and waits." Himself a gentleman *déclassé* with an intense sense of family,[42] Crane would of course "swear by the real aristocrat. The man whose forefathers were men of courage, sympathy and wisdom, is usually one who will stand the strain whatever it may be." Courage, sympathy, wisdom: these are the essential -- the *Western* -- traits, and for Crane they constitute a heroic ideal, a Western stance, that he, for one, would not expect to find in "the society man." ("Time after time, I have seen the social lion turn to lamb and fail -- fail at precisely the moment when men should not fail.")[43] "Wisdom" is perhaps a vague term just here, but not if we recall a sentence from an earlier letter to Miss Crouse: "The final wall of the wise man's thought . . . is Human Kindness of course."[44]

The Nellie Crouse letters, more than any other document, make it clear that Stephen Crane came to learn -- where else but in the American West? -- that "The cynical mind is an uneducated thing."[45] More and more, he came to swear by the "real aristocrat," the man who lives in accord with a code of courage, honesty, sympathy, and kindness. As Wallace Stegner has reminded us, this, for the Modern World, is a "square," supposedly naive, "Western" stance which true Westerners -- whatever their geographic fortunes -- would do well to defend and to preserve in the face of inevitable ridicule. Crane, too, was fully aware, as he mentioned in his November, 1895 letter to Willis Brooks Hawkins, that "the east thinks them [Westerners] ridiculous. When they come to congress they display a child-like honesty which makes the old east laugh."[46] Crane did not laugh. Of course he was himself too honest not to admit to Nellie Crouse that the effort to make oneself "good" is "an incomparably quixotic task for any man to undertake."[47] Yet it is his essential task. In a world so similar, as the following chapter illustrates, to that of Ernest Hemingway -- a world where "Identity is almost as fragile as life itself"[48] -- man's foremost duty is to preserve ideals, *self-created* ideals, for the self. "I do not confront it [life] blithely," Crane told Miss Crouse. "I confront it with desperate resolution. There is not even much hope in my attitude. I do not even expect to do good. But I expect to make a sincere, desperate, lonely battle to remain true to my conception of my life and the way it should be lived, and if this plan can accomplish anything, it shall be accomplished."[49] Although it would be difficult to find -- even in Ernest Hemingway -- a more tough-minded or a more heroic stance toward life than the stance which Crane presented to Miss Crouse, the preoccupation of numerous critics with Crane's "ironic vision"[50] has obscured his being affirmative about anything at all. Clearly, though, the author whose "supreme ambition" was to preserve "his quality of personal honesty"[51] was neither uncommitted nor nihilistic. In his review (1897) of Quida's *Under Two Flags*, as a matter of fact, one finds Crane sounding quite as *Western* as Wallace Stegner:

> The characters in this book abandon themselves to virtue and heroism as the martyrs abandoned themselves to flames. Sacrifice appears to them as the natural course. Pain, death, dishonor, is counted of no moment so long as the quality of personal integrity is defended and preserved. Certainly we may get good from a book of this kind. It imitates the literary plan of the early peoples. They sang, it seems, of nobility of character. To-day we sing of portieres and champagne and gowns.
> ....
> [W]ith all the cavilling of our modern literary class, it is good to hear at times the song of the brave . . . . [It] voices . . . the old spirit of dauntless deed and sacrifice which is the soul of literature in every age, and we are not growing too tired to listen, although we try to believe so [VIII, 677, 678].

As John Berryman has said, "there is something charming here: [Crane] knew himself. History, grammar, gods, an elaborate society, were nothing. A hero, so long as you didn't call him one and concentrated on his hanging shirt-tail, was worth having."[52] Such was the heroism that, by the time of his review, Crane had already seen in "straight out-and-out" Westerners and had dramatized in several Western stories; such also was the heroism that he confessed to Nellie Crouse -- but never to anyone else -- was the aim of his own life.

In his letters to Nellie Crouse, Crane was of course being self-consciously masculine ("an intensely practical and experienced person," he assured her -- fearing that she might think of him as only a "poet"),[53] but this was intrinsic to his Western stance in any case. It was not a stance that he needed to assume. The Stephen Crane who played poker, wore cowboy breeches, and loved horses and horse-riding -- galloping, once, at full speed through English darkness[54] -- and who went to the West because, along with other reasons, he wanted to "see a cowboy ride" and "to be in a blizzard of the plains"[55] was not one who left doubts about his masculinity. Everywhere -- from his distaste for "the cut-and-dried curriculum of the college" ("I preferred base-ball")[56] to his thirst for adventure in the West to his obsession with war to his defense of Dora Clark to his wish to buy a ranch in Texas -- we see the intrinsically honorable and generous Crane "yearning," as George W. Johnson has said, "to touch reality and remain a gentleman."[57] (One of his most intimate friends, Joseph Conrad, observed that "there was in Crane a strain of chivalry which made him safe to trust with one's life.")[58] His solution was the Western stance: the moral redefinition of the "real aristocrat" as one unconcerned with, or superior to, "superficial culture." Above all, the real aristocrat was -- as Crane explicitly told Miss Crouse -- a man of physical courage. One wonders what Miss Crouse thought of "One Dash -- Horses," which Crane sent her, or what she might have thought of "The Five White Mice" or of "A Man and Some Others." Yet these Western stories dramatize what was for Stephen Crane the essence of *real* aristocracy: courage in the face of great physical danger. By far the most brilliant insight into Crane's sensibility is still Thomas Beer's remark that "the mistress of this boy's mind was fear. His search in aesthetic was governed by terror as that of tamer men is governed by the desire of women."[59] This is why Crane could not stay safely in the American East and play "the man of fashion" for Miss Crouse; it is also why he wrote some fine Western stories which take the protagonist outside of -- or at least to the very edge of -- society and which focus upon an extreme physical test, an ordeal.

Joseph Conrad was, for example, absolutely right to find "A Man and Some Others" "an amazing bit of biography" and to "admire it without reserve." By an interesting coincidence, Conrad read this story while he was also reading the story that is widely held to be Crane's masterpiece: "The Open Boat." He was of course highly excited and impressed by both stories -- affirming, though, that "A Man and Some Others" is the better of the two -- and he wrote to Crane, saying: "I am envious of you -- horribly. Confound you -- you fill the blamed land-scape -- you -- by all the devils -- fill the sea-scape . . . . I want to swear at you, to bless you -- perhaps to shoot you -- but I prefer to be your friend."[60] Conrad's judgment was accurate.[61] Not only are these two stories "immense," but they share the same vision. Max Westbrook is the only critic I know of who has understood the "philosophic superficiality of the men's complaints against the universe"[62] in "The Open Boat" (1897). The correspondent's ruminations about fate's cruelty and about nature's indifference are treated ironically, are in no way the message of the story. The message is that reality in any case can not be touched by the intellect, but rather by experience; and on the sea -- as on the Western plains -- "romantic concepts about nature's love and fair play do not hold up when put to the test of brute experience."[63] Still, this vision is neither naturalistic nor nihilistic: it is Westen and sacral -- sacral in the sense that reality, *both* nature's indifference and the brotherhood of the men, is felt rather than intellectualized or romanticized.[64] Exactly as Crane had earlier said of the Nebraskan farmers, the men in the open boat were "driven to bay by nature, now the pitiless enemy"; like the farmers, they learned to "depend upon their endurance, their capacity to help each other, and their steadfast and unyielding courage" (VIII, 412, 420). By the story's conclusion they have touched reality: they have experienced sacred energies in themselves and in the universe. "When it came night, the white waves paced to and fro in the moonlight, and the wind brought the sound of the great sea's voice to the men on the shore, and they felt that they could *then* be interpreters" (V, 92; emphasis mine).

Similarly, in "A Man and Some Others" (1896) an "eddycated" Easterner, a stranger to the Southwestern plains, comes to interpret -- that is, to *experience* -- the message of the elements, "a message of the inconsequence of individual tragedy -- a message that is in the boom of the sea, the sliver of the wind through the grass-blades, the silken clash of hemlock boughs" (V, 60). Again, this is a Western, *sacral* vision which shows just how far Crane really was beyond a merely formulaic celebration of Western heroic traits: beyond the kind of ethnocentric neo-romanticism which caused Theodore Roosevelt to complain to the story's author that "the frontiersman," Bill, should have "come out on top; it is more normal that way!"[65] Bill, the hero, is not a conventional Western hero; he is a man with a desperate past, "a man who had often stormed the iron walls of the city of success, and who now sometimes valued himself as the rabbit values his prowess" (V, 59). And he has now been told that he must get off the range or be killed by Jose " -- and the others."

> As his Mexican friend tripped blithely away, Bill turned with a thoughtful face to his frying-pan and his fire. After dinner he drew his revolver from its scarred old holster, and examined every part of it . . . . Bill loved it because its allegiance was more than that of man, horse, or dog. It questioned neither social nor moral position; it obeyed alike the saint and the assassin. It was the claw of the eagle, the tooth of the lion, the poison of the snake; and when he swept it from its holster, this minion smote where he listed, even to the battering of a far penny. Wherefore it was his dearest possession, and was not to be exchanged in southwestern Texas for a handful of rubies [V, 57-58].

But while Bill's love of his revolver is striking and is also importantly related to Crane's own life, this story is hardly the formulaic celebration of the Western six-gun mystique which Roosevelt would have preferred. Primordial energies are tapped and unleashed; an Easterner is initiated into understanding and into manhood; the heroic is dramatized and defined.

Crane begins the superbly rendered final section of the story by remarking ironically that "It is sometimes taught that men do the furious and desperate thing from an emotion that is as even and placid as the thoughts of a village clergyman on Sunday afternoon. Usually, however, it is to be believed that a panther is at the time born in the heart, and that the subject does not resemble a man picking mulberries" (V. 66). Suddenly, Bill upreared like a great and bloody spirit of vengeance, his face lighted with the blaze of his last passion. The Mexicans came swiftly and in silence.

The lightning action of the next few moments was of the fabric of dreams to the stranger . . . . The rush of feet, the spatter of shots, the cries, the swollen faces seen like masks on the smoke, resembled a happening of the night.

And yet afterward certain lines, forms, lived out so strongly from the incoherence that they were always in his memory.

He killed a man, and the thought went swiftly by him, like the feather on the gale, that it was easy to kill a man.

Moreover, he suddenly felt for Bill, this grimy sheep-herder, some deep form of idolatry. Bill was dying, and the dignity of last defeat, the superiority of him who stands in his grave, was in the pose of the lost sheep-herder [V, 66-67].

A tough-minded, sacral, *Western* vision, as I have said, of primordial reality. The vast distancing Western landscape proclaims "the inconsequence of human tragedy" (V, 62); Bill's last blaze of passion proclaims the existence of primordial energies, the possibility of human dignity, courage, heroism.

"A Man and Some Others" is the strongest of Crane's truly Western writings; but "The Five White Mice" (1896) and "One Dash -- Horses" (1895) present a similar Western stance, a similar testing of the protagonist-hero. Once, at a saloon in San Antonio, "A red-haired man swung his elbow against Crane's arm to get a revolver from his belt and aim it at an enemy, before the bartender threw a seidel and spoiled the show."[66] Shortly later, in Mexico, Crane found himself literally riding for life across the plains, pursued by bandits.[67] These experiences went into his stories, where the stereotyped actions (the fast-draw and the ride-for-life) are made real, are treated seriously and are rendered compellingly. During the stark confrontation, at midnight, in a little Mexican street, the New York Kid, clearly a Crane-surrogate,

suddenly knew that it was possible to draw his own revolver and by a swift manoeuver face down all three Mexicans. If he was quick enough he would probably be victor. If any hitch occurred in the draw he would undoubtedly be dead with his friends. It was a new game; he had never been obliged to face a situation of this kind in the Beacon Club in New York . . . .

> He thought of the weight and size of his revolver and
> dismay pierced him . . . . Some of the eels of despair lay wet
> and cold against his back.
>   But at the supreme moment the revolver came forth as
> if it were greased and it arose like a feather. This somnolent
> machine, after months of repose, was finally looking at the
> breasts of men.
>   Perhaps in this one series of movements, the Kid had
> unconsciously used nervous force sufficient to raise a bale of
> hay . . . . The revolver gleamed in the darkness with a fine
> silver light [V, 49-50].

Did young Steve aim the gun at the hazing sophomores? We will never
know. What we do know is that Crane was serious about the courageous and
skillful use of the revolver as a test, a symbol of manhood. The New York
Kid's "grace under pressure" -- together with the inwardness and the
immediacy with which Crane renders this experience -- is central to Crane's
Western stance. For it is clear that Crane went West, along with other
reasons, precisely to seek this "new game." Like Hemingway, he had a deep
temperamental need to test himself, "to make of danger a kind of mystic
ceremony, or rite, or crucible."[68] Surviving the test -- as Crane did when, in
Mexico, he faced a menacing bandit -- made him a Westerner.

"You know the Mexican incident," Crane wrote to Miss Crouse,
enclosing a clipping of "One Dash -- Horses." "It was very strange."[69] Indeed
it was. For the incidents of this story actually happened to Crane -- not just
the ride across the plains but also the confrontation in the hut. During a tour
of rural Mexico, Crane and his guide had gone to sleep in the back room of a
tavern when, as J. C. Levenson relates, "experience caught up with
imaginings. A local bandit, Ramon Colorado, drunk and looking for trouble,
thrust aside the curtain between the two rooms and peered into the dark for
the rich American. Crane sat up in his blanket, instinctively grasped his
revolver under the covers, and stared stonily at the man who wanted to rob
and probably kill him."[70] Exactly this experience is rendered in the story:

> "Well, I would kill him, then!"
> "No, you must not!"
> "Yes, I will kill him! Listen! I will ask this American
> beast for his beautiful pistol and spurs and money and saddle,
> and if he will not give them -- you will see!"
> ....

> Suddenly the clamor of voices ceased. There was a silence -- a silence of decision. The blanket was flung aside, and the red light of a torch flared into the room. It was held high by a fat, round-faced Mexican, whose little snake-like mustache was as black as his eyes, and whose eyes were as black as jet. He was insane with the wild rage of a man whose liquor is dully burning at his brain . . . .
>   . . . . The American did not move. He was staring at the fat Mexican with a strange fixedness of gaze, not fearful, not dauntless, not anything that could be interpreted. He simply stared.
>   . . . Ah, well, sirs, here was a mystery. At the approach of their menacing company, why did not this American cry out and turn pale, or run, or pray them mercy? The animal merely sat still, and stared, and waited for them to begin. Well, evidently he was a great fighter; or perhaps he was an idiot. Indeed, this was an embarrassing situation, for who was going forward to discover whether he was a great fighter or an idiot?
>   To Richardson, whose nerves were tingling and twitching like live wires and whose heart jolted inside him, this pause was a long horror; and for these men who could so frighten him there began to swell in him a fierce hatred -- a hatred that made him long to be capable of fighting all of them, a hatred that made him capable of fighting all of them. A 44-caliber revolver can make a hole large enough for little boys to shoot marbles through, and there was a certain fat Mexican with a mustache like a snake who came extremely near to have eaten his last tamale merely because he frightened a man too much [V, 15, 16-17].

Throughout Crane's life -- in imagination and in reality -- one finds him grasping a revolver, sometimes in the face of imminent death. It seems clear, too, that he could imagine himself using the revolver, that he did in fact almost use it -- on the hazing sophomores, on the Mexican bandit. I find this to be singular, to reveal a stance that deserves serious study.

"The Bride Comes to Yellow Sky" (1898) and "The Blue Hotel" (1898) are the remaining Western stories in which the testing of the protagonist is prominent. In one a true Westerner dramatizes the legendary courage of the heroic marshal. In the other a would-be Western hero becomes brave only with drink and disasterously lacks the self-assurance, unpretentiousness, and magnanimity of a true Westerner. In both of these stories Crane is concerned, however, as much with depicting historical change -- the *modernization* of Yellow Sky and of Fort Romper--as with dramatizing a testing of the protagonist. The modernization theme -- the "Easternizing" of the West -- is very strong in many of Crane's Western sketches and Western stories, as I have aimed to show in Chapter 8. It would be difficult, for example, to find a more penetrating one-sentence synopsis of the Westward Movement than the one which Crane includes at the beginning of "Moonlight on the Snow" (1899): "And from the East came both the sane and the insane with hope, with courage, with hoarded savings, with cold decks, with Bibles, with knives in boots, with humility and fear, with bland impudence" (V, 179).[71] "Moonlight on the Snow," "The Bride," and "The Blue Hotel" are very fine stories indeed, but they are not centrally related to Stephen Crane's Western stance.   What they show, rather, is that Crane, like anyone emotionally involved in the American myth of the West, was saddened, enraged, and embittered by the advance of modernity.

My purpose in this chapter has been to focus upon Stephen Crane's personal involvement in and commitment to a Western stance as it is dramatized in his life and in his writings. I still believe that he envisioned his ideal self as a Jack Potter. And I still wish that he had been able to buy that ranch in Texas.

Chapter 9

Notes

1. "Stevie and Co.," *New York Herald Tribune Books*, January 2, 1927, p. 1.
2. John Berryman, *Stephen Crane* (New York: William Sloane Associates, 1950), p.13.
3. Thomas Beer, *Stephen Crane: A Study in American Letters* (New York: Alfred A. Knopf, 1923), p. 54.
4. Lyndon Upson Pratt, "The Formal Education of Stephen Crane," *American Literature*, 10 (January, 1939): 468.
5. Edwin H. Cady, *Stephen Crane* (New York: Twayne, 1962), p. 28.
6. *Stephen Crane: Letters*, ed. R. W. Stallman and Lillian Gilkes (New York: New York University Press, 1960), pp. 154-155. Hereafter cited as *Letters*.
7. Berryman, p. 205.
8. Beer, p. 113, mentions the ranch and the spurs. For a photograph of Crane in his den at Ravensbrook, see illustration number 17 in R.W. Stallman, *Stephen Crane, A Biography* (New York: George Braziller, 1968).
9. The major book-length critical studies of Stephen Crane are the following: Cady, *Stephen Crane*; Eric Solomon, *Stephen Crane: From Parody to Realism* (Cambridge: Harvard University Press, 1966); Marston LaFrance, *A Reading of Stephen Crane* (Oxford: Claredon Press, 1971); Milne Holton, *Cylinder of Vision: The Fiction and Journalistic Writing of Stephen Crane* (Baton Rouge: Lousiana State University Press, 1972); and Frank Bergon, *Stephen Crane's Artistry* (New York: Columbia University Press, 1975). Not one of these critics believes that Crane was essentially serious in his stance toward the West.
10. A young man trying to get himself killed, Crane stood on the front line in Cuba in a long, white raincoat, drawing fire. No one could get him down, until Davis thought of the answer: "I knew that to Crane, anything that savored of a pose was hateful, so . . . I called, 'You're not impressing anyone by doing that, Crane.' As I hoped he would, he instantly dropped to his knees. When he crawled over to where we lay, I explained 'I knew that would fetch you,' and he grinned, and said, 'Oh, was that it?'" *Notes of a War Correspondent* (New York: Charles Scribner's Sons, 1911), p. 125. Cf. Berryman, pp. 223-24; and Cady, pp. 63-64.
11. "When I Knew Stephen Crane," in *Stephen Crane: A Collection of Critical Essays*, ed. Maurice Bassan (Englewood Cliffs, N.J.: Prentice-Hall, 1967), pp. 17, 12-13. First printed in *The Library* (Pittsburg), 23, June 1900, pp. 17-18.
12. The Linson drawing first appeared on the copyright page of *Stephen Crane in the West and Mexico*, ed. Joseph Katz (Kent, Ohio: Kent State University Press, 1970).
13. In a review of *Stephen Crane's Artistry*, published in *Western American Literature*, 12 (Winter, 1978): 335-337.

14.   This tradition is represented mainly by the critics listed in note 9, but cf. also Jean Cazemajou, *Stephen Crane* (Minneapolis: University of Minnesota Press, 1969).

15.   "Stephen Crane, Eastern Outsider in the West and Mexico," *Western American Literature*, 13 (Fall, 1978): 243-257. I wish to thank Jamie Robertson for providing me with a copy of his essay prior to its publication.

16.   Beer, p. 114; Berryman, p. 97.

17.   Crane's niece recalled that "the one time I remember him talking animatedly and at length was when he returned from his trip to Mexico." Edith Crane to Louis Zara, December 14, 1958, in the Rare Book Room of the Ohio State University Library. Printed in Katz, ed. *Stephen Crane in the West and Mexico*, p. xxiii.

      Corwin Knapp Linson also remembered that the evening when Crane returned from the West "was a riot of talk. For once his tongue found freedom." *My Stephen Crane*, ed. Edwin H. Cady (Syracuse,N.Y.: Syracuse University Press, 1958), p. 87.

18.   Beer, p. 34; Berryman, pp. 232, 249, 250; Cady, p. 66.

19.   Cf. Berryman, pp. 97-113, especially pp. 98-99.

20.   Cady, p.45.

21.   Beer, p. 234.

22.   Berryman, p.102.

23.   *Letters*, p. 54.

24.   *Ibid.*, pp. 133, 115-116.

25.   Wallace Stegner, *The Sound of Mountain Water* (Garden City, N.Y.: Doubleday, 1969), p.184.

26.   Numbers within parentheses or brackets with quotations from Stephen Crane indicate volume and page in *The University of Virginia Edition of the Works of Stephen Crane*, ed. Fredson Bowers (Charlottesville: The University Press of Virginia, 1969-1975).

27.   Stegner, p. 200.

28.   Beer, pp. 113-114; Berryman, p. 99.

29.   *Letters*, pp. 69-70.

30.   Writing to Nellie Crouse on January 6, 1896, Crane remarked that "in the spring I am wanting very much to go to Arizona to study the Apaches more. There is a man in Boston who has been unwise enough to ask me to write a play for his theater and I wish to have some Apaches in it. For instance the music of their scalp dance is enough to set fire to a stone church." *Letters*, pp. 97-98.

31.   *Ibid.*, p. 126.

32.   *Ibid.*, p. 86.

33.   See the introductory remarks in *Stephen Crane's Love Letters to Nellie Crouse*, ed. Edwin H. Cady and Lester G. Wells (Syracuse, N.Y.: Syracuse University Press, 1954), pp. 17-23; and see LaFrance, *A Reading of Stephen Crane*, pp. 165-171.

34.   In the "Introduction" to his edition of *The Western Writings of Stephen Crane* (New York: New American Library, 1979), Frank Bergon briefly relates one of the Nellie Crouse letters to Crane's Western trip (p. 19). And he includes two of the letters in his edition.

35.   *Letters*, pp. 86, 101.

36.   *Ibid.*, 86, 97.

37. *Ibid.*, p. 86.
38. *Ibid.*, p. 114.
39. *Ibid.*, p. 111.
40. *Ibid*, pp. 115, 116.
41. *Ibid.*, p. 70.
42. For evidence of Crane's intense pride in his family, see the letter that he wrote to John Northern Hilliard on January 2, 1896. *Letters*, pp. 93-96. Cf., also, Berryman, p. 7.; and Beer, p. 219. The most complete analysis of Crane as a gentleman *declassé* is in Cady, *passim*.
43. *Letters*, pp. 114, 115.
44. *Ibid.*, p. 99.
45. *Ibid.*, p. 99.
46. *Ibid.*, p. 70.
47. *Ibid.*, p. 116.
48. J. C. Levenson, "Introduction," *The University of Virginia Edition of The Works of Stephen Crane*, V, p. xvii.
49. *Letters*, p. 105.
50. Marson LaFrance, for example, argues that the ironic vision is central to all of Crane's writings as well as to Crane's own life -- that "the essential Crane should continue to elude the investigator of the influences upon his life until the ironic vision is recognized as a constant factor" (*A Reading of Stephen Crane*, p. 251 and *passim*). Cf. also Robertson, *passim*.
51. *Letters*, p. 110.
52. Berryman, p. 155.
53. *Letters*, p. 101.
54. Berryman, p. 248.
55. Beer, p. 113.
56. *Letters*, pp. 95, 109.
57. "Stephen Crane's Metaphor of Decorum," *PMLA*, 78 (June, 1963): 251.
58. Beer, which includes Conrad's "Introduction," pp. 9-10.
59. Beer, p. 117.
60. *Letters*, p. 154. In a letter to Edward Garnett, Conrad expressed his view that "A Man and Some Others" is "of course" better than "The Open Boat." *Letters*, p. 155.
61. Crane himself agreed. In a letter to Paul Revere Reynolds, he affirmed that "A Man and Some Others" is "one of the best stories that I have done." *Letters*, p. 130.
62. "Stephen Crane: The Pattern of Affirmation," *Nineteenth-Century Fiction*, 14 (December, 1959), p. 222.
63. *Ibid.*, p. 223.
64. Max Westbrook has defined and illustrated "sacrality" in Western American literature in "The Practical Spirit: Sacrality and the American West," *Western American Literature*, 3 (Fall, 1968): 193-205 and in *Walter Van Tilburg Clark* (New York: Twayne, 1960), *passim*. See especially Chapter 2, titled "The Western Esthetic," of *Walter Van Tilburg Clark*.
65. *Letters*, p. 128.
66. Beer, p. 115.
67. See Berryman, pp. 104-106.

68. Philip Young, *Ernest Hemingway* (New York: Rinehart, 1952), p. 162.
69. *Letters*, p. 101.
70. Levenson, p. xxxvii.
71. For a perceptive analysis of the modernization theme in "Moonlight on the Snow," see George Monteiro, "Stephen Crane's 'Yellow Sky' Sequel," *Arizona Quarterly*, 30 (Summer, 1974): 119-126.

CHAPTER 10

Stephen Crane's "Code" and Its Western Connections

Hemingway's heroes, as Robert Penn Warren has said, "are not defeated except upon their own terms . . . . [A]nd certainly they [maintain], even in the practical defeat, an ideal of themselves, some definition, formulated or unformulated, by which they have lived." Warren is describing of course the famous Hemingway Code, which, as he says, is the means by which Hemingway's "heroes make one gallant, though limited, effort to redeem the incoherence of the world."[1] I would like to suggest that what is true of Hemingway's heroes is no less true of Stephen Crane's heroes, even though this important aspect of Crane's sensibility -- his building of a clearly formulated heroic stance toward the world -- continues to be neglected in Crane studies. It almost seems that Philip Young's and Daniel Hoffman's brief discussions,[2] excellent as they are, of the temperamental and the artistic likenesses in Crane and Hemingway have been accepted as definitive statements of the relationship between these two writers. Certainly no one is likely to improve upon Young's remark that "Crane's whole dark view of existence, of man damaged and alone in a hostile, violent world, of life as one long war which we seek out and challenge in fear and controlled panic . . . is all an amazing forecast of Hemingway."[3] But this is only a starting point: recognizing the essential similarity in the sensibilities of two of our classic fictionists, we should go on to do for Crane what Young has already done for Hemingway: we should trace the ways in which the protagonists in Crane's literature -- as well as Crane himself in his own life -- front the "dark view of existence" which the two writers shared. In other words, we should make an effort -- and that is an aim of this chapter -- to understand and to define Stephen Crane's "code."

Defining Stephen Crane's "code" will reveal, too, its Western connections. For Stephen Crane -- man *and* artist -- was, as the previous chapters have been arguing, changed dramatically by his 1895 journey to the American West -- a journey which evoked from him a new and a traditionally

Western stance toward the world.   Clearly, the traits and values which
Chapter 9 found central to Crane's Western stance -- self-reliance, stoicism,
honesty, courage, magnanimity -- are directly connected to, are an integral
part of his code: the essential distinction being that Crane's code is a more
carefully formalized ideal, that -- exactly as with Hemingway -- it is a
conscious, deliberate response to what Willa Cather tellingly referred to as
Crane's bitter "arraignment of the wages of life."[4] The arraignment which
Crane presented to Cather (then "just off the range" and a Junior at the state
university) occurred at Lincoln, Nebraska, when (February, 1895) Crane was,
as Chapter 9 has pointed out, on the very threshold of his westering
experience. Neither in appearance nor in attitude had he, as yet, begun to
form his later Western stance of endurance, of courage, and of magnanimity
which Willa Cather -- of all people -- would have admired, but which she
found, just then, so lacking.   What Willa Cather found, instead, was a
"moody," a "profoundly discouraged," a "deeply despondent" young man with
a heart more bitter than any that she had ever known and with "eyes that
seemed to be burning themselves out."[5] Only later -- only during and after
his exciting, educative, fructifying travels through Nebraska, through Texas,
and on to Mexico City -- can we begin to discover the code which Stephen
Crane created as a response to his dark judgment of the wages of life. As I
have stressed in Chapter 9, it is especially in his love letters to Nellie Crouse
that we see Crane's newly adopted Western stance; it is also in a letter (26
January 1896) to Miss Crouse that Crane himself presented a clear-cut,
explicit formulation of his code of life. The time before one's death may, he
told Miss Crouse, "be a short time or a long one but at any rate it means a
life of labor and sorrow. I do not confront it blithely. I confront it with
desperate resolution. There is not even much hope in my attitude. I do not
even expect to do good. But I expect to make a sincere, desperate, lonely
battle to remain true to my conception of my life and the way it should be
lived, and if this plan [this code] can accomplish anything, it shall be
accomplished."[6] Sincere, desperate, lonely: these adjectives provide an
index to Stephen Crane's stance toward the world and, additionally, explain
the need that he felt for a *code* by which to give meaning to man's sufferings
and to his desperate isolation. As with Hemingway, fidelity to one's code

demands unceasing effort, alertness, self-honesty, self-reliance, and self-discipline. "When I speak of a battle" -- Crane stressed in his letter to Miss Crouse -- "I do not mean want, and those similar spectres. I mean myself and the inherent indolence and cowardice which is the lot of all men . . . . I [have] fought the world and [have] not bended nor moved an inch but this other battle -- it is to last on up through the years to my grave and only on that day am I to know if the word Victory will look well upon lips of mine."[7] Clearly, the newly Westernized Stephen Crane -- as revealed in his letters to Nellie Crouse -- was committed to a brave and, indeed, a heroic quest exactly like that which Earl Rovit has analyzed in Hemingway's life and in Hemingway's writings:[8] a quest to defend and preserve the self, to establish identity, to combat the un-meaning and the chaos continuously threatened both from within and from without: from an undisciplined self and from the incoherence of the external world. The Victory that both Crane and Hemingway surely gained could come only from a sincere, life-long battle to create and to define the self and to remain true to one's ideals -- one's code -- for the self.

The code of life which a Western-changed Stephen Crane presented so cogently to Nellie Crouse can be seen as an operating force, too, in the new kind of fiction which his westering experience inspired -- so much so that one is left wondering why Crane's code has been so slighted or so distorted: why, for example, the single critical article on "The Crane-Hemingway Code" should propose that "for Crane there was no formal code of the Hemingway type," that "Crane's code is unlike Hemingway's in that it does not include the concept of a hero."[9] To answer this question is, I think, to identify a fundamental problem that has characterized Crane studies for as long as I can see: the urge to pigeonhole him as a Naturalist, or as an Impressionist, or as an Existentialist, and so forth. He was no doubt all of these things -- and more; but this is not to say that he can be pigeonholed, and it *is* to say that the critical tradition of treating his literature as if it were a monolithic whole has led inevitably to serious distortions. This is especially true when it comes to studying Crane's building of a heroic code of life; for it must, of course, be granted that his important *early* works -- *Maggie, George's Mother, The Red Badge of Courage* -- are essentially deterministic and anti-heroic.

Heroism requires control and courage, embodies a stance from which ideals for the self are defended and preserved whatever the cost may be; but in Crane's early fiction we see the characters reacting *to* the world rather than courageously fronting it; instead of seeing them shape their lives, we see their lives being shaped for them; they exhibit no ability (or will) to apprehend reality, no capacity to live without illusions, no self-discipline, no self-control -- in short, no self-created code of life. Maggie Johnson is simply, like Dreiser's Carrie Meeber, "A Waif amid Forces"; George Kelcey is equally self-deluded and equally helpless to direct or to control his life -- the antithesis, in fact, of the code-directed heroes who emerge in Crane's later writings. The case of Henry Fleming is of course more complex, but it is clear enough, I think, that Crane's dominant attitude toward Fleming's conduct is bitingly, almost fiercely ironic. Still, it is hardly fair to use these early works, important as they are, as a basis for any final assessment of Crane's view of or attitude toward life and human possibilities. The evidence is strong, in fact, that Crane himself -- almost as soon as he had written them -- was dissatisfied with the deterministic, amoral vision of life rendered by his early stories. As I have stressed in Chapter 9, a central impulse behind his very journey to the West was clearly the search for a tougher, a more honest stance toward the world than he had found anywhere in the East. His early sardonic, irony-ridden works behind him, he was, just then, ripe to create both in himself and in his literature new standards for human performance. The fact that Crane *did* create new standards is evidenced, for example, in his response (November, 1896) to a letter questioning him about *Maggie*:

> I do not think that much can be done with the Bowery as long as the [people there] are in their present state of conceit. A person who thinks himself superior to the rest of us because he has no job and no pride and no clean clothes is as badly conceited as Lillian Russell. In a story of mine called 'An Experiment in Misery' I tried to make plain that the root of Bowery life is a sort of cowardice. Perhaps I mean a lack of ambition or to willingly be knocked flat and accept the licking.[10]

Certainly there is a firm moral stance here that people, in the Bowery or elsewhere, are directly accountable for their lives and for the *way* those lives are lived -- expressed by a man who, travelling in the West, had seen, on Nebraskan plains, a defiant people who dared to "depend upon their endurance, their capacity to help each other, and their steadfast and unyielding courage."[11] Even before he left for the West, Crane had in fact manifested a similar dissatisfaction with deterministic philosophy in his clearly painful attempt at the end of *The Red Badge of Courage* to *believe* in Henry Fleming's heroism -- even though the novella itself does not render a real basis for such a belief. And however intense Crane's irony toward Henry is in most of *The Red Badge*, it should be noted, too, that he does treat Henry's courage nonironically in "The Veteran" (1896) and that the *other* important soldiers, especially "the tattered soldier" (simple, humble, selfless -- truly brave and heroic),[12] of *The Red Badge* do stand as prototypes of the kind of heroes and the kind of heroism which Stephen Crane came to affirm once he had himself, in the American West, both seen and experienced man's potential for heroic conduct.

What is important, then, is that Western-inspired "code" ideals of self-reliance, generosity, endurance, honesty, and courage -- ideals of which we have only a glimpse in *The Red Badge* and of which we have no glimpse at all in the early Bowery stories -- became central to Crane's fiction after his Western trip. And this is true even when -- as, say, in "The Blue Hotel" (1898) or in "Death and the Child" (1897) -- a code of discipline and of courage is violated by the main characters of the story. For surely the stories which do not overtly dramatize Crane's code still implicitly (or even, as in "The Blue Hotel," explicitly) argue *for* the code: they show the despicableness, the shabbiness, the meaninglessness of lives which fail to maintain the ideals collectively embodied in the code. This is quite evident, for example, in the Easterner of "The Blue Hotel," in Peza of "Death and the Child," or in Caspar Cadogan of "The Second Generation" (1899). In the last story particularly we have a portrait of an individual who does not measure up to Crane's code for man: who fails to achieve -- or even to understand the need for -- the code virtues of discipline, of responsibility, and of courage. Faced with "the inestimable privilege of sitting in a wet trench and slowly but surely starving to death" (VI, 276-277),[13] Caspar violates the very essence of Crane's code for human performance by exclaiming, "'I can't stand it . . . . I can't'" (VI, 277). In the world of Crane's heroes -- as Hemingway's -- certain things are just not done -- and one of these is to surrender to life's pressures, in whatever form that they may take, and to say that you "can't stand it"; this, to tragically aware heroes or heroines who understand the crucial need for a code of life, is embarrassing and, as Hemingway famously put it, "messy." Not surprisingly, then, Crane pointedly dramatizes the inadequacy of Caspar's performance, and does so in the final scene of the story. This scene is a discussion between Caspar and his father during which Caspar's attempts to defend his conduct gradually reveal to his father the truth about that conduct; and in the last paragraph of the story the truth is bluntly presented: "'Oh, well, Caspar,' interrupted the Senator. Then he seemed to weigh a great fact in his mind. 'I guess--' He paused again in profound consideration. 'I guess--' He lit a small, brown cigar. 'I guess you are no damn good'" (VI, 284).

The most famous -- justly so -- of Crane's stories portraying men who, like Caspar Cadogan, betray the code and thereby their own manhood is "The Blue Hotel." Certainly this story dramatizes the importance -- indeed, the imperativeness -- of the code: of an ideal of responsibility and courage in man's conduct and in his relationship to other men.[14] The Easterner makes the point explicitly enough at the story's conclusion: "'Fun or not . . . Johnnie was cheating . . . . I saw him. And I refused to stand up and be a man. I let the Swede fight it out alone. And you [the cowboy] -- you were simply puffing around the place and wanting to fight. And then old Scully himself! We are all in it! . . . We, five of us, have collaborated in the murder of this Swede'" (V, 170). We would not wish, of course, to accept the Easterner's judgment of himself and of the others if this judgment were not dramatized by the story itself, but it is clear that the action of the story -- or, more exactly, the moral *vision* which the story's action renders -- *does* lead inevitably to the Easterner's pronouncement. To argue, as some critics have,[15] that the Easterner's statement weakens the story or even contradicts the story's intrinsic meaning is to miss the point completely. What Crane is showing is not that a seemingly indifferent universe eliminates meaning from human conduct but rather that such a universe makes responsible, courageous, code-directed conduct unspeakably important. If man's life on "a whirling, fire-smitten, ice-locked, disease-stricken, space-lost bulb" (V, 165) is to have meaning at all, man himself must by his own life-code -- by a resolute fidelity to his own self-created ideals -- make that meaning. The Swede, through his own fearfulness, self-centeredness, and self-conceit, is responsible for his own death, yes -- but so too, as the Easterner correctly understands, are the rest of the story's characters. All of them could have and *should* have acted more responsibly, more magnanimously, more courageously. And of course the entire action of the story is triggered by the Swede's initial fear and cowardice. More clearly than any other of Crane's stories, "The Blue Hotel" shows that Crane was fully as intrigued by the phenomenon of *fear* as was Hemingway; and no story shows more clearly that for Crane -- as for Hemingway -- nothing is more despicable and more destructive to human values, to *dignity*, than the failure to achieve the "grace under pressure" which is, above all else, a mastery of fear. If -- as I argued in Chapter 8 -- "The Blue Hotel" is not really a Western story, it is nevertheless a story which compellingly dramatizes the crucial need in man's life for a *Western code* of sympathy, honesty, magnanimity, and courage.

While Stephen Crane's later fiction occasionally portrays characters who fail to measure up to his code of manliness, of magnanimity, and of courage, it is equally true that it also portrays truly heroic characters who do live up to the code. Certainly a clear-cut code of discipline, endurance, responsibility, and courage is directly dramatized and affirmed in another classic story, "The Open Boat" (1897) -- even though there are critics who argue that the conduct of the men in this story is a product of their environment[16] or that Billie's death erases all meaning from their conduct and from their experience.[17] Obviously, environment in this story is what Crane once called (with reference to *Maggie*) "a tremendous thing";[18] equally obvious is the fact that, caught in a hostile environment, the men conduct themselves in accordance with the ideals of Stephen Crane's code. "*Nous ferons notre petit possible*," as General Golz famously summarized Hemingway's code;[19] likewise the men in the open boat: against overwhelming odds they bring the unselfishness, the discipline, and the courage which alone make dignity and meaning in man's life. It is this courage, this heroism, this human solidarity -- this "subtle brotherhood of men" (V, 73) -- which Crane dramatizes and celebrates: "there was this comradeship, that the correspondent [a clear Crane-surrogate], for instance, who had been taught to be cynical of men, knew even at the time was the best experience of his life" (V, 73). To claim that Billie's death -- cruel and ironic as it is -- makes this experience meaningless is equivalent to claiming that the death of Catherine in *A Farewell to Arms* makes her and Frederic's love relation meaningless. With regard to the latter, Robert Penn Warren pointedly comments: "In the end, with the death of Catherine, Frederic discovers that the attempt to find a substitute for universal meaning in the limited meaning of the personal relationship is doomed to failure . . . . But this is not to deny the value of the effort, or to deny the value of the discipline, the code, the stoic endurance, the things that make it true -- or half true -- that 'nothing ever happens to the brave.'"[20] As "the white waves [pace] to and fro in the moonlight, and the wind [brings] the sound of the great sea's voice to the men on the shore," it is their experience of the value of Crane's code which enables the three survivors to feel "that they could *then* be interpreters" (V, 92; my emphasis). They have, to be sure, discovered the pain, the tragedy, perhaps even the absurdity of human existence: more importantly, they have discovered that man's capacity for endurance, for discipline, for comradeship, and for courage does inform his life with a vital though limited meaning. In the words of Hemingway's Santiago, they have discovered that "A man can be destroyed but not defeated."[21]

"The Open Boat" is perhaps Crane's most vivid and most compelling -- certainly it is his most sustained -- dramatization of his code of discipline, manliness, stoicism, and courage; we can, however, see this code operating in most of Crane's writings after *The Red Badge of Courage*. Crane's Western stories, as we have seen, nearly all dramatize and celebrate legendary Western virtues of self-reliance, manliness, openness, and physical courage. In the American West, it bears repeating, Crane found a people who dared, as did the men in "The Open Boat," to "depend upon their endurance, their capacity to help each other, and their steadfast and unyielding courage." This discovery profoundly changed both Crane's vision and his fiction, and it was, I am convinced, the single most important influence upon his building of a code of life. Certainly the protagonist-heroes -- the New York Kid,

Richardson, Bill, Tom Larpent, Jack Potter -- in Crane's Western stories display a genuine, unaffected manliness and courage that is entirely lacking in Crane's earlier protagonists. And the superb Western story titled "A Man and Some Others" (1896) classically dramatizes the workings of a code identical to Hemingway's, presents a hero (the isolated outcast typical of Hemingway) who goes down on his own terms: who fronts a desperate situation with independence and pride and will -- so that at the story's conclusion the reader, like the Eastern tyro-stranger, is made to feel "for Bill, this grimy sheep-herder, some deep form of idolatry. Bill was dying, and the dignity of last defeat, the superiority of him who stands in his grave, was in the pose of the lost sheep-herder" (V, 66-67). What the Eastern stranger suddenly understands about Bill is what the young lieutenant, Manolo Prat, of "The Clan of No-Name" (1899) suddenly understands about himself upon making his very deliberate decision to fight and to die even though "every part of him seemed to be in panic-stricken revolt": "He was of a kind -- that seemed to be it -- and the men of his kind, on peak or plain, from the dark northern ice-fields to the hot wet jungles, through all wine and want, through all lies and unfamiliar truth, dark or light, the men of his kind were governed by their gods, and each man knew the law and yet could not give tongue to it; but it was the law . . . and always with the law there is only one way" (VI, 130-131). In Crane's world as in Hemingway's, it is this wordless, inborn understanding of man's obligation to courage that, above all else, defines the hero, that marks the superiority of those who are governed by their gods -- by their deep, inward knowledge of the law, of the code -- and who stand in their graves. If -- as my earlier chapters suggest -- Stephen Crane envisioned his ideal self as a Jack Potter, it seems clear, too, that in the final years of his short life he increasingly understood his actual self and his actual life-situation to be akin to that of his lost sheep-herder: isolated, lonely, desperate, trapped -- but determined to hold on to his code (his pride and his will and his courage) and to stand in his grave.

The code that Crane's hero knows, yet to which he can not give tongue, is central, as I have indicated, to Crane's later war stories. It is even central to a social satire like *The Monster* in which the independence, courage, and magnanimity of one man, Dr. Trescott, are contrasted to the cowardice, small-mindedness, and cruelty of the (Eastern) townspeople. The crucial point is that once Stephen Crane had journeyed to the American West and had discovered, in himself and in others, man's capacity for real bravery he never again treated it with the scornful irony so characteristic of *The Red Badge of Courage*. True, there *is* irony in a story like "A Mystery of Heroism" (1895; written in Mexico), but it is a gentler, a more sympathetic irony -- an irony suggesting that human motivation and conduct can be absurd *and heroic* at the same time. Granted all the silliness and all the "mystery" surrounding Collins's conduct, one must remember that he *does* return to give water to the dying officer -- an act of genuine kindness and courage. Moreover, this story is very much the exception among Crane's later war stories; the others treat heroism entirely nonironically, and they celebrate, as much as Hemingway ever did, that ideal of conduct which Edmund Wilson defined as Hemingway's "principle of courage, of honor, of pity . . . of sportsmanship in its largest human sense."[22]   More specifically, these stories, as well as Crane's war dispatches like "Regulars Get No Glory," affirm and even eulogize the soldier's acceptance of duty and of discipline: his professionalism. This is seen in the "bronzed and steady" officer of "Death and the Child," in the "strictly military Gates" of "Virtue in War" (1899), and especially in the conduct of the men, both officers and regulars, in what is perhaps Crane's best war story (excluding *The Red Badge*), "The Price of the Harness" (1898).

The *price* of the harness, of being in military uniform, is of course death. But it is clear that for Crane war is simply, as with Hemingway, a metaphor for life itself: what counts is man's conduct -- man's code of life -- as he fronts the onrush of death. The men in "The Price of the Harness" conduct themselves in strict accordance with their self-created codes. There is, for example, a "young staff officer" whose dedication to his ideal of battle-conduct is clearly admired:

> He heeded nothing because he was busy -- immensely busy and hurried with a multitude of reasons and desires for doing his duty perfectly. His whole life had been a mere period of preliminary reflection for this situation, and he had no clear idea of anything save his obligation as an officer. . . . [T]raditions of fidelity and courage which have been handed to

him from generation to generation, and which he has
tenaciously preserved despite the persecution of legislators and
the indifference of his country, make it incredible that in battle
he should ever fail to give his best blood and his best thought
for his general, for his men, and for himself. And so this young
officer . . . failed to heed the wails of the wounded man, even
as the pilgrim fails to heed the world as he raises his illumined
face toward his purpose -- rightly or wrongly, his purpose -- his
sky of the ideal of duty; the wonderful part of it is that he is
guided by an ideal which he has himself created, and has alone
protected from attack [VI, 101-102].

There is an unmistakable sense, here, as in Hemingway, that the discipline of
a profession is, in the words of Robert Penn Warren, "an index to a moral
value,"[23] a means by which certain individuals -- heroes, heroines -- impose a
self-created, albeit limited and finite, coherence upon a world of chaos and
casualty. A similar professional discipline is clearly displayed, too, by the
privates of this story: equally with the officers, they are uncompromisingly
committed to the code of the soldier, to preserving an ideal of battle-conduct
that they refuse to betray. Thus, for example, Crane's description of Nolan's
emotions at the point of the regiment's attack:

He sprang to his feet, and stooping, ran with the others.
Something fine, soft, gentle, touched his heart as he ran. He
had loved the regiment, the army, because the regiment, the
army, was his life -- he had no other outlook; and now these
men, his comrades, were performing his dream scenes for him;
they were doing as he had ordained in his visions. It is curious
that in this charge he considered himself as rather unworthy.
Although he himself was in the assault with the rest of them, it
seemed to him that his comrades were dazzlingly courageous.
His part, to his mind, was merely that of a man going along
with the crowd [VI, 110].

So we find Stephen Crane affirming, once again, the quiet, disciplined, self-
reliant *and* selfless heroism that is celebrated in "The Open Boat." For
Jimmie Nolan as for Billie the price of heroism is death, yet their courage in
its face affords the same final Victory that Crane told Nellie Crouse he
hoped himself -- at death -- to achieve.

Like *The Red Badge of Courage*, then, Stephen Crane's code was a
creation "born of pain -- despair, almost."[24] Despair, *almost* -- for the

scornfulness, bitterness, and cynicism of his early writings did give way under the impact of his inspiriting Western experience to a more mature, a more affirmative assessment of the human condition -- painful and grim as he always found it essentially to be. Shortly after his Western journey, halfway through the single decade of his creative life -- and filled himself, as always, with what, in Mexico, he had called "the modern desperate rage at the accident of birth"[25] -- he urged Nellie Crouse to understand that pessimism is "ridiculously cheap," that "The cynical mind is an uneducated thing."[26] And in the literature that followed his educative life- and vision-changing westering experience, he, like Hemingway, affirmed man's capacity to make his own meanings in a universe that *appears* ultimately meaningless. These meanings came from man's fidelity to a self-created code of generous, resolute, responsible, courageous conduct -- a code that Stephen Crane learned in the American West.

Chapter 10

Notes

1. Warren, "Hemingway," *The Kenyon Review*, 9 (Winter, 1947): 2, 11.
2. Young, *Ernest Hemingway: A Reconsideration* (New York: Harcourt, Brace & World, 1966), pp. 191-196; Hoffman, *The Poetry of Stephen Crane* (New York: Columbia University Press, 1957), pp. 266-269.
3. Young, p. 193.
4. Cather, "When I Knew Stephen Crane," in *Stephen Crane: A Collection of Critical Essays*, ed. Maurice Basan (Englewood Cliffs, N.J.: Prentice-Hall, 1967), p. 15. First printed in *The Library* (Pittsburgh), June 23, 1900, pp. 17-18.
5. Cather, pp. 14, 15.
6. *Stephen Crane: Letters*, ed. R.W. Stallman and Lillian Gilkes (New York: New York University Press, 1960), p. 105. Hereafter cited as *Letters*.
7. *Letters*, p. 105.
8. *Ernest Hemingway* (New York: Twayne, 1963), *passim*.
9. W.M. White, "The Crane-Hemingway Code: A Reevaluation," *Ball State University Forum*, 10 (1969): 18. Earle Labor's "Crane and Hemingway: Anatomy of Trauma" *Renascence*, 11 (Summer, 1959): 189-196 is a comparative study of *The Red Badge of Courage* and *A Farewell To Arms*. Max Westbrook has published two articles which treat generally, but not specifically, the theme of a code in Crane's work: see "Stephen Crane: The Pattern of Affirmation," *Nineteenth-Century American Fiction*, 14 (December, 1959): 219-229; and "Stephen Crane and the Personal Universal," *Modern Fiction Studies*, 8 (Winter, 1963): 351-360. An important, specific discussion of Crane's code within the context of his religious background and historic period may be found in Robert W. Schneider's "Stephen Crane and the Drama of Transition: A Study in Historical Continuity," *Journal of the Central Mississippi Valley American Studies Association* [now *American Studies*], 2 (Spring, 1961): 1-18. A brief but important analysis of the code of conduct in Crane's later war stories appears in Marston LaFrance, *A Reading of Stephen Crane* (Oxford: Oxford University Press, 1971), pp. 181-186. Philip Durham's piece on "Ernest Hemingway's Grace under Pressure: The Western Code," *Pacific Historical Review*, 45 (August, 1976): 425-432, is an unsuccessful, cursory attempt to identify and clarify the Western connections of Hemingway's code.
10. *Letters*, p. 133.
11. From Crane's Western sketch titled "Nebraskans' Bitter Fight for Life," in *Stephen Crane in the West and Mexico*, ed. and intro. Joseph Katz (Kent, Ohio: Kent State University Press, 1970), p. 14.
12. Cf. Leland Krauth, "Heroes and Heroics: Stephen Crane's Moral Imperative," *South Dakota Review*, 11 (Summer, 1973): 1988.
13. Numbers within parentheses or brackets with quotations from Stephen Crane indicate volume and page in *The University of Virginia Edition of the Works of Stephen Crane*, ed. Fredson Bowers (Charlottesville: The University Press of Virginia, 1969-1975).

14.   Cf. Donald B. Gibson "'The Blue Hotel' and the Ideal of Human Courage," *Texas Studies in Literature and Language*, 6 (Autumn, 1964): 388-397.

15.   Robert Wooster Stallman, ed. and intro., *Stephen Crane: An Omnibus* (New York: Knopf, 1952), pp. 482-483; William Bysshe Stein, "Stephen Crane's Homo Absurdus," *Bucknell Review*, 8 (May, 1959): 173-174.

16.   White, p. 18.

17.   Stein, p. 172.

18.   *Letters*, p. 14.

19.   *For Whom The Bell Tolls* (New York: Scribner's, 1940), p. 430.

20.   Warren, p. 22.

21.   *The Old Man and The Sea* (New York: Scribner's, 1952), p. 103.

22.   *The Wound and The Bow: Seven Studies in Literature* (Boston: Houghton Mifflin, 1941), p. 220.

23.   Warren, p. 23.

24.   *Letters*, p. 78.

25.   From Crane's Mexican sketch titled "Above all Things" in Katz, ed., *Stephen Crane in the West and Mexico*, p. 75.

26.   *Letters*, p. 99.

SECTION IV

THE SOUTH:
WILLIAM FAULKNER

CHAPTER 11

The Adamic Hero and the Southern Myth:
Faulkner's Isaac McCaslin and Quentin Compson

The American westering dream of escaping time and history and of achieving a rebirth into innocence and into "new youth" is a major American myth. Under D. H. Lawrence's famous definition, it "is the true myth of America."[1] And it is a myth that holds a special poignancy for an American Southern writer like William Faulkner who inescapably faces the irreconcilable opposition of the American Adamic, Western myth of transcendence and of rebirth and the Southern myth: a place-myth that emanates an intense consciousness of time and of the harsh realities of historical change; a place-myth that focuses upon and that defends the older South as a more integrated, a more humanistic, and therefore a more attractive and a more desirable society than the prevailing American progressive and industrial society. The fact that Faulkner *can* -- in one of his greatest works: *Go Down, Moses* -- imaginatively render both our Western myth and our Southern myth stems, I believe, from the fact that both place-myths are in their own ways intensely opposed to the dominating American capitalistic civilization as embodied in the myth of the Midwest. I would argue, further, that the special tension and the intensity of *Go Down, Moses* derives (much as we have earlier seen of *The Scarlet Letter*) precisely from the fact that Faulkner is compellingly dramatizing two opposing (Western and Southern) American place-myths at once. Like Hawthorne, Faulkner in his art must finally make a choice between the place-myths that his fiction embodies; and it is important to recognize that Faulkner's fable about Isaac McCaslin (the following chapter will show that this is true of the entire tradition in our classic fiction) does *not* affirm the American Western, Adamic myth. Like all of our classic fictionists, Faulkner finally denies the American westering dream of transcendence, of rebirth; he affirms, instead, the Southern myth: time, history, society, family can not be (*should* not be) escaped; any attempt to do so is doomed to failure, leads not to innocence but, more often than not, to its opposite. Faulkner's Isaac McCaslin does indeed *almost* become an Adamic hero, and one way clearly to see Faulkner's affirmation of the Southern myth rather than the Western myth is to compare Isaac McCaslin to another important Faulkner character: Quentin Compson.

Revealing as the relationships between Isaac and Quentin are, only R. W. B. Lewis has suggested these relationships in a single sentence wherein he *contrasts* Isaac and Quentin by way of categorically affirming Isaac's heroic stature: "[T]he repeated attacks of Quentin Compson on the history of his country may be fruitfully contrasted with the disciplined exposition of Isaac McCaslin, and Quentin's suicide with Ike's honorable long career."[2] Not surprisingly, the author of *The American Adam* has written by far the most sensitive and most perceptive analysis of Ike's initiation and rebirth in the wilderness -- an analysis which supports Frederic I. Carpenter's assertion that "almost the whole American myth of a lost paradise and the subsequent achievement of grace has found symbolic embodiment in . . .'The Bear.'"[3] For both Lewis and Carpenter, in other words, Ike is unquestionably an Adamic hero in the sense that Lewis has classically defined: "the hero as a self-created innocent," as "a radically new personality" -- "an individual emancipated from history, happily bereft of ancestry, untouched and undefiled by the usual inheritances of family and race."[4] Correctly, though, the notion that Isaac is a truly westering, Adamic hero has been challenged.[5] Moreover, Mr. Lewis is simply wrong in suggesting that the relationships between Quentin's and Ike's understanding of American (and specifically Southern) history and between Quentin's suicide and "Ike's honorable long career" lie *only* on the side of contrast. There are, in fact, striking and disturbing similarities between the lives, the motivations, and the goals of Quentin and of Ike -- similarities which force us to wonder just how "fruitfully" Quentin's suicide may be contrasted with Ike's "long career." And clearly to see the similarities between the lives of Isaac and of Quentin we must examine two major themes, themes that are intrinsic to the place-myths of the West and of the South: the theme of innocence and the theme of time.

In his important essay on the meaning of innocence in American literature, Frederic I. Carpenter argues that American literary heroes "have sought . . . to regain their paradise by following some ideal pattern, or by adopting some conscious strategy of innocence" and that "Confusion occurs when this strategy of innocence -- the conscious American effort to regain paradise -- is described as if it were the naive impulsiveness of an unfallen Adam."[6] And, as I have indicated, both Carpenter and R. W. B. Lewis find in Isaac McCaslin an archetypal instance of "the conscious American effort to regain paradise" by "adopting some conscious strategy of innocence." "This [Ike's] innocence" -- Lewis says -- "is an achievement, not merely a gift; it is gained through discipline and submission; it is announced in a ritual. This innocence is nothing less than conscience itself."[7] Lewis and Carpenter are right: there *is* a truly Western and Adamic, a Thoreauvian, toughness to Ike's innocence -- a toughness won from his successful initiation, under Sam Fathers's tutelage, into the sacred ritual of the hunt and into man's sacramental relation to nature. And we must say the very opposite of the innocence of Quentin Compson.

Clearly, the innocence that Quentin embodies, or yearns for, is utterly negative -- revealing, as it does, a cowardly fear of experience; a refusal to accept responsibility for his own actions; and, ultimately, a lack of will for *any* positive action. Obsessed with his negative notion of innocence as a timelessly pure and untainted state, Quentin is incapable of love and, consequently, of any effective moral action. For Quentin's neurotic obsession with sex as an epitome of the world's, of history's, imperfection and corruption prevents his ever seeing Caddy as anything other than a symbol -- which, of course, is another way of saying that he never loved her. As Faulkner tells us in the Appendix he prepared for Malcolm Cowley's *The Portable Faulkner*, even Caddy "Loved her brother despite him . . . loved him not only in spite of but because of the fact that *he himself was incapable of love*, accepting the fact that he must value above all not her but the virginity of which she was the custodian" (p. 10; emphasis mine).[8] Of the many ironies in *The Sound and the Fury*, one of the most significant is surely the fact that Benjy's, the idiot's, love for Caddy is more real and more human than Quentin's intellectualized and abstract love "not [for] her but [for] the

virginity of which she was the custodian." And this irony is even more telling
when we remember that both brothers do, in fact, desperately long for the
same thing: for a Caddy immune from time and circumstance -- from
change, from physical maturity, from sexuality. The difference is that Benjy
wants Caddy preserved from time because she is *Caddy* (just the sound of
these two syllables sets him moaning with the anguish of Caddy's loss), while
Quentin wants her preserved from time because of his perverted, life-denying
conception of innocence: an ahistorical, atemporal, vacuum-like innocence
that is accessible only to a child -- or to an idiot like Benjy, who has the mind
of a child. So if there is a bitter irony in the fact that only Benjy and not
Quentin was capable of loving Caddy, there is an even bitterer and, for
Quentin, more damning irony in the fact that the innocence for which he so
desperately longed was in fact the innocence of an idiot.[9]

Ike's innocence is not identical to the innocence to which Quentin
aspired; but this is not to say that there are no similarities between Ike's
innocence and Quentin's, or that Ike's innocence does not partake of the
negativity and the weakness of Quentin's. Like Quentin, Ike was, for
example, primarily, and selfishly, concerned with *peace*, with escaping the
struggles, the responsibilities, and the sorrows of living in a historical world
of imperfection and of change. As he tells his cousin, Cass, during their
midnight conversation in the commissary, "I have got myself to have to live
with for the rest of my life and all I want is peace to do it in" (p. 288).[10] All
that Quentin wanted was peace, too -- an escape from the present and from
history; a freezing, a timeless isolating, of childlike innocence; but, Faulkner
implies, such a peace can be gained only at the ethical price of withdrawal
from life itself: Quentin's suicide or Ike's "relinquishment" of his inheritance.
For when on his twenty-first birthday Ike relinquishes his inheritance, his act
is, ultimately, of a kind with Quentin's refusal even to live beyond his twenty-
first birthday. So without in the least ceasing to sympathize with Ike's agony
and Ike's failure, we must acknowledge that, like Quentin's agony and
Quentin's failure, they are essentially of his own making. This is to say that
the innocence which Ike achieved in the wilderness -- the same innocence,
really, which Thoreau consciously and ritualistically achieved in *Walden* --
was *not* the innocence into which he weakly withdrew after his twenty-first

birthday. In the wilderness -- and only in the wilderness -- Isaac *is* an Adamic hero: a hero who, through courage and discipline, through "pride and humility," achieves innocence and copes with evil: "He felt [fleeing Memphis] the old lift of the heart, as pristine as ever, as on the first day; he would never lose it, no matter how old in hunting and pursuit: the best, the best of all breathing, the humility and the pride" (p. 233). Certainly the very meaning of the ritual of the hunt, as taught to Ike by Sam Fathers, is an initiation into evil, a spilling of innocent blood. And when Sam marks Ike's forehead with the blood of Ike's first buck, he marks Ike with guilt and, consequently, with maturity and with responsibility. Only as an old man, in "Delta Autumn," could Ike put into words what as a boy he knew intuitively: "*I slew you; my bearing must not shame your quitting life. My conduct forever onward must become your death*" (p. 351). And, in what is perhaps the most moving passage of Ike's entire initiation story, we see him, at eighteen, revisiting the graves of Old Ben and of Sam, and suddenly encountering a six-foot-long rattlesnake:

> the old one, the ancient and accursed about the earth, fatal and solitary and he could smell it now: the thin sick smell of rotting cucumbers and of something else which had no name, evocative of all knowledge and an old weariness and of pariah-hood and of death. At last it moved. Not the head. The elevation of the head did not change as it began to glide away from him, . . . an entity walking on two feet and free of all laws of mass and balance and should have been because even now he could not quite believe that all that shift and flow of shadow behind that head could have been one snake: going and then gone; he put the other foot down at last and didn't know it, standing with one hand raised as Sam had stood that afternoon six years ago when Sam led him into the wilderness and showed him and he ceased to be a child, speaking the old tongue which Sam had spoken that day without premeditation either: "Chief," he said: "Grandfather" [pp. 329-330].

This, clearly, is a recognition of evil that is as deep and absolute as any that one could ask of a tragic hero -- an evil at the very heart of things, in the heart of the wilderness itself. More importantly, it is an evil inherent in the human heart: "'Chief,' he said: 'Grandfather.'"[11] Significantly, this episode occurs *during* Ike's mystical vision of the deathlessness of Sam, of Old Ben, and of the wilderness; and it is immediately followed by his discovery, at the story's conclusion, of a hysterical Boon Hogganbeck, madly beating his gun under the gum tree. The unmistakable implication is that Ike, at eighteen and in the wilderness, *has*, unlike Boon, achieved the kind of tough, mature innocence which is rightly praised by critics like Carpenter, Lewis, and Bowling. He has achieved this innocence because, for one thing, he has learned from Sam that sacramental and mystical view of life which Faulkner evokes so powerfully in his description of Ike's visit to the graves of Sam, of Lion, and of Old Ben ("the knoll which was no abode of the dead because there was no death, not Lion and not Sam: not held fast in earth but free in earth and not in earth but of earth, myriad yet undiffused of every myriad part . . . : and Old Ben too, Old Ben too; they would give him his paw back even, certainly they would give him his paw back: then the long challenge and the long chase, no heart to be driven and outraged, no flesh to be mauled and bled -- " [pp. 328-329]). But if Sam taught Ike to be a mystic -- not simply to believe in immortality but to *experience*, to apprehend, sacred, primordial reality (witness also Ike's earlier, solitary mystical vision of Old Ben) -- he taught him, as well, to be a humanist, even a tragic humanist; and this, of course, is the meaning of the snake-confrontation which, as I have said, occurs *during* Ike's mystical vision at Sam's grave. Thus Ike is simultaneously aware of two worlds: of an archaic, timeless, primordial, eternal world beyond death and evil; and of a temporal world that is, by definition, filled with death and with evil. And this is why, unlike Boon, he can recognize the evil of the temporal world -- and even the fact that he, with Boon, is an accomplice in that evil -- without being reduced to Boon's hysteria.

But the Isaac McCaslin who, at eighteen, pays a last visit to the graves of Sam and of Old Ben is not the same Isaac McCaslin who, at twenty-one, repudiates his heritage. And it is precisely here that Ike's similarity to Quentin Compson becomes particularly telling and conclusive in regard to the question of Ike's stature as an Adamic, westering hero. For, as I have said, it is clear that once Ike turned from the wilderness to the "tamed land" -- from the mythic American West to the historic American South -- his one thought, as with Quentin, was to achieve "peace," the negative, empty, sterile peace found only by living outside time and outside history. This is an innocence that carries a vengeance, an innocence that in fact victimizes Ike, just as Quentin was victimized, driven to suicide, by his mad quest for a kind of innocence that does not exist in the temporal, historical world. And it is on just this point that R. W. B. Lewis's otherwise excellent analysis of Ike's initiation is seriously misleading. "The action in Section Four" -- Lewis argues -- "is made possible by the experience preceding it: the ritual in the wilderness *contains* the decision in the commissary."[12] This is not true: in the wilderness, as shown by the snake-confrontation, Ike learned to face evil, to accept his own complicity in evil -- to understand that to be "taintless and incorruptible" as (Faulkner tells us in the story's opening sentences) "only Sam and Old Ben and the mongrel Lion were" (p. 101) is (in Old Ben's case) to be "fierce and ruthless not just to stay alive but ruthless with the fierce pride of liberty and freedom" (p. 295), or (in Sam's case) to be "an old man, son of a Negro slave and an Indian king, inheritor on the one hand of the long chronicle of a people who had learned humility through suffering and learned pride through the endurance which survived the suffering, and on the other side the chronicle of a people even longer in the land than the first, yet who now existed there only in the solitary brotherhood of an old and childless Negro's alien blood and the wild and invincible spirit of an old bear" (p. 295). Lewis rightly points to the story's opening sentences as an important clue to the "profound dialectical transformation" that "the quality of innocence undergoes" in "The Bear"[13] -- but, again, he is misleading in claiming that Ike, too, remains "taintless and incorruptible" in the way that Sam and Old Ben were. If Sam and Old Ben taught Ike anything at all, it was that, to borrow Emerson's words in "Self-Reliance," "Your goodness must have some edge to it, -- else it is none." But Ike's story from twenty-one on is the story of a man whose goodness loses its edge; of a man who, like Quentin, becomes quixotic and impotent in his attempt to preserve, to renew, to redeem lost values; and of a man who withdraws, if not into death, at least into a life almost deathlike in its emptiness and ineffectiveness.

I am saying, of course, that Ike should not have rejected his inheritance any more than Quentin should have rejected his life. For Ike the land is tainted, for Quentin Caddy becomes tainted; Ike forgets, as Quentin never knew, that a quest for innocence through mere escape from evil, from time, is weak and cowardly. We have seen that Quentin's obsession with innocence made him, quite simply, incapable of love. But Ike, we know, loved Sam Fathers ("whom he had revered and harkened to and loved and lost and grieved" [p. 326]). And there is reason to believe that Ike also loved his wife ("they were married, they were married and it was the new country, his heritage too as it was the heritage of all, . . . his too because each must share with another in order to come into it and in the sharing they become one: for that while, one: for that little while at least, one: indivisible, that while at least irrevocable and unrecoverable, living in a rented room still but for just a little while and that room wall-less and topless and floorless in glory" [pp. 311-312]). But Ike's marriage -- his love, even, for his wife -- lasted "but for just a little while." In 1895 Ike is "husband but no father, unwidowered but without wife" (p. 281), and he is so from a failure of love. Ike allows his obsession with abstract principles and his urge to escape change, time, and evil to wreck his marriage, just as Quentin allows his obsession with Caddy as a custodian of "honor" to destroy his capacity to love her as a person. Even before his marriage Ike knew intuitively, when he visited Sam's and Old Ben's graves, that, whatever "brief unsubstanced glory" might come from marriage, "the woods would be his mistress and his wife" (p. 326). Inevitably, then, Ike denies his wife's wish to own the inherited farm -- even as he, like Quentin, begins to see sex itself as something like Original Sin: a fall from taintlessness into time: "and still the steady and invincible hand and he said Yes and he thought, *She is lost. She was born lost. We were all born lost*" (p. 314). We may have been born lost; to love is to accept that state of imperfection and of lostness rather than, like Isaac or like Quentin, to try to escape it by fleeing to a private world, to an unreal dream, of timeless innocence.

Faulkner leaves little doubt, indeed, that Isaac failed quite as seriously, as disastrously as Quentin. In "Delta Autumn" an old Isaac McCaslin, having once again made his annual two-week return to the wilderness, lies on an iron cot in a tent ("even this tent with its muddy floor and the bed which was not wide enough nor soft enough nor even warm enough, was his *home*" [p. 352; emphasis mine]) -- lies "looking up at the motionless belly of rain-murmured canvas" and remembering how he had tried to "repudiate the wrong and shame, at least in principle, and at least the land itself in fact, for his son at least: and did, thought he had: then (married then) . . . , the first and last time he ever saw her naked body, himself and his wife juxtaposed . . . against the same land, that same wrong and shame from whose regret and grief he would at least save and free his son and, saving and freeing his son, lost him" (pp. 350, 351). Just as Quentin asked, essentially, of Caddy that she not mature sexually, so Ike expected "a rented cubicle [as opposed to the McCaslin farm that he 'relinquished'] in a back-street stock-traders' boarding-house" (p. 351) to remain "wall-less and topless and floorless in glory." Both Quentin and Ike, in short, made impossible demands of life; when life would not meet those demands, they lost the courage and the will to live -- which is to say, too, that they lost the capacity to love. Witness especially the scene between Ike and Roth Edmond's mistress -- who, as Ike discovers to his "amazement, pity, and outrage" (p. 361), is the granddaughter of Tennie's Jim, Carothers McCaslin's grandson. Standing before an eighty-year-old Isaac McCaslin is, then, one more instance of the incestuous miscegenation -- and of the callous attempt, on the white man's part, literally to purchase immunity from crime -- that he had discovered, at sixteen and to his horror, in the deeds of his grandfather, and which he (Isaac) had spent a lifetime trying to expiate, or at least to escape: "she moved her hand, the single hand which held the money, until he touched it. He didn't grasp it, he merely touched it -- the gnarled, bloodless, bone-light bone-dry old man's fingers touching for a second the smooth young flesh where the strong old blood ran after its long lost journey back home. 'Tennie's Jim,' he said. 'Tennie's Jim'" (p. 362). Thus there is no escape; Ike's attempt, by withdrawal, by "relinquishment," to expiate "the wrong and the shame" has been in vain. Indeed, Roth's mistress places most of the blame for Roth's callousness and irresponsibility upon Ike himself:

> "I would have made a man of him. He's not a man yet. You spoiled him. You, and Uncle Lucas and Aunt Molly. But mostly you."
>
> "Me?" he said. "Me?"

"Yes. When you gave to his grandfather that land which didn't belong to him, not even half of it by will or even by law" [p. 360].

And, again, Ike's very withdrawal, his very obsession with "the wrong and the shame," has ironically but inevitably, wastefully, tragically destroyed his capacity to love. Ike, at eighty, is outraged by a woman's simple request for love (not money): he is no longer outraged by his own relation's abuse of such love. To Roth's mistress Ike can only exclaim:

> "Marry a black man. You are young, handsome, almost white; you could find a black man who would see in you what it was you saw in him . . . . Then you will forget all this, forget it ever happened, that he ever existed -- . . . . "

> "Old man," she said, "have you lived so long and forgotten so much that you don't remember anything you ever knew or felt or even heard about love? [p. 363]"

Thus the result of Ike's lifelong effort to find "peace" -- an effort that is, ultimately, no more successful than the desperate, quixotic, half-mad, life-denying, self-murdering effort of Quentin Compson.

Having emphasized the failures of Isaac and of Quentin, I want to emphasize also that, given Faulkner's view of the world -- his *Southerner's* view of the world -- they are understandable failures, failures with which Faulkner clearly sympathizes. For we cannot fully understand what happens to Ike and to Quentin without examining another major thematic concern of Faulkner's work: his ontology of time. Ike and Quentin are victims of time, and so are innumerable other Faulkner characters. They are so because Faulkner's very world-view presupposes, as Karl E. Zink has said, that "reality is less a matter of time and space than a condition of the consciousness." For Faulkner, real time, true time, is never simply linear or chronological: "the past," to quote Zink again, "is not experience, dead because it occurred weeks or years ago; the past is the total timeless, spaceless consciousness, and, as such, recurs whenever it crosses the mind."[14] And, as Jean-Paul Sartre points out, nothing is clearer or more important in Faulkner's work than the fact that his fictional technique, his refusal (best exemplified in *The Sound and the Fury*, but important, too, in *Go Down, Moses*) to tell his stories chronologically, derives from his "metaphysics of time" -- a metaphysics wherein the true, the ontological, present is "not the ideal limit whose place is neatly marked out between past and future," but rather a present that inheres in the human consciousness and that is "essentially catastrophic," "leaking at every seam," ceaselessly subject to "sudden invasions of the past."[15]   Quite simply -- to quote another French critic, Jean Pouillon -- "Faulkner's people are real only in their pasts. They do not rethink their pasts, they simply live them."[16] And they have no choice, because it cannot be stressed too strongly that for Faulkner ontological time *is* consciousness: to be in true, or real, time is simply to be conscious; and what one is inevitably, inescapably conscious *of* is the past. This, as I have said, makes consciousness itself for the American Southerner a cruel expiation, or curse, or doom. This is the fatalistic, tragic concept of time held by Mr. Compson in his discussions with Quentin: "was" is "the saddest word of all there is nothing else in the world its not despair until time its not even time until it was" (p. 197).

But if Faulkner believes that real time for the individual is his very consciousness -- that, in Mr. Compson's words, man is "the sum of his climatic [sic] experiences" (p. 142); that, ontologically, time is "a fluid condition" (in Faulkner's own words) "which has no existence except in the momentary avatars of individual people"[17] -- this does not mean that Faulkner denies the reality of a time that is separate from and independent of man's consciousness: of time, that is, in history. The intensity and the tension in Faulkner's work derives, in fact, precisely from clashes between these two kinds of time -- of time in the individual's consciousness and of time in history.   For if time in man's consciousness is neither linear nor chronological, time in history is exactly that: a sequence of events and of changes that is not only linear and chronological but also inexorable and irreversible.   And of course when one speaks of history in connection with Faulkner one means Southern history. More specifically still, one means what Malcolm Cowley calls Faulkner's "Legend of the South":[18] a legend, or myth, that identifies the Old South with certain values and principles such as honor, courage, compassion, and integrity (in short, a society devoted to distinguished and to principled living) -- values and principles that were, after the watershed of the Civil War, gradually submerged in the commercialism of the New South. It is precisely the disintegrative social-historical process that Henry Adams saw happening to *his* Puritan eighteenth-century Quincy heritage in Yankee, mercantile nineteenth-century Boston; and it is a legend familiar to any reader of Faulkner. But it should be emphasized that -- for Faulkner, as for all true Southerners -- this legend, this myth, of the South *is* true: it is history as well as myth. Thus, again, the Southerner -- under William Faulkner's vision -- inevitably, tragically expiates his living in the world, in the South, with his very consciousness: not the Adamic, transcending, *Western* consciousness achieved by Thoreau in *Walden* or *fleetingly* achieved by Isaac McCaslin in "The Bear," but consciousness *as* time, as *was*. Faulkner's characters, that is to say, and Quentin Compson is clearly an archetype, are aware not only that their past *is*, ontologically, their present but also that this past is, historically, truly *passed*, and can never be repeated.   Throughout his death-day monologue, for example, it is only clock-time, chronological time, that Quentin tries desperately to escape: if he could but live in true time, in his consciousness, in his vivid awareness of frozen moments of the past, all would be well. But unlike Benjy, Quentin is intensely aware not only of the past *but also* of history; and it is to evade the latter that he kills himself. Similarly, all is well with Isaac as long as he can achieve an Adamic vision within the timeless, mystical realm of the wilderness; it is only when he is forced to recognize the *simultaneous* reality of history, of the Southern history epitomized in the commissary ledgers, that, like Quentin, he becomes desperate and quixotic and pathetic in his attempt to hold his timeless vision.

    In this sense, then, both Quentin and Isaac are victims of time: neither can reconcile his consciousness -- *his* time -- with the historical reality of change. Both opt for their private timeless visions, refuse to cope with historical change, and consequently deny themselves the full humanity that Dilsey, for example, so superbly embodies. The fact that Ike *survives*, lives to be "past seventy and nearer eighty than he ever corroborated any more" (p. 3), is evidence not of his achieving full humanity but simply of his achieving (or thinking he had achieved), in life, the timeless vision that Quentin could find only in death. Witness the dramatic point in "Delta Autumn" at which Ike "suddenly knew why he had never wanted to own any of [the land], arrest at least that much of what people called progress . . . .

> It was because there was just exactly enough of it. He seemed to see the two of them -- himself and the wilderness -- as coevals, . . . the two spans running out together, not toward oblivion, nothingness, but into a dimension free of both time and space where once more the untreed land . . . would find ample room for both -- the names, the faces of the old men he had known and loved and for a little while outlived, moving again among the shades of tall unaxed trees and sightless brakes where the wild strong immortal game ran forever before the tireless belling immortal hounds, falling and rising phoenix-like to the soundless guns [p. 354].

This is a dream-vision equivalent to Quentin's dream of escaping the "loud world" by claiming he had committed incest with Caddy: *"Then you will have only me then only me then the two of us amid the pointing and the horror beyond the clean flame"* (p. 135).

The essential difference, finally, between Quentin and Ike is simply that Ike *does* achieve an Adamic, westering vision, a transcending of time and of history, whereas Quentin does not. This is especially clear, for example, in the contrast between the successful ritual under which Ike, as a young boy, divests himself of his watch and of his compass in order to gain a vision of Old Ben -- and the unsuccessful, quixotic ritual of Quentin's breaking his watch on the morning of his death-day monologue. Moreover, Old Ben himself -- and, for that matter, Sam Fathers, too -- does not simply represent, he *is* "an anachronism indomitable and invincible out of an old dead time, a phantom, epitome and apotheosis of the old wild life" (p. 193) -- the very kind of apotheosis that, as Mr. Compson understands (cf. p. 195), Quentin himself urgently longs for, but that, in Mr. Compson's Stoic's view (pp. 195-196), is beyond man's capacities and possibilities. Thus, I think that R. W. B. Lewis is right in claiming that "The Bear" *does* mark a turning point in Faulkner's work toward a more hopeful and even toward a religious view of the world[19] -- to the extent that Isaac McCaslin does truly experience a Thoreauvian, mystical apprehension of sacred reality. But this does not change the fact that Isaac is hardly more successful than Quentin in dealing responsibly and courageously with the problems of historical change -- or even that he clings to his religious experience, to his Adamic vision, as an *escape* from the problems of time and of history. And of course there is finally no real escape for Isaac any more than there was for Quentin. This is clearly the whole point of "Delta Autumn," a story that renders the pathos, the tragedy of historical change as powerfully as anything Faulkner wrote, including *The Sound and the Fury.*

When, in the last section of *The Sound and the Fury*, Faulkner places his story of the fall of the Compson family within its social and its historical context, he begins with a remarkable description of Dilsey:

> She had been a big woman once but now her skeleton rose, draped loosely in unpadded skin that tightened again upon a paunch almost dropsical, as though muscle and tissue had been courage or fortitude which the days or the years had consumed until only the indomitable skeleton was left rising like a ruin or a landmark above the somnolent and impervious guts, and above that the collapsed face that gave the impression of the bones themselves being outside the flesh, lifted into the driving day with an expression at once fatalistic and of a child's astonished disappointment, until she turned and entered the house again and closed the door [pp. 281-282].

Life to a child, outside time and outside history, affords much; but (as Henry Adams and William Faulkner, among other of our greatest writers, acutely knew) it is man's fate, modern man's fate -- above all, the Southerner's fate -- to have the intense, vibrant happiness and the wild, sensuously rich freedom of child-life, or of the Adamic dream-state achieved by Thoreau in *Walden*, destroyed by time and by history: to experience Dilsey's astonished disappointment and to share in her fatalism. And of course the measure of Dilsey's tragic humanity and of her heroism lies in her capacity to embody "at once" the astonished disappointment of a child and the fatalism of the Southerner's sense of his entrapment in time. Most important of all is the fact that Dilsey *lives*, does the most she can for the Compsons even as she remains an astonished child and even as she has a clear, a complete awareness of the Compsons' tragic loss and downfall.

And it is Dilsey who, ultimately, is the key to our understanding of Isaac McCaslin and of Quentin Compson -- both of whom were, like Dilsey, astonished children, but neither of whom possessed Dilsey's capacity for innocence *and* endurance. Because at the traditional age for manhood both Isaac and Quentin sought *only* innocence, neither ever truly grew up, neither "endured," and one in fact did not live beyond twenty-one. In Part IV of "The Bear" Ike perceptively sees that the American dream -- the dream that the New World would not repeat the corruption and the evil of the Old -- was doomed from the beginning by man's inherent evil; but he failed, tragically, to see that his own dream of permanent Adamic innocence was likewise doomed. Man cannot be *simply* innocent; neither can he escape involvement in time and in history. If he tries to do either, he will, like Ike, be stabbed in old age with an awareness of his life's failure and futility.

An American writer and a Southern writer, Faulkner powerfully renders both the tragedy of man's entrapment in time and the intensity of man's yearning to transcend time; but he uncompromisingly shows, too, that the heroic figure -- not Isaac and certainly not Quentin, but only Dilsey -- has the courage to live *in* time. This is to say that Faulkner affirms not the Western myth but the Southern myth. And it is to say more: that the hero in Faulkner's fictional world *believes* the Southern myth, understands the tragedy of time and of historical change, but refuses to allow his anguished involvement in time to destroy his will to live.

Chapter 11

Notes

1.   D. H. Lawrence, *Studies in Classic American Literature* (Garden City, N.Y.: Doubleday, 1951), p. 64.
2.   R. W. B. Lewis, "The Hero in the New World: William Faulkner's *The Bear*," *The Kenyon Review*, 13 (Autumn, 1951): 659.
3.   Frederic I. Carpenter, "'The American Myth': Paradise (To Be) Regained," *PMLA*, 74 (December, 1959): 606.
4.   R. W. B. Lewis, *The American Adam: Innocence, Tragedy, and Tradition in the Nineteenth Century* (Chicago: The University of Chicago Press, 1955), pp. 197, 5.
5.   The best analyses of Ike's limitations as a moral hero are the following: Richard P. Adams, *Faulkner: Myth and Motion* (Princeton: Princeton University Press, 1968), pp. 137-154; Melvin Blackman, "The Wilderness and the Negro in Faulkner's 'The Bear,'" *PMLA*, 76 (December, 1961): 595-600; Richard E. Fisher, "The Wilderness, the Commissary, and the Bedroom: Faulkner's Ike McCaslin as Hero in a Vacuum," *English Studies*, 44 (1963): 19-28; Joseph Gold, *William Faulkner: A Study in Humanism from Metaphor to Discourse* (Norman: University of Oklahoma Press, 1966), pp. 49-75; John W. Hunt, *William Faulkner: Art in Theological Tension* (Syracuse, N.Y.: Syracuse University Press, 1965), pp. 137-168; Michael Millgate, *The Achievement of William Faulkner* (New York: Random House, 1966), pp. 201-214; Herbert A. Perluck, "'The Heart's Driving Complexity': An Unromantic Reading of Faulkner's *The Bear*," *Accent*, 20 (Winter, 1960): 23-46; Thomas J. Wertenberker, Jr., "Faulkner's Point of View and the Chronicle of Ike McCaslin," *College English*, 24 (December, 1962): 169-178.
6.   Carpenter, p. 602.
7.   Lewis, "The Hero in the New World," p. 655.
8.   All page references for *The Sound and the Fury* are to the Modern Library Edition (New York, 1946).
9.   Cf. Lawrence E. Bowling, "Faulkner and the Theme of Innocence," *The Kenyon Review*, 20 (Summer, 1958): 474-475.
10.   All page references for *Go Down, Moses* are to the Modern Library Edition (New York, 1955).
11.   It is immensely significant that while "speaking the old tongue which Sam had spoken" Ike utters the one word -- Grandfather -- which takes him back to the dead center of the evil in his own heritage and, by extension, in the heritage of the entire South ("they were all Grandfather all of them" [p. 283]). Surely, then, Sam taught Ike not to shun evil but to accept its reality and its ineradicableness not just in society and his heritage but in the wilderness and in himself.
12.   Lewis, "The Hero in the New World," p. 650.
13.   *Ibid.*, p. 655.
14.   Karl E. Zink, "Flux and the Frozen Moment: the Imagery of Stasis in Faulkner's Prose," *PMLA*, 71 (June, 1956): 299, 300.

15.   Jean-Paul Sartre, "On *The Sound and the Fury*: Time in the Works of Faulkner," in *Faulkner: A Collection of Critical Essays*, ed. Robert Penn Warren (Englewood Cliffs, N.J.: Prentice-Hall, 1966), pp. 87, 88, 90.

16.   Jean Pouillon, "Time and Destiny in Faulkner," in *Faulkner: A Collection of Critical Essays*, ed. Warren, p. 82.

17.   Taken from Faulkner's 1956 interview with Jean Stein. Quoted in Frederick J. Hoffman, *William Faulkner*, 2nd ed. (New York: Twayne, 1966), p. 21.

18.   Malcolm Cowley, "William Faulkner's Legend of the South," *The Sewanee Review*, 53 (Summer, 1945): 343-361.

19.   Lewis, "The Hero in the New World," p. 641.

SECTION V

THE LOSS OF PLACE:

AMERICAN FICTIONISTS, AMERICAN OBSERVERS IN ENGLAND

CHAPTER 12

The American Dream and the Romance Tradition
In American Fiction:
A Literary Study of Society and of Success in America

Classic American fiction, as Daniel G. Hoffman has noted, focuses characteristically upon "archetypal individual experience" rather than upon ordinary, "realistic" experience within a densely rendered social world. Critics of the American novel may emphasize its gothic nature (Leslie A. Fiedler, Jonathan Baumbach); its rendering of the tensions and the contradictions in American culture and in American history (Marius Bewley, Richard Chase); its concern with isolation (Edwin T. Bowden) and with a mythic past (Wright Morris); its creation of new environments through style (Richard Poirier) and its creation of ideal social constructs (A. N. Kaul); its preference for "the stance of wonder" (Tony Tanner) and for "the Adamic vision of life" (R. W. B. Lewis); its essential duplicity (D. H. Lawrence) or its obsession with epistemology (Joel Porte); but upon one thing do they all agree: the American novel is thoroughgoingly anti-realistic; the Romance, as classically defined by Hawthorne, is the central tradition in American fiction.[1] This chapter aims to show that an analysis of the social and the historical relationships between the American dream and the Romance tradition in American fiction is a valuable key to a greater understanding of American society and of the American myth of success.

I

Of all the place-myths inhering in the American dream, perhaps the most important one is that dream of an absolute West of newness and of innocence classically defined by Henry Nash Smith in *Virgin Land* and by R. W. B. Lewis in *The American Adam*. This myth of Adamic innocence and freshness, of "beginning all anew,"[2] is a central myth of our culture, as vibrant, if not as viable, now as it was at the time of Emerson and Thoreau.

But the Adamic myth is not just anti-historical and anti-traditional: it is personal. It throws the individual upon himself; he alone is responsible for his destiny, and for his success. Tocqueville predicted that an egalitarian and progressive society would create intense loneliness -- and this has proved all too true.[3] For it is not just that each individual must define himself, establish his own identity, save his own soul: he must do so in a society which is, theoretically and to a large degree actually, free and equal, in which there are finally no fixed criteria for maturity and for worthiness other than the sheerly economic yardstick of success.[4]

Depending on one's point of view, this severe isolation of the individual in an egalitarian society committed to self-help, self-definition, and success can be seen as either good or bad. Our "Transcendentalists," for example, not only recognized the individual's isolation in American society but also celebrated it. Although Emerson, Thoreau, and Whitman were acutely conscious of and critical of the materialism and the commercialism of American society, they nevertheless affirmed the individual's isolation within that society as a truly exciting historical phenomenon: a chance, as Emerson insisted, for the individual to "Build [his] own world," discover his unlimited regenerative possibilities by withdrawing into his own soul. And certainly there is no greater fable of the American westering dream of rebirth into innocence and into "new youth"[5] than Thoreau's *Walden*, a book which is rivalled only by Faulkner's "The Bear" in its dramatization of the Adamic myth, of the transcending of time and history through a sacral relation with the natural world. "Our truest life" -- Thoreau always affirmed -- "is when we are in dreams awake."[6]

If, however, our nonfiction writers have affirmed the Adamic vision of the waking dream (and even in the twentieth century major poets like E. E. Cummings and Wallace Stevens have continued to celebrate the waking dream), it is hardly true that our *fiction* writers have rendered this vision. Our fictionists have, instead, emphasized the negative rather than the positive, the tragic rather than the redemptive, consequences of the individual's isolation in American society; and the Romance tradition in American fiction is, somewhat paradoxically, not an affirmation but rather a negation of the American dream. This is, of course, a view which directly opposes the views of prominent critics like Frederic I. Carpenter and R. W. B. Lewis who place the Adamic vision at the center of American fiction as well as of American literature in general; but to discover the limitations of Carpenter's and Lewis's views we need only to note that both critics simply do not consider *Huckleberry Finn* in their studies[7] of American literature and of American mythology. And I want to suggest that Mr. Carpenter and Mr. Lewis omit any discussion of *Huckleberry Finn* for a very formidable reason: Huck simply is *not* an Adamic figure -- nor, for that matter, and in spite of the assertions of Mr. Carpenter and Mr. Lewis, is Hester Prynne or Ishmael or Robert Jordan or Holden Caulfield or the narrator of *Invisible Man*, or any number of other classic protagonists in American fiction. A few protagonists -- Leatherstocking, Jay Gatsby, Isaac McCaslin, and Sy Levin are perhaps the most obvious and the most important -- come close to being truly Adamic heroes; but even these, as we shall see, serve more to dramatize the limitations of the Adamic myth than to confirm its validity and its viability. It will be to our advantage, though, to stay with Huck awhile: he is surely a major American literary hero, and understanding his character will reveal much about American fiction and about American culture.

The most insightful statement ever made about Huck Finn is, I believe, that of Leslie A. Fiedler in *Love and Death in the American Novel*:

> He is the product of no metaphysics, but of a terrible break-through of the undermind of America itself. In him, the obsessive American theme of loneliness reaches an ultimate level of expression, being accepted at last not [in the tradition of Emerson and Thoreau] as a blessing to be sought or [in the tradition of Hawthorne and Melville] a curse to be flaunted or fled, but quite simply as man's fate. There are mythic qualities in Ahab and even Dimmesdale; but Huck *is* myth: not invented but discovered by one close enough to the popular mind to let it, this once at least, speak through him. Twain sometimes merely pandered to that popular mind, played the buffoon for it, but he was unalienated from it; and when he let it possess him, instead of pretending to condescend to it, he and the American people dreamed Huck -- dreamed, that is to say, the anti-American American dream.[8]

Here, surely, is the very heart of the matter: "Huck *is* myth" -- "a terrible break-through of the undermind of America itself." Nor does the determination with which most Americans persist in seeing Huck (to borrow Fiedler's effective terminology) as a *Good* Bad boy, rather than as the Bad Bad boy that he actually is, in any way disprove Fiedler's insight: this is in itself simply an expression of the near desperation with which Americans conspire to hide from themselves one of the deepest and one of the most disturbing truths of American life -- its essential loneliness. Wright Morris identifies our plight very succinctly: "Privately, in the depths of our being, we are Huckleberry Finns fleeing from Aunt Sally. Publicly we create and promote the very civilization we privately reject . . . . Nostalgia rules our hearts while a rhetoric of progress rules our words."[9] This, then, explains why *Huckleberry Finn* is not included in Lewis' study of *The American Adam*: far from being an Adamic hero, Huck is indeed "the juvenile pariah" ("idle and lawless and vulgar and bad")[10] that Twain calls him and that, as Morris says, we all privately long to be. For Huck is never really initiated,[11] never really reborn into the Adamic state of consciously achieved innocence, newness, and grace; rather, he quite deliberately chooses to "go to Hell": to become a Faustian hero in absolute and dread-ridden rebellion against American society. No doubt Fiedler is right in saying that it is sometimes difficult to "tell where the American dream ended and the Faustian nightmare began" ("they held in common the hope of breaking through all limits and restraints, of reaching a [mythic] place of total freedom where one could with impunity deny the Fall, live as if innocence rather than guilt were the birthright of all men"), but I think that Fiedler himself has shown, brilliantly and definitively, that *one* place where the dream ended and the nightmare began is within the asocial, anti-realistic, essentially gothic life-experience that is rendered in our classic fiction. And certainly there is no more terrifying insight into Huck Finn's essential life-experience, or predicament, than Fiedler's remark that Huck's burst of pity for the Duke and the King upon finding them "astraddle of a rail" is caused by the fact "that it is his own fate which Huck foresees in their plight, and that it is himself he weeps for. Even so he must end up, too, tarred and feathered, unless he dies like his father, stabbed in the back and set adrift on the river." At another point, in a sentence which strikes to the heart of the experience which is rendered in classic American fiction, Fiedler observes that "Huck is heading for no utopia, since he has heard of none; and so he ends up making flight itself his goal. He flees from the impermanence of boyhood to that of continual change; and, of course, it is a vain evasion except as it leads him to understand that *no* society can fulfill his destiny."[12]

"*No* society can fulfill his destiny": a fitting epigraph for the American novel. The basic proposition of American fiction is, as R. W. B. Lewis has noted, "the proposition . . . that the valid rite of initiation for the individual in the new world is not an initiation *into* society, but, given the character of society, an initiation *away from it*: something I wish it were legitimate to call '*de*nitiation'"[13] -- which is to say, no initiation at all! And it is here that the cultural reasons for some of the major characteristics of American fiction -- its anti-realism, its tendency toward nihilism, its nostalgia, its obsession with adolescence -- are suddenly revealed. "In every culture," as Daniel Hoffman rightly contends, "the concept of maturity implies a full commitment to fixed values; until modern times these values were sacred. Their fixity had been established by supernatural powers, and the passage from childhood to maturity was marked by initiatory rites in which the sacred knowledge that came to the present from the beginning of time was passed on to the initiate."[14] But predominantly in American society there have been no such initiatory rites, there has been no such initiation. As I have mentioned, the only way of establishing identity, the only criterion for maturity, and (seemingly) the only fixed value in American society is "success." Making It is the basic, popular American dream; and the Self-Made Man is the archetypal American hero, just as being On the Make is the only socially sanctioned novitiate for American heroes.[15] This is initiation in America; the spiritual limitations of such an initiation, its utter shallowness *as* initiation, go blithely, or perhaps deliberately, unrecognized by the preachers of our popular creed. At best, the Self-Made Man in America resembles Benjamin Franklin, who, as Melville said, and as Franklin himself cheerfully admitted, "was everything but a poet";[16] more commonly, the Self-Made Man is the American who has "made it," economically, and who wonders why making it has failed to make him happy. No wonder most of our writers have chosen to have *their* heroes "light out for the territory" rather than to have them make it within society! Haunted and often hurt in their own lives by what Alfred Kazin has called "the grinning idiot's face" of success,[17] most of our major fictionists have created heroes who are essentially pariah figures, figures who remain outside society, alone, lost, and with no real hope of spiritual rebirth. The Romance tradition in American fiction stands as a single, massive denial of the American dream.

Of course a nonfiction writer like Thoreau held an equally critical view of the prevailing, popular American dream of success. But the crucial difference is that Thoreau, unlike our fictionists, was able to create a *private* initiation, a private ritual of rebirth,[18] whereby he did truly achieve the Adamic vision, or state, of the "waking dream." Our fictionists, seemingly without exception, have been unable to achieve the same Adamic vision of life. Even those who have come closest -- Cooper, Faulkner, Malamud, for instance -- finally affirm the death of the Adamic dream rather than the dream itself: Natty and Ike and Sy, no matter how determinedly they strive to transcend time and history and to repudiate society by withdrawing into nature, cannot finally escape either the wreckage of time and of history or the encroachment of society.[19] In other words, our fiction writers are unable to affirm either the success ethic of American society itself or the possibility of any ultimate escape from, or of any private rebirth outside of, that society. While it is true, as Richard Poirier has shown, that American fictionists have characteristically striven to create *A World Elsewhere* in which their heroes can achieve the American westering dream of freedom and of spiritual rebirth, it is equally true that they have been unable to *believe* in such a world. The Great Good Place has proved to be a dream indeed, impossible permanently to attain; there is, as Fiedler says, "no absolute raft,"[20] and Nick Adams's tent in the woods of northern Michigan or Ike McCaslin's tent in the woods of northern Mississippi are, as havens of peace in a world without peace, equally as vulnerable and impermanent as Huck's raft. Moreover, of these three characters it is only Ike who retreats to nature with the Thoreauvian purpose of spiritual rebirth; for both Huck and Nick, as Philip Young has shown,[21] the flight to nature is just that: sheer flight, an effort, desperate and at least partially futile, to retain sanity and to survive physically in a world that everywhere threatens that very sanity and survival. Neither Huck nor any of Hemingway's heroes "grow up" -- and for very good reason. To do so is, given Twain's and Hemingway's views of American society, to lose the American dream at the only place that it can ever exist: in boyhood and outside society. Nor is it encouraging to note that sanity itself is, as with Huck and Nick, more often than not a major quest of the American protagonist. "I've lain with madness long enough," Stephen Rojack belatedly concludes in *An American Dream*,[22] and any reader of his story will readily agree -- finding, as well, little reason to hope that things will work out for Rojack in Yucatan. The same kind of hysterical -- if not utterly insane -- quest for the American dream of innocence is dramatized in Updike's *Rabbit, Run*. If, indeed, there is any encouragement at all in our fiction, it is that *some* of our protagonists -- such as Huck Finn, Sy Levin, the narrator of *Invisible Man*, and (to a lesser degree) Holden Caulfield -- realize to their betterment that the Adamic westering dream of rebirth into innocence and into new youth is a false dream indeed; that maturity, humanity, and sanity itself depend upon an open-eyed recognition of and acceptance of guilt and responsibility.

In short, our fictionists have affirmed neither our Adamic dream of newness and of innocence nor our popular dream of success. Implicit within the entire Romance tradition of American fiction is the understanding that success, while it may be a glorification of the self, is hardly an initiation of the self -- at least not if we define initiation, in its classic sense, as a spiritual change which entails a rebirth into maturity and responsibility.[23] Yet, as we have seen, success is the *only* kind of initiation that can be offered by a culture -- like America's -- that is secular, atomistic, competitive, progressive, and egalitarian. This accounts for the notorious "innocence" of the American character (for without a real ritual of initiation there can be no real maturity) as well as for the refusal of our major fictionists to affirm a dream as shallow as the "American dream of innocent success."

II

The "American dream of innocent success" is Leslie Fiedler's apt description of the dream which Scott Fitzgerald compellingly dramatizes in *The Great Gatsby*;[24] and at this point it should be helpful to examine the ways in which this Romance is a key to a firmer understanding of the points that I have been making about initiation, success, the American dream, and the Romance tradition in American fiction. *The Great Gatsby* is of course a compelling and haunting portrayal of what Marius Bewley calls "the Collapse of the American Dream."[25] In my view it is also an utterly *unique* portrayal of the American dream, and Gatsby is an utterly unique character in American fiction. I mean that *The Great Gatsby* is the *only* Romance in American literature to portray the American dream as it actually exists, and has existed, in the popular American imagination -- and that Gatsby himself is an embodiment, practically unique to American fiction, of the materialist-idealist paradox which, as sociologists like David M. Potter have shown,[26] is a central paradox of the American character. For if R. W. B. Lewis is right in saying that *The Great Gatsby* is a vivid example of "the Adamic anecdote," that it "demonstrates once more the dramatic appeal of the hero as a self-created innocent,"[27] it should be noted that this is true only in a very special sense. At first glance, for example, it would seem that Gatsby simply does not aspire to or embody the kind of Adamic innocence to which Cooper's Natty or Faulkner's Ike aspired. If we compare Gatsby to Natty and Ike, a substantial difference is immediately apparent: Gatsby aspires to, and achieves, the popular American dream of success; Natty and Ike self-consciously repudiate the dream of success, retreat from society, take to the woods: all in an effort to achieve a spiritual success, an Adamic innocence. My point, though, is that Gatsby's dream is not *essentially* any less ideal or any less spiritual than Natty's or Ike's -- the main difference being that Gatsby (like so many Americans; like his own creator, himself a Minnesotan who rose from obscurity to near-legendary fame and success) sought to achieve his dream, by material means, *through* society. Nor is this to say that Gatsby is a social climber or that his dream is in any way socially oriented -- only that, as Richard Chase has said, he views "society and its ways . . . not [as] ends but [as] means to a transcendent ideal."[28] The heart of the matter is that Gatsby is a Thoreau who seeks to achieve the Adamic "waking dream" by pursuing the popular American dream of material success.

Of all American writers, then, it seems that Fitzgerald is the only one to have made great literature out of the tragic contradictions (as personified by Gatsby) in the American dream itself. Only Fitzgerald, that is to say, has done justice to, has vividly and memorably rendered, the essential idealism that does in fact lie behind, or beyond, the unquestionable materialism of American life. Most of our other major writers, it seems, have seen only the materialism, only the harsh competitiveness, only the single-minded commitment to Progress; and consequently they have taken their protagonists *out* of society rather than to Gatsby's mansion at West Egg. Of course no more than any of our other classic writers does Fitzgerald approve of or affirm the popular American dream of success; but unlike the others he renders the ironies and tragedies of the dream as well as its shallowness: he shows that while Gatsby may represent "everything for which [we] have an unaffected scorn," we, like Nick Carraway, cannot help but respond affirmatively to his "extraordinary gift for hope, [his] romantic readiness," his "heightened sensitivity to the promises of life."[29] And what makes *The Great Gatsby* a Romance quite as much as *The Scarlet Letter* or *Huckleberry Finn* is the fact that Fitzgerald centers his story not just upon Gatsby but upon Gatsby's ideal aspirations -- remains true, that is, to Gatsby's dream by showing that it *was* a dream. A "realistic" novel like Dreiser's *An American Tragedy* contains, in a thousand pages, less than half of the truth about the popular American dream of "innocent success" which Fitzgerald captured, once and for all, in the short legend of Gatsby. For it is not that Americans dream of money but that for Americans money *is* a dream: a means "to a transcendent ideal."

It is possible, of course, to argue that Gatsby's failure to recognize the shallowness of his dream makes him a more limited character than the more typical heroes of American fiction -- such as Huckleberry Finn or Isaac McCaslin -- who repudiate the American dream of success. This is probably true, but to say that Gatsby is less aware than Huck or than Ike is not to say that he is any less mythic. The point is that Gatsby embodies the popular and the prevailing American success-dream, while Huck and Ike embody the secret, unspoken anti-American dream -- the dream of repudiation and of escape -- for which most Americans privately yearn. For if Americans dream of taking to the woods or to the river like Natty or Huck or Ike, it is quite clear that they also dream of owning a mansion like Gatsby's (Mark Twain *did* own such a mansion).[30] Yet what saves *The Great Gatsby* from being an

All-American success story is, after all, Gatsby's "incorruptible dream" -- a dream which clearly has nothing whatever to do with his "huge incoherent failure of a house" or with the "beautiful shirts" with which he tries, grotesquely, to pay homage to his dream. Gatsby is not a man on the make but a man with a dream; and, astonishingly enough, this dream is, in the final analysis, the same Adamic waking dream that Cooper, Twain, Hemingway, Faulkner, and Thoreau imaged in Natty, Huck, Nick, Ike, and the "I" of *Walden*: the dream of regaining and of freezing in time the intense, innocent, thoroughly affirmative life-experience of youth. "No amount of fire or freshness" -- as Nick Carraway so rightly concludes -- "can challenge what a man will store up in his ghostly heart."[31] But, again, *only* Thoreau, and none of our fictionists, has actually believed in the possibility of repeating the past, of achieving a rebirth into innocence and into new youth. Indeed, the poignancy of the works of Cooper, Twain, Hemingway, Faulkner, and Fitzgerald derives precisely from these authors' belief that the past cannot be repeated, that time and history are inexorable and irreversible. *Walden* is a joyful celebration of an achieved rebirth; the works of our great fictionists are somber accounts of the impossibility of man's escaping history, of living, as it were, before the Fall. Nor is it really true, as Frederic I. Carpenter has argued,[32] that American fictionists traditionally affirm a myth of the regaining of paradise *after* the Fall. Deerslayer and Isaac McCaslin, for instance, are initiated (Deerslayer's killing of an Indian and Isaac's killing of a buck) not into innocence but into guilt, and both live long lives which ultimately dramatize not the possibility of an Adamic rebirth in the wilderness but the *impossibility* of man's escape from history or from guilt; Huck Finn and Nick Adams, far from regaining any paradise, are always, as I have said, just one step ahead of the violence and the evil which threaten their very psychic and physical survival; and Gatsby, of course, lives not to see his dream realized but to have "his Platonic conception of himself . . . broken up like glass against Tom [Buchanan's] hard malice."[33]

III

Gatsby's dream -- America's dream -- of repeating the past and of regaining a lost innocence, freshness, and happiness has always owed its strength and its vibrancy to what Tony Tanner has movingly called "America's brave and exhilarating apostasy from history."[34] But Americans (even the second-generation Puritans, for example, or the later Thomas Jefferson, and certainly all reflective Americans since the Civil War) have generally realized that to apostatize from history is not the same as to escape from history. This is why, as Wright Morris has shown,[35] America, the most "progressive" nation in the world, is, paradoxically, an overwhelmingly nostalgic nation. Conscious of their entrapment in time and history, Americans yearn for a mythic past of innocence and of newness. Like Gatsby, we "stretch out our arms" for "the orgiastic future that year by year recedes before us" and are "borne back ceaselessly into the past."[36] American writers appear to have shared this nostalgia, this search for a mythic past, and this, too, helps to explain why American fiction itself is essentially mythic, Romances rather than novels. It is generally accepted that novels, by definition, render an actual, social, contemporary world; and it is this world which American fictionists, no less than Americans in general, have cared neither to face nor to believe in. Our *belief* lies with the dream, which itself lies either in some mythic past or in some equally mythic future -- but never in the present. Likewise, the essence of despair for American fictionists, as for Americans in general, has always been an awareness of the inescapableness of the present, of man's entrapment in time, of the harsh facts of historical change. Even during the afternoon when Gatsby and Daisy were reunited, she inevitably "tumbled short of his dreams"; it was only during his first discovery of Daisy or only when he could gaze, in anticipation, at the green light at the end of her dock far across the bay that "he could suck on the pap of life, gulp down the incomparable milk of wonder."[37] And the cause of Fitzgerald's own Crack-Up was, as Wright Morris has perceptively remarked, "neither fatigue nor the aimless wandering, but the paralysis of will that grew out of the knowledge that the past was dead, and that the present had no future."[38] A similar conviction about the death of an ideal past has, as a matter of fact, driven a disturbingly large number of our writers to crack-ups, or to the verge of crack-ups. Cooper, as D. H. Lawrence and Leslie Fiedler have shown,[39] indulged in the most obvious kind of wish fulfillment in the Leatherstocking saga in an effort to escape the oppressive realities of his life within American society; Melville, in the words of Maxwell Geismar, "wandered to the brink of nervous collapse and insanity" when he realized, in the early 1850s, how fully he, as an artist, was ostracized in a nation committed to the values of Wall Street;[40] Mark Twain retreated to a hopeless cynicism and fatalism once he realized that his pre-Civil-War dream-image of Hannibal was forever lost -- did not in fact ever exist; Hemingway withdrew to a private world of adolescence, ritual, and stoicism in an effort to retain the order and sanity which he found so threatened by the adult, public world -- an effort which led to a crack-up quite as severe as Fitzgerald's and, ultimately, to suicide; and as for Faulkner, his tale, as Robert Penn Warren has said, "is one of the anguish of time, the tension of change."[41] Quentin Compson, a close projection of Faulkner's own youthful self, commits suicide in order to escape his agonized awareness that the Southern past is dead and that modernity holds no future; Isaac McCaslin retreats to a mystical communion with the wilderness in an effort to escape the encroachment of history -- an effort that ends, inevitably, in failure and in personal tragedy; and of all Faulkner's characters it is perhaps only the servant Dilsey who has the courage to "endure," to live in the present and to face the harsh facts of historical change in spite of her experience -- quite as intense as Quentin's or Isaac's or Gatsby's -- of "a child's astonished disappointment" at the wreckage and the irreversibility of time.[42] Faulkner himself -- in spite of what he may have said in his sentimental Stockholm address -- clearly could never bring himself to believe in our modern world and was, to borrow Fitzgerald's words, "borne back ceaselessly into the [mythic, Southern] past."

And it is finally with Faulkner, even more than with Twain or with Fitzgerald, that the relationships between the American dream and the Romance tradition in American fiction are most vividly illustrated. No American writer has given to his fiction a fuller or a more densely specified geographic, economic, social, and historical texture than Faulkner has given to his saga of Yoknapatawpha County; yet Faulkner's fiction -- no less than Hawthorne's or Melville's or Twain's -- is actually not realistic but mythic, not novels but Romances. And it is so because Faulkner is not finally or essentially writing about a region or a society or economics or history but about myth, the Southern myth, and about the individual's relation to that myth. It should be added at once that the Southern myth is a fundamental *American* myth -- an essential part of the American dream itself. For Wright Morris is surely right in stressing that the American mind has always been, paradoxically, both progressive and nostalgic. Even pre-Civil-War America (the North included) was, as W. J. Cash has put it, "an age . . . that . . . was not only ready but eager to believe in the Southern legend -- that . . . fell with a certain distinct gladness on this last purely agricultural land of the West as a sort of projection ground for its own dreams of a vanished golden time."[43] And if this was true of pre-Civil-War America, how much more -- as writers like Twain, Fitzgerald, and Faulkner have vividly shown -- has it been true of post-Civil-War America! In spite of his hatred of the South and of slavery, Twain could never forget that boyhood in a pre-Civil-War, Southern slave-holding town was the happiest life that he had experienced or could imagine. Fitzgerald was simultaneously ashamed and proud of the fact that his father was a Southerner who embodied the essential Southern values which made it impossible for him (the father) to be economically successful in a Northern, progressive, industrial society. And Faulkner -- well, Faulkner has singlehandedly made the myth of the South one of the central realities of American life. But, again, Faulkner surely could not have done so if a deep, crying *need* for the Southern place-myth had not already existed in American life itself -- just as the incredible success of the Leatherstocking Tales resulted from the urgent need which Americans felt to *believe* in the westering myth which these tales embodied.[44] The unquestionable grasp which the Southern myth has upon the American imagination -- even, I would venture to say, the secret envy with which Americans look to the South and its principled, stubborn commitment to a backward-looking, English-oriented, conservative, aristocratic, agrarian way of living -- is in itself the clearest possible proof of the persistence with which Americans continue to dream the anti-American, anti-progressive dream. On this point the words of Wright Morris bear repeating: "Nostalgia rules our hearts while a rhetoric of progress rules our words." Thus, it is hardly surprising that the celebrated sense of *doom* in Faulkner -- and its cogency for American readers -- derives precisely from his belief not only that the past was better but also that it is dead and can never be repeated; it is, quite simply, a historical doom -- the same kind of doom which Hawthorne rendered in his fable of the first-generation Puritans or which Melville projected in his epic of the white whale. And in Faulkner's "The Bear," itself as great a dramatization of the failure of the American dream as *The Great Gatsby*, Isaac McCaslin explains that the new-world westering dream was doomed even before American history began -- that history simply has been an acting out of the doom -- by the evil and the greed which "'Grandfather and his kind, his fathers, had brought into the new land . . . from that old world's corrupt and worthless twilight as though in the sailfuls of the old world's tainted wind which drove the ships --'."[45]

IV

If the Romance tradition in American fiction tells us anything about American life and about the American dream, it is, first of all, that isolation and loneliness pervade our society. It is not, as David Riesman has argued, just in the twentieth century, but always, that we have been a "lonely crowd." Commercially and materially, American democracy has produced a dominant civilization, but it has not produced a coherent *culture* within which individuals are meaningfully related by their commitment to certain fixed values and beliefs. This absence of a real culture -- a culture that offers the individual a true rite of initiation and, consequently, a true solidarity with his society -- has caused our fictionists to write Romances which concentrate on the individual's attempt to find a coherent and meaningful world *outside* society. For the only fixed value of a society committed to Progress is success, and none of our great fictionists have accepted or endorsed this value in their literature -- although many have been trapped and damaged by it in their lives.

Second, the Romance tradition reveals the deep, but private, ambivalence of Americans toward the American dream. To repudiate society and to repudiate success is, in effect, to repudiate the American dream as it exists on its popular, prevailing level; yet Americans have always been ready and even anxious to join Huck on his raft. All of the important protagonists of American fiction have been questers of values more meaningful than the American dream of success, and Americans have been more than willing *imaginatively* to join them in their quests. Of course, as D. H. Lawrence has pointed out,[46] Americans usually hide this subversion even from themselves by reassuring themselves and others that our classics are just "children's books."

Finally, the Romance tradition constitutes a thoroughgoing denial of the American dream in practically all of its social, historical, political, and mythological forms. For if our fictionists have denied the popular dream of success, they have also denied the Jeffersonian dream of a perfect democracy and of an escape from history; and they have denied the Adamic westering dream of rebirth into innocence and into new youth. The single most forceful reminder that the Romance tradition in American fiction stands as a denial of the American dream is, however, simply this: the *one* attitude toward the American dream -- the nostalgic dream of a paradisic, mythic past -- which our classic fictionists share with Americans in general is in itself an illustration of the extent to which Americans feel that the dream has been betrayed in the present.

Chapter 12

Notes

1. Daniel G. Hoffman, *Form and Fable in American Fiction* (New York: Oxford University Press, 1965), p. 353; Leslie A. Fiedler, *Love and Death in the American Novel*, 2nd ed. (New York: Dell, 1966); Jonathan Baumbach, *The Landscape of Nightmare: Studies in the Contemporary American Novel* (New York: New York University Press, 1965); Marius Bewley, *The Eccentric Design: Form in the Classic American Novel* (New York: Columbia University Press, 1959); Richard Case, *The American Novel and Its Tradition* (New York: Doubleday, 1957); Edwin T. Bowden, *The Dungeon of the Heart: Human Isolation and the American Novel* (New York: Macmillan, 1961); Wright Morris, *The Territory Ahead: Critical Interpretations in American Literature* (New York: Atheneum, 1963); Richard Poirier, *A World Elsewhere: The Place of Style in American Literature* (New York: Oxford University Press, 1966); A.N. Kaul, *The American Vision: Actual and Ideal Society in Nineteenth-Century Fiction* (New Haven: Yale University Press, 1963); Tony Tanner, *The Reign of Wonder: Naivety and Reality in American Literature* (Cambridge: Cambridge University Press, 1965); R. W. B. Lewis, *The American Adam: Innocence, Tragedy, and Tradition in the Nineteenth Century* (Chicago: University of Chicago Press, 1955); D. H. Lawrence, *Studies in Classic American Literature* (New York: Thomas Seltzer, 1923); Joel Porte, *The Romance in America: Studies in Cooper, Poe, Hawthorne, Melville, and James* (Middletown, Connecticut: Wesleyan University Press, 1969).
2. Taken from Hester's impassioned exhortation -- "Begin all anew!" -- to Dimmesdale in the forest scene of *The Scarlet Letter*. Hawthorne's refusal to affirm Hester's dream of freedom and of a new life is a dramatic example of a central point in this chapter: the fact that our classic fictionists have traditionally denied the American westering dream. Cf. Chapter 3 of this book.
3. Cf. Bewley, *The Eccentric Design*, p. 293.
4. Cf. Hoffman, *Form and Fable*, p. 7.
5. Taken from D. H. Lawrence's famous definition of "the true myth of America. She starts old, old, wrinkled and writhing in an old skin. And there is a gradual sloughing of the old skin, towards a new youth. It is the myth of America." *Studies*, p. 64.
6. Henry David Thoreau, *A Week on the Concord and Merrimack Rivers* (New York: New American Library, 1961), p. 256.
7. Carpenter, *American Literature and the Dream* (New York: Philosophical Library, 1955); Lewis, *The American Adam*.
8. *Love and Death*, pp. 286-287.
9. *The Territory Ahead*, pp. 24, 25.
10. Mark Twain, *The Adventures of Tom Sawyer* (New York: New American Library, 1959), p. 46.
11. Cf. Leslie A. Fiedler's remark that "it is hard finally to believe in Huck's having been initiated into anything; if he is at all different at the end of the book from where he is at the start, it is only in

possessing a few more nightmares; but in such treasures he was rich enough to begin with." *No! in Thunder: Essays on Myth and Literature* (Boston: Beacon Press, 1960), p. 279. Cf. also Chase, *The American Novel*, pp. 144-145.

12.   *Love and Death*, pp. 143, 286, 465.
13.   *The American Adam*, p. 115.
14.   *Form and Fable*, pp. 79-80.
15.   Cf. Norman Podhoretz, *Making It* (New York: Random House, 1967).
16.   Melville's statement appears in *Israel Potter* and is quoted in Hoffman, *Form and Fable*, p. 39. In his *Autobiography* Franklin explains that his father discouraged his efforts at poetry "by ridiculing my performances and telling me verse-makers were generally beggars. Thus I escaped being a poet and probably a very bad one." *Autobiography and Other Writings of Benjamin Franklin*, ed. Russell B. Nye (Boston: Houghton Mifflin, 1958), p. 11.
17.   "Fitzgerald: An American Confession," in Kazin, *The Inmost Leaf* (New York: Harcourt, Brace, 1941), p. 120.
18.   For the importance of *Walden* as a ritual of rebirth, see Charles Roberts Anderson, *The Magic Circle of Walden* (New York: Holt, Rinehart and Winston, 1968); and Sherman Paul, "Resolution at Walden," *Accent*, 13 (1953): 101-113.
19.   See, for example, David W. Noble, "Cooper, Leatherstocking and the Death of the American Adam," *American Quarterly*, 16 (1964): 419-431.
20.   *Love and Death*, p. 354.
21.   *Ernest Hemingway: A Reconsideration* (New York: Harcourt, Brace & World, 1966), pp. 211-260.
22.   Norman Mailer, *An American Dream* (New York: Dell, 1964), p. 243.
23.   Cf. Hoffman, *Form and Fable*, pp. 79-81.
24.   *Love and Death*, p. 315.
25.   "Scott Fitzgerald and the Collapse of the American Dream," in Bewley, *The Eccentric Design*, pp. 259-287.
26.   "The Quest for the National Character," in *The Reconstruction of American History*, ed. John Higham (New York: Harper & Row, 1962), pp. 197-220.
27.   *The American Adam*, p. 197.
28.   *The American Novel*, p. 165.
29.   F. Scott Fitzgearld, *The Great Gatsby* (New York: Scribner's, 1925), p. 2.
30.   As Henry Nash Smith has noted, the Hartford house where Twain lived while dreaming the story of Huckleberry Finn "was three stories high and contained a score of rooms. On the outside were a half-dozen balconies, two towers, a portecochere, and a broad veranda. With the furnishing, it cost more than $120,000 at a time when the dollar had perhaps three times its present purchasing power." "Mark Twain," in *Major Writers of America*, ed. Perry Miller (New York: Harcourt, Brace & World, 1962), II, p. 49. See also Justin Kaplan, *Mr. Clemens and Mark Twain* (New York: Pocket Books, 1968), pp. 207-210. As Kaplan points out (p. 209), Twain's mansion "was a fulfillment of dream," in that it "was a classic American success story, a reminder that it was possible to be born in a two-room clapboard

house in Florida, Missouri, a village of one hundred inhabitants, and to become world-famous, marry a rich and beautiful woman, and live a life of domestic bliss in a house that was the marvel of Hartford."

31. Fitzgerald, p. 97.
32. "'The American Myth': Paradise (To Be) Regained," *PMLA*, 74 (December, 1959): 559-606.
33. Fitzgerald, pp. 99, 148.
34. *The Reign of Wonder*, p. 113.
35. *The Territory Ahead, passim*, especially the discussion of Norman Rockwell ("Abuse of the Past"), pp. 113-129.
36. Fitzgerald, p. 182.
37. *Ibid.*, p. 112.
38. *The Territory Ahead*, p. 163.
39. Lawrence, *Studies*, pp. 55-73; Fiedler, *Love and Death*, pp. 162-214.
40. "The Shifting Illusion: Dream and Fact," in *American Dreams, American Nightmares*, ed. David Madden (Carbondale: Southern Illinois University Press, 1970), p. 46.
41. "Faulkner: The South, the Negro, and Time," in *Faulkner: A Collection of Critical Essays*, ed. Robert Penn Warren (Englewood Cliffs, N.J.: Prentice-Hall, 1966), p. 251.
42. William Faulkner, *The Sound and the Fury* (New York: Modern Library, 1946), p. 282.
43. *The Mind of the South* (New York: Random House, 1941), p. 64.
44. Cf. Fiedler, *Love and Death*, p. 187.
45. William Faulkner, *Go Down, Moses* (New York: Modern Library, 1940), p. 259.
46. *Studies*, pp. 11-13.

CHAPTER 13

American Observers in England, 1820-1920:
A Cross-National Perspective on American Culture
and the American Character

Analysts of American culture and of the American character have placed understandable and substantial importance upon what foreign observers have said of America, but surprisingly little use has been made of what *American* observers have had to say about other countries. Certainly reasons are readily available for studying America from the perspective provided by American observers of other countries -- and especially of England. I would point, first of all, to the *quality* of the books that Americans have written on England: during the period, roughly, of one century between Washington Irving's *The Sketch Book* and George Santayana's *Soliloquies in England*, several of America's major literary and philosophical figures wrote books on their observations of English culture and of the English character -- books which are, in at least two or three cases, quite as penetrating and perspicacious as the most important books on America by foreign observers, including Tocqueville.[1] Second, there is the essential fact that the historic origins of American society and of American culture are, after all, basically *Anglo*-American and that to understand America one needs to understand England. Contemporary analysts of American society such as Louis Hartz and Seymour Martin Lipset have persuasively argued that an understanding of America's English heritage is essential to an understanding of American culture and of the American character.[2] The major American writers of the nineteenth and early twentieth centuries, at least, did not need to be reminded of this fact. Indeed, all of the writers to whom I shall refer were acutely aware that England is, as Hawthorne put it in the title of his book, *Our Old Home* and that there is, in spite of many differences, a deep-rooted continuity and affinity between the English and the American cultures. Emerson, for example, stated flatly that "The American is only the continuation of the English genius into new conditions, more or less propitious."[3]   And Henry James felt that "the English-American world" is simply "different chapters of the same general subject."[4] Third, and last, it should be noted that all of these books are addressed primarily to Americans and that they are, either implicitly or explicitly (and it is usually explicitly), concerned quite as much with America as with England -- an inevitable consequence of their being written *by Americans*.   For, of course, the experience of another culture challenges the American observer and forces him to sharpen and to objectify his attitudes toward and his ideas about American culture -- so that if foreign observers must come to America to discover America, American observers must leave.

In what follows, then, I shall (1) identify the major responses to England found in American observers from 1820 to 1920 and (2) analyze these responses *from an American point of view*: that is, I shall show why I think that these responses are a revealing and a valuable index to important aspects of American culture and of the American character.[5]

In regard to their responses to England, it can be said at once that there is an arresting and a highly suggestive keynote pervading the works of all the American observers: namely, their scarcely concealed or, as with Emerson or with Santayana, entirely open *envy* of English life and of English society. Even Hawthorne, by far the most hostile of the American observers, admits that London was "the dream city of my youth" and that he "found it better than my dream."[6] And Hawthorne wrote a letter to Longfellow in which he tried to persuade him to move to England, explaining that "A man of individuality and refinement can certainly live far more comfortably here . . . than in New England."[7] Envy on the part of the American observers is suggestive, of course, for the simple reason that one envies in another country qualities which are either nonexistent or, at least, less common in one's own country.   And more suggestive still is the fact that what the Americans envy most, sometimes begrudgingly but more often magnanimously, about England is the English *people* themselves. They may not always *like* the English, but they do envy, admire, and earnestly respect them. This is so because, as nearly all of the American observers note, the English, and particularly the English aristocracy, undeniably embody the most admirable of human traits -- traits like practical ability, unsentimentality, candor, self-sufficiency, energy, learning, courage, and devotion to privacy and to domesticity and to distinctive living: a cluster of virtues which for George Santayana is summarized by that greatest of all virtues: manliness.[8]   Indeed, nearly all of the American observers were immediately struck by (and Hawthorne, alone, responded negatively to) what Henry James calls "that explosive personal force in the English character," that "latent capacity . . . for great freedom of action" -- or, in other words, by the "superior richness of [the English] temperament."[9]   From Emerson there is pure admiration and delight in the fact that "They are oppressive with their temperament, and all the more that they are refined."[10]   Irving states, quite simply, that he does "not know of a finer race of men than the English gentlemen.   Instead of the softness and effeminacy which characterize the men of rank in most countries, they exhibit a union of elegance and strength . . . which I am inclined to attribute to their living so much in the open air, and pursuing so eagerly the invigorating recreations of the country. These hardy exercises produce . . . a manliness and simplicity of manners."[11]   Similarly, Cooper notes that the Englishmen "are simple, masculine in manner and mind, and highly cultivated," that they "have the merits of courage, manliness, intelligence, and manners."[12]   And, at another point in his book, Emerson describes the English nobles as "high-spirited, active, educated men" who "have that simplicity, and that air of repose, which are the finest ornament of greatness."[13]

Since there are, as the above quotations indicate, so many traits in the English character which win the admiration and respect of the American observers, it will be helpful to separate them in order to analyze more clearly their relevance to an understanding of American culture and the American character. And among the traits which I think deserve special consideration are those coming under the headings of *candor, independence, individuality*; for these are traits which, as our observers are painfully aware, are embarrassingly lacking in the American character. Independence and "rugged individualism" in the American character is an overworked myth which Martineau and Tocqueville were exposing even during the times of Irving and Cooper, and which discerning Americans in the twentieth century have long since ceased to believe. But, for the American observers, the independence and sturdiness of the English character was a deep, massive, and ever-present reality. Emerson, America's famous celebrant of "Self-Reliance," was perhaps the observer most forcefully impressed by the integrity and stolidity of the British, so much so that he devoted a separate chapter to the Englishman's characteristic love and practice of "Truth":

> They are blunt in saying what they think, sparing of promises, and they require plain dealing of others. When they unmask cant, they say, "The English of this is," etc.; and to give the lie is the extreme insult . . . . In the power of saying rude truth, sometimes in the lion's mouth, no men surpass them. On the king's birthday, when each bishop was expected to offer the king a purse of gold, Latimer gave Henry VIII a copy of the Vulgate, with a mark at the passage, "Whoremongers and adulterers God will judge"; and they so honor stoutness in each other that the king passed it over. They are tenacious of their belief and cannot easily change their opinions to suit the hour.[14]

In short, these Englishmen, to quote Emerson again, "have in themselves what they value in their horses -- mettle and bottom . . . . They require you to dare to be of your own opinion, and they hate practical cowards who cannot in affairs answer directly yes or no. They dare to displease, nay, they will let you break all the commandments, if you do it natively and with spirit. *You must be somebody* [emphasis mine]; then you may do this or that, as you will."[15] And although it is only near the end of his book that Emerson begins explicitly to contrast the English to the Americans, one cannot help reading in every expression of his deep admiration for the independence and integrity of the English character the despairing lament: how unlike America! For *there* is a country where people are all too ready to "change their opinions to suit the hour" and where anyone who has the courage to *be somebody* and to express his own opinion can, to say the least, hardly hope to be rewarded by popular approval or by personal freedom.

Emerson, of course, is just one observer, but his description of the independence and "invincible stoutness"[16] of the English is far from unique among the American observers. Irving, too, noted that while Americans are governed "entirely by public opinion" the English are distinguished by "their freedom of opinion" and by their "love for what is blunt."[17] And Cooper was virtually obsessed with the absolute contrast between the freedom of opinion in England and the slavery *to* opinion in America. Of all the American observers, Cooper is the one who is most like the English themselves in his daring to be direct and blunt in describing the lack of independence and of individuality in American society as compared to English society:

> The English are to be distinguished from the Americans, by greater independence of personal habits . . . . In England a man dines by himself in a room filled with other hermits, he eats at his leisure, drinks his wine in silence, reads the paper by the hour; and, in all things, encourages his individuality and insists on his particular humours. The American is compelled to submit to a common rule; he eats when others eat, sleeps when others sleep, and he is lucky, indeed, if he can read a paper in a tavern without having a stranger looking over each shoulder. The Englishman would stare at a proposal that should invade his habits under the pretence of a common wish, while the American would be very apt to yield tacitly . . . . The Englishman is so much attached to his independence that he instinctively resists every effort to invade it, and nothing would be more likely to arouse him than to say the mass thinks differently from himself; whereas the American ever seems ready to resign his own opinion to that which is made to seem to be the opinion of the public. I say "seems" to be, for so manifest is the power of public opinion, that one of the commonest expedients of all American managers is to create an impression that the public thinks in a particular way, in order to bring the common mind in subjection.[18]

Surely not even Tocqueville has made a more lucid or a more penetrating description of the "tyranny of the majority" in America, and this is by no means the only passage in which Cooper makes such a statement. In his chapter on "The Press," for example, Cooper notes the readiness with which Americans, in contrast to the English, accepted a book which had been "written *up*" by booksellers who were afraid of a loss: "In England these puffs . . . have had no visible effect, while I see, by the journals at home, that the work in question is deemed established, on this authority!"[19] And near the end of his chapter on the "Comparative Merits" of the English and the American societies, Cooper states flatly that "The besetting, the degrading vice of America, is the moral cowardice by which men are led to truckle to what is called public opinion."[20]

Once the American observers were aware, as they immediately were, of the impressive and undeniable independence, individuality, and integrity -- in a word, the *freedom* -- of the English people, they were forced to confront that great irony and failure of American democracy: the fact that a political system devoted to the freedom and equality of all individuals has created little freedom and few individuals. In other words, the observers were forced to evaluate the relative merits of aristocracy and of democracy and to wonder if England's hierarchical class structure did not indeed lend itself to greater personal freedom and independence -- which is to say, also, to greater individuals and to greater individual achievements -- than were to be found in America's democratic and egalitarian social structure. Thus Emerson remarks that "The American system is more democratic, more humane; yet the American people do not yield better or more able men, or more inventions or books or benefits, than the English."[21] For Emerson, in short, as for nearly all of the American observers, the overriding, extenuating, and truly awe-inspiring glory of the English class system is the *men* it has produced:

> It was pleaded in mitigation of the rotten borough, that it worked well, that substantial justice was done. Fox, Burke, Pitt, Erskine, Wilberforce, Sheridan, Romilly or whatever national men, were by this means sent to Parliament, when their return by large constituencies would have been doubtful. So now we say that the right measures of England are the men it bred; that it has yielded more able men in five hundred years than any other nation; and, though we must not play Providence and balance the chances of producing ten great men against the comfort of ten thousand mean men, yet retrospectively, we may strike the balance and prefer one Alfred, one Shakespeare, one Milton, one Sidney, one Raleigh, one Wellington, to a million foolish democrats.[22]

This, as Emerson would say of the English, is speaking the truth even in the lion's mouth: it is hardly the kind of statement calculated to please the "foolish democrats" of American society. Like all of our observers, Emerson dared to say what he thought, and like all, or nearly all, of them he was severely disturbed by the comparative lack of individuality, distinction, refinement, and manliness in American society: "I have sometimes seen them [Englishmen] walk with my countrymen when I was forced to allow them every advantage, and their companions seemed bags of bones."[23] Santayana put the whole problem in one sentence when, sixty-six years later, he said that "America will not be a success, if every American is a failure."[24] In "free," democratic America men and women are led about by the nose by the force of public opinion because they are afraid of disagreeing with the supposedly sacred majority. This is to say that the tendency of American democracy is, as Cooper stresses, "to destroy all individuality of character and feeling, and to concentrate every thing in the common identity," while England, supposedly a nation lacking in freedom because of its undemocratic class structure, is, in Santayana's words, "the paradise of individuality, eccentricity, heresy, anomalies, hobbies, and humours."[25] So it would seem in the long run, as Henry James remarks, that "conservatism has all the charm and leaves dissent and democracy and other vulgar variations nothing but their bald logic."[26] The central, perplexing problem facing the American observers was, then, simply this: why is it that the English system, in spite of its lack of real *political* freedom, has created a nation of far greater *personal* freedom than the American system has?

It seems to me that Henry James provides an immensely important insight into the problem of individuality and freedom in American society when he suggests that the English are freer than Americans precisely *because* they are more rigidly bound by certain clearly defined values, customs, proprieties, and traditions -- because, in a word, they are more *responsible*:

> No one in England is literally irresponsible; that perhaps is the shortest way of expressing a stranger's, certainly an American's, sense of their cohesion. Every one is free and every one is responsible. To say what it is people are responsible *to* is of course a great extension of the question: briefly, to social expectation, to propriety, to morality, to 'position', to the conventional English conscience, which is, after all, such a powerful factor. With us there is infinitely less responsibility; but there is also, I think, less freedom.[27]

What James means is that the famous *manners* of the English -- their aloofness, their formality, their aggressive sense of independence and of superiority, their unthinking acceptance of certain customs and traditions -- are their way, either conscious or instinctive, of preserving their *personal* privacy and freedom. Indeed, next only to their awareness of the

Englishman's independence and integrity, the American observers are most impressed by his single-minded and fierce devotion to *privacy*. The English, in other words, are intensely aware of a cardinal fact that seems to have escaped Americans -- the fact that there can be no real freedom without privacy. And the Englishman's rigid adherence to his country's complex system of customs, proprieties, and moralities is simply his way of defending and of testifying to the right of each individual to live *privately* as he pleases. To put it in the simplest terms, the English have established and have preserved a system within which , if everyone follows certain rules, all individuals can retain their private dignity and independence. Of all the observers, George Santayana is the most perceptive and the most articulate in describing this devotion to privacy which underlies the Englishman's adherence to an elaborate system of social and moral proprieties. The key to British manners and to the British character is, in Santayana's analysis, the Englishman's absolute devotion and fidelity to his "inner man":

> All the Englishman's attitudes and habits -- his out-of-door life,his clubs, his conventicles, his business -- when they are spontaneous and truly British, are for the sake of his inner man in its privacy. Other people, unless the game calls for them, are in the way and uninteresting . . . . There is a comfortable luxuriousness in all his attitudes. He thinks the prize of life worth winning, but not worth snatching. If you snatch it, as . . . Americans seem inclined to do, you abdicate the sovereignty of your inner man, you miss delight, dignity, and peace; and in that case the prize of life has escaped you.[28]

Part and parcel of the Englishman's fidelity to his"inner man" -- to the kind of privacy, independence, and self-sufficiency which bring "delight, dignity, and peace" -- is the overwhelming influence of the *home* in English life. Again and again the American observers are struck by the primacy and even the sacredness of the home as a value and as an institution in English society. Henry James makes reference not simply to "English domestic virtue" but to "the *sanctity* [emphasis mine] of the British home."[29]. And from the perspective gained by his visit to England, Oliver Wendall Holmes came to understand that "We in America can hardly be said to have such a possession as a family home."[30] Hawthorne, too, was forcefully impressed by "the multitudinous idea of an English home" and declared it to be "an institution which we Americans have not." As for his own English experience, Hawthorne confessed to having "acquired a home-feeling there, as nowhere else in the world."[31] Irving was enchanted by "this sweet home-feeling, this settled repose of affection in the domestic scene," which he felt was the most salient characteristic of English rural life.[32] And Emerson observed that "Domesticity is the taproot which enables the nation to branch wide and high. The motive and end of their trade and empire is to guard the independence and privacy of their homes. Nothing so much marks their manners as the concentration on their household ties."[33] In like manner, Santayana affirms that the greatness of the English, as of the Greeks, lay in the fact that "their home remained their ideal. They were scarcely willing to settle in foreign parts unless they could live their home life there."[34] Still further examples could be cited, but it will be more to the point to begin to analyze the cultural implications of the Englishman's devotion to home and to home-life. For, as Emerson said, it is the home which is the main "motive and end" of the entire English enterprise and system and which provides one of the main keys to the English character.

That the home is an essential part of the Englishman's devotion to privacy and to independence has just been noted, but the significance of the home in English life extends still further. The home also, I think, explains the Englishman's deep-rooted conservatism and traditionalism, his strong desire for property and wealth, and, as we learn from Santayana, his impressive and attractive dedication to health, to hygiene, and to vitality. And in each of these cases we will be able to note a clear and striking contrast to American traits and to American values. For example, we learn from the American observers that the Englishman's desire for property and for wealth is quite as intense and consuming as the American's -- but we also learn that the Englishman pursues property and wealth *as a means for privacy*, while I think that the same can hardly be said for Americans. The English, as Emerson puts it, "wish neither to command nor obey, but to be kings in their own houses"; and, in Emerson's view, it is precisely this "predilection for private independence" which has caused wealth and property to reach an "ideal perfection" in England:

> The English are a nation of humorists. Individual right is
> pushed to the uttermost bound compatible with public order.
> Property is so perfect that it seems the craft of that race, and
> not to exist elsewhere. The king cannot step on an acre which
> the peasant refuses to sell. . . . There is no freak so ridiculous
> but some Englishman has attempted to immortalize by money
> and law. . . . With this. . . . passion for independence, property
> has reached an ideal perfection. . . . The rights of property
> nothing but felony and treason can override. The house is a
> castle which the king cannot enter. The Bank is a strong box to
> which the king has no key. . . . Vested rights are awful things,
> and absolute possession gives the smallest freeholder identity
> of interest with the duke. High stone fences and padlocked
> garden-gates announce the absolute will of the owner to be
> alone.[35]

In short, while wealth and property have in America traditionally been ends
in themselves -- have been equated, that is, with the American dream of
success -- they are in England a means to privacy, independence, and
individuality: quite literally, as Emerson notes, an Englishman's home *is* his
castle -- a place where his own values and the laws of his country combine to
allow him to be totally independent and totally alone.[36]

The love of the home also explains other salient traits in the English
character. For the Englishman's devotion to domesticity, privacy, and
independence is surely one of the main reasons, if not *the* reason, for English
conservatism and traditionalism. Clearly, if one's center of values lies in
one's home and in one's property, one's political and social views will be
strongly marked by a desire to preserve and to protect the individual
freeholder's absolute right to the exclusive, independent use an enjoyment of
his property. As Santayana has shown, however, English conservatism and
traditionalism is far more than mere selfishness: it is the determination to
preserve a distinctive, vital way of living which the Englishman instinctively
honors as his supreme aim in life. "When," as Santayana says,

> [the Englishman] has taken his exercise and is drinking his tea
> or his beer and lighting his pipe; when, in his garden or by his
> fire, he sprawls in an aggressively comfortable chair; when,
> well-washed and well-brushed, he resolutely turns in church to
> the east and recites the Creed (with genuflexions, if he likes
> genuflexions) without in the least implying that he believes a
> word of it; . . . when he makes up his mind who is his best
> friend or his favorite poet; when he adopts a party or a

> sweetheart; when he is hunting or shooting or boating, or
> striding through the fields; when he is choosing his clothes or
> his profession -- never is it a precise reason, or purpose, or
> outer fact that determines him; it is always the atmosphere of
> his inner man.

And as Santayana goes on to explain, the Englishman's inner atmosphere is neither simple "physical well-being" nor "the vision of any ideal"; rather, "It is a mass of dumb instincts and allegiances, the love of a certain quality of life, to be maintained manfully." In other words, the Englishman is loyal, he is conservative, he is traditional out of the love of, and out of the determination to maintain, "a certain quality of life" -- a life in which home, with all its connotations of dignity, independence, privacy, and peace, is "the center of his physical and moral comfort, his headquarters in the war of life, where lie his spiritual stores."37

Again, I find the contrasting English and American traits and values quite striking: Americans are conservative, certainly; but it is, I think, hardly out of "the love of a certain *quality* [emphasis mine] of life." Indeed, "quality" for Americans is too often only that which can be measured in pecuniary terms; the English values of privacy, of independence, and of distinctive living are quite overlooked. With the cardinal exception of the South -- and especially, as other chapters have been suggesting, of the mythic older South -- it is only in their desire to protect their pocketbooks, and to pursue the American myth of success, that Americans are conservative. "The worst tendency we have at home" -- said Cooper in England -- "is manifested by a rapacity for money."38 Or to recall Santayana's infinitely telling distinction, the English insist upon winning the prize of life, while Americans try vainly to snatch it.

Finally, the centrality of the home in England is directly linked to a third major English trait: English vigor, vitality, and robustness. This is so because, as the American observers note, the English home is necessarily a rural home. Any Englishman who can afford it, any member of the nobility certainly, has a country home. And surely any American -- the inheritor, supposedly, of a rugged frontier tradition -- cannot help being struck by the near-worshipful testimonies which one after another of the American observers gives to the superior heartiness and vitality of the English.

Americans like to think that their present softness is due only to the physical comforts and conveniences of modern life and that in earlier times, at least, they were a uniquely hearty and vigorous people. But the testimonies of the American observers emphatically belie this idea. Emerson, for example, was so struck by the "impressive energy" of the English that in his lectures to them he "hesitated to read and threw out for its impertinence many a disparaging phrase which I had been accustomed to spin about poor, thin, unable mortals; so much had fine physique and the personal vigor of this robust race worked on my imagination." In another passage Emerson observes that the English "have more constitutional energy than any other people"; that they "live jolly in the open air, putting a bar of solid sleep between day and day"; and that they "walk with infatuation."[39] Similarly, Henry James observed that in comparison to Americans the English have "a much higher relish for active leisure": "A large appetite for holidays, the ability not only to take them but to know what to do with them when taken, is the sign of a robust people, and judged by this measure we Americans are sadly inexpert." The most striking single example of the English appetite for holidays and for active leisure was, James felt, the eagerness with which the people boated on the Thames: "In its recreative character [the Thames] is absolutely unique. I know of no other classic stream that is so splashed about for the mere fun of it. There is something almost droll and at the same time almost touching in the way that on the smallest pretext of holiday or fine weather the mighty population takes to the boats. . . . Nothing is more suggestive of the personal energy of the people and their eagerness to take, in the way of exercise and adventure, whatever they can get."[40] And, in what amounts to a summary statement for the other American observers, Oliver Wendell Holmes answers affirmatively his own question as to whether or not the English are "taller, stouter, lustier, ruddier, healthier, than our New England people": "If I gave my impression, I should say they are. Among the wealthier class, tall, athletic-looking men and stately, well-developed women are more common, I am compelled to think, than with us."[41]

Once again, their English experience has awakened within the American observers, and within their readers, a clearer, a more objective understanding of certain American traits and values. For in spite of

America's celebrated frontier tradition, all of the observes came to realize[42] that England was, in Santayana's words, "a beautifully healthy England" ("domestic, sporting, gallant, boyish, of a sure and delicate heart")[43] in a way that America was not. And it is Santayana, of all the observers, who is the most perceptive in his understanding of why this is so -- why the English are not only more independent, more private, and more distinctive but also more energetic than the Americans. As Santayana admits, the English are quite as aggressive and unashamed as Americans in their love of physical comfort,[44] and this is *one* of the reasons that they place such a high value on their homes. But Santayana also notes that besides physical comfort, and infinitely more than this, the English value vitality. Indeed, the single most important key to the English character is, in Santayana's view, the Englishman's complete devotion to hygiene and to health: "In manners of hygiene the Englishman's maxims are definite and his practice refined. He has discovered what he calls good form, and is obstinately conservative about it, not from inertia, but in the interests of pure vitality."[45] Thus it is that the Englishman values his home and his precise, decorous, formal home-life not only for its physical comforts, its privacy, and its domestic affection and intimacy but also as a source of vitality. This is a striking contrast to Americans, who have always valued physical comfort but who have never (with the significant exception, perhaps, of the older South) really valued vitality.

If, as Emerson affirmed, "The American is only the continuation of the English genius into new conditions, more or less propitious," a study, from an American point of view, of the exceptionally fine and challenging books by American observers in England from 1820 to 1920 can only cause one to conclude that the new conditions have proved less than propitious. Indeed, the final, the essential import of the books by the American observers is to give credence to the assertion of a brilliant English writer on America, D. H. Lawrence, that "Men murdered themselves into this [American] democracy."[46] Even in 1828 Cooper realized that "There is undeniably a cant obtaining the ascendancy at home, that is destructive of all manner, in conducting the ordinary relations of life, and which is not free from danger." This cant, as Cooper identified it, was the all too typical fanaticism of Americans in regard to democracy and to equality -- a fanaticism which leads them even to deny that one man might have "higher tastes, more learning, better principles, more strength, more beauty, and greater natural abilities than the another." Their English experience, in short, forced the American observers to recognize that American democracy produces mediocrity. To quote Cooper again (at separate points in his book): "The prevailing characteristic of America is mediocrity." "Our standard, in nearly all things, as it is popular, is necessarily one of mediocrity."[47] Consequently, the American observers were literally at a loss to find any English traits or English values which were not clearly superior to American traits and to American values. The English were more independent, more individualistic, more learned, more refined, more candid, more courageous; they placed higher value on privacy and vitality and distinguished living, and less value on mere material possessions and comfort; they were, in short, more manly and more civilized than Americans. This left very little on which Americans (to whom, as I said at the beginning, the observers' books were mainly addressed) could congratulate themselves; and it is interesting to note, in conclusion , that nothing is more indicative of the superiority of English traits and of English values than Hawthorne's desperate and pathetic attempts to find *something* superior in American culture. Like Cooper and Emerson and James, Hawthorne was struck by the harshness and cruelty of the life of the English lower classes;[48] and on this issue he does make some very effective points against the English. Otherwise, however, we see him turning to such unbecoming and silly assertions as that Lord Nelson did *not* have English traits, that "the kind of excellence that distinguished" Leigh Hunt was *American* rather than English, that American women are more ethereal than English women, and that American gingerbread is superior to English gingerbread.[49]

One only hopes that the superiority of American culture does not rest, in the final analysis, upon the ethereality of its women or upon the superiority of its gingerbread.

Chapter 13

Notes

1. As works worthy of comparison with Tocqueville's *Democracy in America*, I would cite Cooper's *Gleanings in Europe: England*, Emerson's *English Traits*, and Santayana's *Soliloquies in England*.
2. I am referring to Hartz's demonstration of the importance of seeing American culture as a "fragment" of English culture, and to Lipset's demonstration that the American value system was derived mainly from America's Puritan and Revolutionary heritage. Louis Hartz, *The Founding of New Societies: Studies in the History of the United Sates, Latin America, South Africa, Canada, and Australia* (New York: Harcourt, Brace and World, 1964); Seymour Martin Lipset, *The First New Nation: the United States in Historical and Comparative Perspective* (Garden City, New York: Doubleday, 1967).
3. Ralph Waldo Emerson, *English Traits* (Boston: Phillips Sampson, 1856), p. 42.
4. Percy Lubbock, ed., *The Letters of Henry James* (New York: Scribner's, 1920), I, p. 143.
5. It is a notable fact that there are virtually no real differences in the reports of American observers. The uniformity of their impressions surely argues for the validity of their observations of England.
6. Nathaniel Hawthorne, *Our Old Home* (Boston and New York: Houghton Mifflin, 1907), p. 362.
7. Quoted in Oliver Wendell Holmes, *Our Hundred Days in Europe* (Boston and New York: Houghton Mifflin, 1887), p. 311.
8. "The *man* is he who lives and relies directly on nature, not on the needs or weaknesses of other people. These self-sufficing Englishmen, in their reserve and decision, seemed to me truly men, creatures of fixed rational habit, people in whose somewhat inarticulate society one might feel safe and at home." George Santayana, *Soliloquies in England and Later Soliloquies* (Ann Arbor, MI: The University of Michigan Press, 1967), p. 5.
9. Henry James, *English Hours*, ed. Alma Louise Lowe (New York: The Orion Press, 1960), pp. 74, 75, 102.
10. Emerson, p.303.
11. Washington Irving, *The Sketch Book of Geoffrey Crayon, Gent.* (New York: Dutton, 1963), p. 58.
12. James Fenimore Cooper, *Gleanings in Europe: England*, ed. Robert E. Spiller (New York: Oxford University Press, 1930), pp. 192, 238.
13. Emerson, pp. 187, 188.
14. *Ibid.*, pp. 120, 121, 123, 124.
15. *Ibid.*, pp. 106-107.
16. *Ibid.*, p. 134.
17. Irving, pp. 52, 53, 301.
18. Cooper, pp. 384-385.
19. *Ibid.*, p. 269.
20. *Ibid.*, p. 388.
21. Emerson, p. 306.
22. *Ibid.*, pp. 305-306.

23. *Ibid.*, pp. 303-304.
24. Santayana, p. 64.
25. Cooper, p. 359; Santayana, p. 30.
26. James, p. 44.
27. *Ibid.*, pp. 75-76.
28. Santayana, p. 37.
29. James, p. 81.
30. Holmes, pp. 177-178.
31. Hawthorne, pp. 312, 314. Randall Stewart, ed., *The English Notebooks of Nathaniel Hawthorne* (New York: Modern Language Association of America, 1941), p. 104.
32. Irving, p. 61.
33. Emerson, p. 112.
34. Santayana, p. 33.
35. Emerson, pp. 145, 146, 166-167.
36. "How sedulously he plants out his garden, however tiny, from his neighbors and from the public road! If his windows look unmistakably on the street, at least he fills his window-boxes with the semblance of a hedge or a garden, and scarcely allows the dubious light to filter through his blinds or lace curtains. . . . He is quite willing not to be able to look out,. . . . if only he can prevent other people from looking in." Santayana, p. 37.
37. *Ibid.*, pp. 30-31, 37.
38. Cooper, p. 172.
39. Emerson, pp. 75, 110.
40. James, pp. 26, 78.
41. Holmes, p. 294.
42. As is often the case, Hawthorne is on this point an example of a biased observer whose very bias reveals what he tries to conceal. Clearly impressed by the heartiness of the English, Hawthorne still tries to depreciate English robustness by giving it another name such as "earthliness" or "coarseness." See, for example, Hawthorne, pp. 378-379.
43. Santayana, p. 3.
44. *Ibid.*, p. 38.
45. *Ibid.*, p. 36.
46. D. H. Lawrence, *Studies in Classic American Literature* (Garden City, New York: Doubleday, 1951), p. 63.
47. Cooper, pp. 254, 304-305, 382.
48. See Cooper, pp. 311, 353-354; Emerson, pp. 174, 299; James, pp. 43, 29-30, 170-171; and Hawthorne, pp. 477-479, 519-522, 524, 526.
49. Hawthorne, pp. 374, 392-393, 465, 567-569.

INDEX

STUDIES IN AMERICAN LITERATURE